Saga Hillbom

Princess of Thorns

Princess of

Thorns

ISBN: 978-91-519-3832-5

I would like to thank Robin for her unfailing critique and support, Eleanor for mirroring my enthusiasm, and the Richard III Society for all their hard work

'Tant le desiree'
I have longed for it so much

Written in Richard III's hand along with his name on a page of the 12th century chivalric romance *Ipomedon*, the 'best knight in the world', most likely before 1470

'For God's sake, let us sit upon the ground,
And tell sad stories of the death of kings:
How some have been deposed; some slain in war;
Some haunted by the ghosts they have deposed;
Some poison'd by their wives; some sleeping kill'd;
All murder'd: for within the hollow crown
That crowns the mortal temples of a king
Keeps death his court'

Shakespeare, William. *King Richard the Second* (Act 3, Scene 2)

Significant historical figures as of 1482

Children who died in infancy are not included, nor are figures of lesser importance at the beginning of the story

HOUSE OF YORK

Richard Plantagenet, late Duke of York, Edward IV's father (b. 1429, d. 1460)

Edward IV, King of England and Lord of Ireland (b. 1442)
      His children by Elizabeth Woodville:

Edward, Prince of Wales, frequently referred to as Ed (b. 1470)

Richard, Duke of York, frequently referred to as Dickie (b. 1473)

Elizabeth (b. 1466)

Mary Plantagenet (b. 1467)

Cecily (b. 1469)

Anne (b. 1475)

Katherine (b. 1479), frequently referred to as Kate

Bridget (b. 1480)
      His brothers:

Edmund, Earl of Rutland (b. 1443, d. 1460)

George, Duke of Clarence (b. 1449, d. 1478)

Richard, Duke of Gloucester, frequently referred to as Uncle Richard (b. 1452)

HOUSE OF LANCASTER

Henry VI, late King of England (b. 1421, d. 1471)

Marguerite d'Anjou, his queen (b. 1445)

Edward of Westminster, Duke of Cornwall, their son (b. 1453, d. 1471)

HOUSE OF TUDOR

Edmund Tudor, Earl of Pembroke (b. 1430, d. 1456)

Margaret Beaufort, Countess of Pembroke, widow of Edmund (b. 1443)
Henry Tudor, their son (b. 1457)
Jasper, Edmund's brother (b. 1431)

NEVILLE

Richard Neville, Earl of Warwick, frequently referred to as the Kingmaker (b. 1428, d. 1471)
Anne Beauchamp, his wife (b. 1426)
      Their children:
Isabel Neville, Duchess of Clarence (b. 1451, d. 1476)
Anne Neville, Duchess of Gloucester (b. 1456)

Cecily Neville, Duchess of York, Edward IV's mother, the Kingmaker's aunt (b. 1415)

WOODVILLE AND GREY

Elizabeth Woodville, Queen of England, (b. 1437)
      Her children by her first marriage:
Thomas Grey, Marquis of Dorset (b. 1457)
Richard Grey (b. 1458)
      Her siblings:
Anthony, Earl Rivers (b. 1442)
Edward, Lord Scales, frequently referred to as Ned (b. 1454)
Catherine Woodville, Duchess of Buckingham (b. 1458)

OTHER PERSONAGES

Thomas Kyme, an esquire (b. 1465)
Elizabeth Shore, commonly known as Jane Shore, Edward IV's long-term mistress (b. 1445)
William Hastings, Edward IV's close friend and advisor (b. 1431)
Thomas Stanley, King of Mann, married to Margaret Beaufort (b. 1435)
John Howard, Earl of Surrey (b. 1425)
Henry Percy, Earl of Northumberland (b. 1449)

John de Vere, Earl of Oxford (b. 1442)
Henry Stafford, Duke of Buckingham (b. 1455)

Prologue

RICHARD WIPED THE blood from his split lip with the back of his hand. Even now, a full month after the battle of Tewkesbury, it was still a raw source of irritation.

The two-year-old girl wiggling on his lap turned her wide eyes to his face and gazed in astonishment through honey-coloured lashes and strands of fine-spun hair that had escaped her short braids. She stretched out a chubby hand to point at his lip.

'Yes. Not nice,' Richard conceded and made a small grimace at his oldest brother across the room.

Cecily had begun to emerge as his favourite niece with her curiosity and sometimes brazenness even for her slight age, but Richard had never been particularly comfortable with children in general. They understood so little, yet often more than one expected, and could be horridly unpredictable. At least now, after the flight to Flanders and the return to England as well as the battles of Barnet and Tewkesbury, he felt no need to distance himself from youngsters. At eighteen, Richard knew his brother Edward finally saw him as an adult and an equal after the daunting time they had spent together in exile. Duke of Gloucester, Constable of England, Chief Justice of North Wales, Chamberlain of Wales, Great Chamberlain and Lord High Admiral of England—these were burdensome offices for a boy his age, but he cherished them, for they proved just how great his brother's trust in him had grown.

The solar at Baynard Castle was emblazoned with dull gold from the tapers and cressets lining the wall, the mild air of a summer evening saturated with the scent of wax and leather.

Though a room large enough for echoes, it held a certain intimacy at this hour, the three sons of York and the princess sitting secluded with the exception of a few servants.

'It is a good thing she has not seen the wound on your arm, little brother,' King Edward said now, and grinned. 'Nearly slashed the limb off your shoulder!'

'I doubt not she could take the gore of war better than most grown men.'

As if challenged by his words, Cecily twisted around, tugging at the sleeve of Richard's velvet doublet in a futile attempt to see said gore.

George, Duke of Clarence, gave an audible sigh and extended a slender hand to accept the cup of Venetian glass that one of the servants offered him.

'What, George?' said the King. 'Would you have us speak of *your* so-called bruises instead?'

Clarence's cornflower-blue eyes at once flashed cold. 'It was your decision, not mine, to give Rich command of the vanguard—*again*. Your Grace.' He added the last words through his teeth.

'I had every reason. Unlike some, his loyalty has never failed me.'

'Pox on you, Edward. If you intend to admonish me, I'd rather you had not pardoned me to begin with.'

Richard watched the exchange between his brothers in tense silence. He knew Clarence did not mean what he said, but had spoken merely out of pride, out of caprice. And the King…the King's patience was not without limits, yet it endured impressively where his blood kin was concerned. Family. Family above everything; the House of York above everything. That was what their father had imprinted in their minds since they were no older than Cecily was now.

In a low, guarded voice, Richard said, 'Let's not quarrel now. Lancaster is defeated, never to rise again, thank God all-merciful. We ought to celebrate.'

This truth broke laughter from King Edward's lips. 'How right you are! A feast is called for, tomorrow, and now we shall have an abundance of fine wine and fine wenches on that!'

Richard immediately regretted his suggestion, for a celebration in the King's eyes invariably meant food, drink, and women, all in greater quantities than could be considered sane by any standard. Perhaps this was not the ideal moment to mention he would rather spend the evening reading *The Canterbury Tales* and writing a letter to the girl he had long hoped to wed.

George seemed to read his thoughts. 'Why, you look thwarted. If it's Anne Neville, you'd do best to forget her. Whore to the Lancaster prince—'

In a twitch of blind fury, Richard knocked over his own cup, and Cecily gasped as the crimson liquor spilled down on her chemise. After a heartbeat of terror, her clucking giggles filled the room.

To Richard's relief—but not surprise—King Edward was enraged with Clarence rather than with his younger, favourite brother. The issue of Anne Neville was a sensitive one, since the man who married her would obtain half of the inheritance otherwise controlled by her sister's husband, George, Duke of Clarence. Still, this was neither the time nor the place to sort out the rivalry.

Richard lifted Cecily off his lap and put her down on the floor. After granting her father a goodnight kiss, she sped to the door, where her nursemaid was waiting to lead her by the hand back to her two sisters and little brother in the nursery.

Once she was out of sight, the King did indeed order for more wine and his three latest fancies. While his liege lord popped a succulent grape between the equally succulent lips of a fair-skinned woman, and George stared grudgingly into his beloved malmsey wine, Richard exchanged his chair for the window seat. From there, he watched the two men through a candlelit haze. Edward, who loved everything in life with charming indulgence, from his eerily beautiful wife and children to the heat of battle and the sins of the flesh. George, who appeared to love very little save himself, who had betrayed them to Lancaster before turning his coat again.

One question foremost hovered in Richard's mind. How, in God's sacred name, could one prevent the thorns of the Yorkist White Rose from turning inwards on its own house, infecting and shredding.

Chapter I

I FANCY RUBIES but I prefer diamonds. Father must have let it slip his mind, though I did remind him not once but thrice.

The clamour in the great hall is deafening. Minstrels plucking at lute strings and virginals mingle with the constant choir of chatter from the courtiers and the scraping of knives against wooden trenchers. Fragrant perfume of lavender and the aroma of roasted meat press up my nostrils, intoxicating, clinging silks and flashes of sun-chinked hair blending in a palette of colours before my eyes. How many feasts such as this have I attended in my life? Hundreds, no doubt, yet the atmosphere never fails to imbue me with mirth, a mirth only slightly dampened with disappointment this time.

Uncle Richard bends down to kiss me on both cheeks, a flicker of discomfort cracking through his composure and the felicity in his pebble-grey eyes. I have never heard him complain about the pain in his back, except to my father; he is too proud. Of course, none holds as dear a place in his heart as Father does, none save his own wife and children. The King was always the brightest shining star, the man who won the intimate trust of men and women alike through smiles and banter. At least it was thus when he arrived in London twenty years hence to claim his crown—I dare not say when the people's love begun to waver. Perhaps it was when the years took their toll and he grew licentious, or perhaps it was when he drowned his and Uncle

1

Richard's treacherous brother Clarence in a barrel of malmsey wine.

'What say you of your gift? The King's Grace thought it might suit you.' My uncle nods at the jewel-encrusted casket firmly clasped in my hands. The mahogany has turned russet gold in the light from the chandelier, the rubies glistening on the lid like countless beads of blood.

'Well, it is very pretty, Uncle.'

'But?'

I should have known he would detect the note of hesitation in my voice. He is too attentive to be fooled by my smile.

'But...but Elizabeth received one with diamonds when *she* turned thirteen.' I swallow. 'And I told Father I wanted one like that, too. I told him three times.'

A subtle smile pulls at the corner of Uncle Richard's mouth. 'Yes, I remember. I am afraid that's the lot of those later born.'

The glance we exchange contains more than would be prudent to speak: the eternal tinge of envy in us both regarding our older siblings, who appear to have been granted the whole world and more on a golden platter. The difference is that he has long since accepted his place in the shadow of the sun, and been handsomely rewarded for it, while I find it impossible to dull my resentment towards my sister Elizabeth. Her strawberry-blonde locks, her poise and effortless grace, her ability to wipe her face blank of emotion when need be... She is perfection incarnate, sublime, three years my senior, and I suspect God made us with a cruel twinkle in his eye. It is bordering on heresy to think such a thing, but there can be no other explanation.

Mary is also older, yet she was never a headache to me, having been pallid and sickly all her life. Kind, it is true, but not much more than that. The younger girls—Anne, Kate, and darling baby Bridget—are all half my age or less and a sweet throng of wide-eyed children. It is difficult to imagine them ever growing into adulthood, difficult to think of them as future queen consorts, though that is what we all are: links in the dynastic chain of York that Father hopes to snare Europe with. Scotland shall be mine, so they tell me, if the fighting ever ceases. If, not when. France will be Elizabeth's, hence she has been styled *Madame la Dauphine* for many years.

My gaze wanders to the high table where the King and Queen are seated. Father has his arm on the wrought oak armrest of his chair, his wife's fingers laced with his like ivy around iron bars, his thumb stroking her knuckles out of habit. Their trenchers are still heaped with venison and honeyed plums—his markedly more so than hers. Few can compete with Father in wining and dining, and perchance one ought not to attempt it, for the sake of one's own health.

Not even lovely Elizabeth can hold a candle to Ed and Dickie. They are, after all, boys. Now, they tumble around the great hall, swinging their wooden swords, re-enacting some glorious battle, their doublets of gold-stitched black damask crumpled. Eleven and eight years of age respectively, they should have left childish games behind, but where is the harm? At times, I cannot help but giggle at the thought of the Prince of Wales and the Duke of York forsaking their grand titles along with their manners for an hour or two. They have been brought up in separate households for the sake of Ed's education, but are quick to revive the familiarity whenever they meet.

Dickie's eyes sparkle when he catches sight of me, and he speeds towards me, stumbling over his own feet in a flurry to escape the perils of Ed's wooden sword.

'Cece!' He latches onto me, clutching my skirts. A mere moment later, though, both he and his brother have resumed their game, before the poor esquire tasked with keeping them under close guard hauls them in.

I struggle to stifle the smile tickling me. I wish I could press Dickie close to me to protect him from the feigned battle; I wish I could join them and disregard all restrictions. I wish… However, if they can barely escape chiding for this kind of rowdy behaviour, I could never. I am of marriageable age, as incongruous as it feels, and the Holy Virgin would weep to see me abandon modesty, as Elizabeth reminded me this very morning

'They are growing up fast, Cecily.' Uncle Richard brushes away a wisp of ebony hair from his high cheekbone. 'Not fast enough, I fear. Every day the Prince of Wales spends at Ludlow with Anthony Woodville is a day lost to abhorrent influence.'

I reach up to adjust my hennin ever so slightly; I can never keep it from tipping, the gauze veil fluttering around my face. The jagged relationship between the nobles, foremost among them Richard, Duke of Gloucester and Lord of the North, and the Woodville clan headed by Mother's beloved brother Anthony, is a truth widely accepted at court. I rarely dare utter my own qualms regarding the Woodvilles, not when Mother is listening, but at this moment I am safe from reproach.

'I know it. Though surely, Anthony is an admirable man if one were to place him next to his nephew.'

'You see more than I give you credit for. Yes, I wager Dorset will be the end of us, the way he encourages the King's vices.'

I gnaw on my lip, eager to blot out the images crowding in my mind. My half-brother Dorset and William Hastings may not be keen on one another, but they have both found common ground with Father in his debauchery, lining up harlots for sharing like pearls on an endless necklace. Queasy, I flit to an easier topic.

'How is the north these days?'

'With God's good grace, I hope to capture the Scottish stronghold of Berwick shortly. Then, the invasion must proceed.' Uncle Richard touches his cup to his lips but does not drink.

'And what of my marriage?' The hennin is slipping again. 'Why all this warring when an advantageous alliance can be obtained through diplomacy?'

He scoffs, a shadow crossing his eyes for a fragmented moment. 'You know not what you speak of, dear niece.' He regains his chivalric disposition. 'I do what His Grace decrees, and I am certain you cannot doubt your own father's methods for enhancing the weal of England.'

'But *you* doubt his methods at times, do you not?'

To my relief, Uncle Richard simply arches a crescent dark eyebrow and emits a soft laugh. 'There have been moments, yes, though we are united in this Scottish endeavour. I do promise you this: if a Scottish king does not eventually wed you, I shall make them repay your dowry for certs.'

I bask in his piercing gaze, absorbing the satisfaction of not being dismissed as a frivolous little girl grown too big for her boots. The dowry—twenty-thousand marks paid in instalments in advance—would be a dire loss indeed.

'Richard! Brother! Won't you lead our dearest daughter in a merry dance? It is her fourteenth birthday, after all,' the King calls from his grand chair.

Ha! I have never been his dearest daughter, and I am thirteen, but I say nothing of it. That voice alone could command a stormy sea to turn mellow.

'As you wish, Sire.' Uncle Richard bows his head, but the King is once more occupied with devouring the rich dishes lining the table.

The Duke of Gloucester turns to me instead. 'And what tune shall we have?'

'Something fit for the *saltarello*.'

'I see.' He gestures to the minstrels, who are already tapping their drums impatiently.

To my delight, the courtiers withdraw to the corners of the great hall, clearing a circular space for the performance. I cannot recall a time when I did not dance, truly, I cannot. Mother's most frequent praise is regarding my so-called natural graces—graces she no doubt wish would appear on other occasions, too, but it is only music that can lure them forth. And to perform the *saltarello* gracefully is a distinguishing feat, for the skipping steps and lively turns are an art in themselves.

I bend my knee in a curtsey, mirroring my uncle, and so the dance begins. I flash Father my brightest smile in an attempt to hold his attention, and succeed for a moment.

Uncle Richard's face, though, is a mask of solemn concentration. He can rule his domains with steadfast resolve, he can deal the blows of justice in the name of the King, he can read all the knightly manuscripts—but dancing is not one of his skills.

I skip and jump and twist and turn to the joyous tune, the hem of my embroidered kirtle flashing beneath my murrey gown. If only I were older, or taller for my tender age, I might cut a fine figure. As the dance draws to a close, I curtsey once more to the high table.

Mother smiles, the lines around her eyes deepening. People say she was the most stunning damsel in all of England once; now, the years and the hardships, not to speak of twelve child beds and countless infidelities, have carved a weariness on her face. But when she smiles...when she smiles, it is as if the sun has broken through a crust of clouds, the sharpness in her dragon-eyes glossed over. Men could die for that smile, and I doubt not some have done just that.

The musicians pick another melody and the courtiers swarm the dance floor once more.

Uncle Richard clears his throat. 'I must be gone, Cecily. My wife is ardent for my return, and Scotland will not wait forever—it is as adversary as when I left.'

'I thought you would stay longer.' I push down my dismay. 'God grant you victory, and do give my greetings to your Anne.'

He smiles, as he does so often when I refer to his wife as 'your Anne', and is gone.

I am left with a hotly brewing blend of emotions in my chest. If my uncle is victorious in his endeavour, as he certainly will be, Father will have to find me another husband than the then-defeated Scottish Prince James. I would not mind that. It is not James—a boy I have never met—in particular whom I yearn for, but the wondrous thing that is a coronet. Yes, as long as I can still wed a prince or in the very least a duke, I do pray Scotland perishes to our English swords.

That same eve, as Agnes—one of my women, low in birth but high in spirit and often my sole confidante—liberates my hair from the hennin and brushes out the wealth of burnished gold, I recount to her every single moment of the feast. These intimate nights are dear to us both. Agnes can gorge in gossip and I can prattle mindlessly on without fear of being scolded. With logs crackling in the fireplace, spewing sprinkles of ember and fire, and the lush tapestries in my bedchamber remedying the chill of stone walls, it is little wonder I feel as if my heart is enveloped in pure warmth.

Agnes' eyes dart from my head to our reflection in the silver mirror and back again. 'And what did the White Boar of Gloucester say of your betrothal? Still not looking reliable, hmm?'

My hair tangles in the comb as I twist around to look at her. 'You speak too boldly.'

6

'Pardon, then, love.' An amused smirk. 'You ne'er really minded before, now, did you? You suffer from the same tendency.'

I roll my eyes. She is right. Almost every evening she speaks out of turn for a woman in her position, and always, always I overlook it and the cycle repeats itself. In truth, I wish for her to speak thus; she is nigh on twenty years old, far more worldly than I could ever hope to be, and her honesty makes her irresistible to me. Another mistress might have dismissed her long ago, yet I cannot think of anyone who would share the same understanding with me.

'No, not particularly reliable. I...I almost think it won't ever come to pass. They cannot seem to make proper peace, but then that is only what one ought to expect from those savage Scots.'

'Won't you be queen then, love?'

I knit my brows. 'I must be. My father the King's Grace will find someone else. I know it. If not a queen, then perchance duchess. My uncle was a dear today, he truly was, though he is not as marvellous a dancer as he is a magnate.'

'Pah! His brother of Clarence was the prettiest dancer I ever saw, except for you, love, and no merry-go-round could 'ave saved that churl,' Agnes grumbles, pulling the brush through my hair in long, energetic strokes.

'Of course not. One does not defect to Lancaster and the ungodly without facing retribution. He was a fool, Agnes, a fool worse than the jugglers who entertained us last Michaelmas. And to think he loved malmsey! Well, loved it a little too much until it was a little too late.'

I count to seventy-three before she begins to braid my hair with flick fingers, a crease of concentration on her forehead.

I study my cuticles intently, desperate not to retire to my bed. 'I wish I was more like you.'

'What for? You're as beauteous as the White Rose you so adore.'

'Not that.' I am beauteous enough. Accomplished enough. There is a difference between reaching the mark and truly shining. 'I mean...I mean I wish I could always speak as freely as you and not cause a fair scandal.'

7

'And I wish I had your fancy slippers and all the rest of the sparkly things. Want to trade?'

A giggle escapes me. 'No, no I suppose not.'

'Thought so.'

In May, my sister Mary is taken gravely ill at the Palace of Placentia, Greenwich. The fever holds her in a merciless grip, and the physician claims her pulse is faint as a fluttering moth. Her throat swells to twice its normal size, reminding me of the exotic snake that one of Father's favoured merchants brought from the Far East. When it swallowed a dead rabbit in a single bite, its pasty yellow body bloated enough to make me nauseated for a full evening.

When Mary opens her mouth, it is coated in a thick, grey mass, just like her nostrils. She cannot speak, cannot swallow. Her breaths are shallow and quick, constantly interrupted by fits of barking coughs, and her hair lies slicked with sweat against her temples.

Mother is sunk down on the edge of the bed, stroking Mary's cheek, helpless.

I stand outside the locked door, peering through the keyhole, Anne and Kate cramming to share my view.

'Move, Cece, move!' Kate squeals. She has not yet turned three and would have to be hoisted up to be able to see anything.

'Hush! Mother is with her.' I put a firm hand on Kate's tiny shoulder to keep her from bouncing with curiosity. 'And you do not want to see it. It's ghastly.'

'Why? *Why?* Is she going to die?'

'I...no.' I bend down and scoop up Kate in my arms, turning from the door. Anne trots diligently at my heels as the three of us flee from the odours of disease, slippers clicking against the polished stone floor.

Mary is buried in Saint George's chapel at Windsor. I weep with my sisters, but my own tears contain only a sliver of the sorrow in our mother's dry eyes. I always thought Mary too little—too shy, too boring, too sickly—yet that is what made her the greatest object of our mother's care and concern. Yes, Mother has doted on Mary like a fragile pet as long as I can remember.

Father does not attend the funeral, just as tradition would have it, and regardless, he is caught up in the preparations for the invasion of Scotland. The situation has turned on its axis, because King James' disaffected brother, the Duke of Albany, has landed in England and travelled to Fotheringhay to sign a treaty with Father. Albany is to be our puppet king upon the throne of Scotland, and in exchange for English military aid to depose James, he vows to wed me if he manages to annul his current marriage.

Uncle Richard joins the two other men at Fotheringhay, and together, he and Albany depart for Scotland with an army of twenty-thousand men-at-arms and an assemblage of English lords. Among said lords are not only Uncle Richard's northern counterpart the Earl of Northumberland, but Dorset and one of my maternal uncles, Edward Woodville. I can only imagine the chafing against raw nerves. Father, though, is not part of the chain of command, not this time. He may have been the most awe-inspiring warrior in this land during his youth, taller than most and with the strength and unhesitating courage of a lion, but that is a fading image at best. The wine and food that used to fuel his rampages now accumulate at his midsection; his indulgences have made the years come quicker and more cruelly to him than nature might have deemed fit. It has been thus for a decade now, his decline creeping on ever since he settled to rule a peaceful kingdom after reclaiming his crown from Lancaster in 1471. At last, he tasks his younger brother to do what he himself is no longer capable of: heading an invasion. I believe it is wise, and I tell him as much.

In August, the entire enterprise collapses. James III is huddled up in Edinburgh Castle, held prisoner by his own lords but safe nonetheless, and Albany is at odds with the Scottish nobility. The possession of a king, or at least a man likely to become king, is as vital to a coup as blood is to the human body. Moreover, my uncle lacks the resources to besiege Edinburgh—or rather, the royal coffers do not contain enough resources, Father having spent lavish sums on luxuries not even I fancy myself. At least, that is what I discern from the hushed voices I hear behind closed doors and how I see the courtiers arch their eyebrows.

Uncle Richard does capture Berwick, the pivotal stronghold that the Lancastrians surrendered to Scotland once upon a time. Father sings his praise for days on end, and I am dangerously tempted to tell him God's honest truth: his brother could have done so much more if given reasonable circumstances.

I have now been twice betrothed to a Scottish claimant, and I am heartily weary of it. Albany has abandoned his vow to marry me, swapping sides once more to reconcile with his brother. I cannot help but to think of him as the Scottish Clarence.

'Father told me Uncle Richard extracted an agreement from Edinburgh to repay my dowry,' I say as Mother and I stroll through the garden at Greenwich.

The lawns stretch out before us like lush green carpets, soaked in dew and morning sun. The air is heavy with the scent of roses velvety to the touch.

Mother's face twists. 'Yes, Gloucester can be so frightfully *handy*, my sweet.'

My sweet. That is what she called Mary, always. It appears the nickname has passed on to me, although it would have suited Anne better.

'Did you hear the news, Lady Mother? Did you hear about the French Woman?'

Marguerite d'Anjou, the ill-fated Lancastrian Queen, has finally wasted away in her native land after her cause died with her son and heir on the battlefield of Tewkesbury.

Mother licks her peachy lips, calling to mind a sated cat. 'Yes, I heard. God has called her to him at last. Methinks it was the first and only time he touched that wretched strumpet's soul. Don't drag your skirts in the dew, Cecily, please.'

I grab the folds of my gown and hitch up the hem above the grass we are treading over, perhaps a little too high, struggling to glide forward like Mother.

As we approach the palace, I cannot contain myself any longer. 'You must be pleased. Marguerite lost and you won, did you not?'

'Edward won the crown—I won in my marriage. Never forget that. Women win through whose wedding band they put on their finger, not through whom they slay on the battlefield. If you cannot alter the rules of the game, you must learn to master them.'

'I will, Lady Mother.'

Elizabeth Woodville has indeed won, for never before did England see an impoverished widow catch the all-consuming eye of a king, not to mention a king five years younger than she, and the enemy of her late husband. As long as Father lives, England is at the Woodvilles' feet. Perhaps that is why England has not grown to love her.

Chapter II

T
HE FISHING TRIP my father takes in late March the following year turns out not to be as inconsequential as we assumed; mayhap it put his humours in imbalance. The physicians cannot pronounce a definitive diagnosis, and as the King takes to his bed on Easter Sunday, the court is like a choir of chattering monkeys. Some speak of poison, others of a fever or chill. Still others blame his escalated debauchery and indulgence in food and drink and women, indulgences encouraged by certain close advisors and in-laws. I do not know which rumour to credit. I only know one thing: Father was expected to live for many more years, having always had a reputation for being virile and strong, and his heir is not mature enough to rule on his own. England has had boy-kings before, rarely successful.

The last one, Henry VI, was an infant when the crown passed to him, and look where that got us, with our territories in France lost. Of course, nothing much improved after Henry of Lancaster came of age, because never was there a man more unlike his lion for a father, never was there a man less interested in ruling England or less capable of doing so. Indeed, he always preferred the chapel to the presence chamber, would rather sit idly under a tree than visit his wife's bed or confer with his despairing councillors, and then came the bouts of catatonic stupor.

Ed, on the other hand, is a clever boy, a promise of greatness with duty in his eyes and confidence in his step, but it was no more than a year since he played with Dickie in the great hall.

Unlike when Mary was ill, we are allowed to visit Father's bedside, for the physicians have not noted anyone else catching his ailments during the ten days since Easter Sunday. Mother is as pale as if it was she who had been subject to bloodletting in search for a cure, her lips pressed tight, gaze pinned to her husband's massive hands. Those hands are dear to all of us, but she must know them better than anyone else.

'Don't fret, Lis,' he mutters. 'You will be the mother of the King. Our son will not deny you any comfort…'

'I know. I know.' She nods. 'Don't leave me, Edward, not after all this. Not after everything I have lost for your sake—'

I frown. Did she not once speak to me about winning? Perhaps she means something else, perhaps she means the hardships, her own father and brother perishing. There was a price to pay for glory, I suppose.

Father beckons for Elizabeth to come closer. She is an oasis of serene, cool grace, yet I know she is feeling as wretched as the rest of us, if not more. It burns my eyes more than the tears I myself cannot hold back.

The King clasps her slim hand. 'I'm sorry…about France. That bastard Louis…'

'No matter, Papa. I shall rejoice to wed whomever Lady Mother sees fit. And I'll pray for you, Papa…' Her voice trails off before it can begin to tremble.

'Good girl.'

Even through my curtain of tears, I feel the tiniest inkling of glee, and shame over that inkling. Elizabeth is no longer styled *Dauphine*, but like me, she is presently unspoken for on the marriage market.

Father calls each of us forth, placing a faint kiss on our cheeks. 'Anne…' he says when I dip down to receive his blessing.

'No, Papa. Cecily.'

'Hmm.'

I know he loves me. I also know Elizabeth and his sons are the only children who bear a truly distinct mark in his love.

Dickie, always the wide-eyed angel and soon to be heir presumptive to his brother Ed, receives his due farewell.

Finally, Father says, 'Dorset…Hastings…Come hither.'

Mother's eldest son from her first marriage, the Marquess of Dorset, and my father's chief advisor, William Hastings, obey after a moment's hesitation. Both are imposing figures in their robes of heavy black brocade and gold chains; however, Dorset is more than a score of years younger and markedly more handsome. The acrimonious glances passing between them are clear for all to see, but at least they maintain greater sobriety and discretion here than in their usual habitat of wine-sodden carousing.

'I would have you shake hands...like brothers. This dispute...is one to be had by beggars and bawds. Unity. My son needs...needs unity in his government.'

Hastings crinkles his nose ever so slightly.

'Now! Shake hands, damn you.'

This they do, over the rise and fall of their King's chest, though there is a familiar twinkle of mendacity in Dorset's almond eyes.

'Richard? Where is Rich?'

Mother stiffens visibly at the mention of the man I know she has so little affection for. 'He is in the north and methinks you know it.'

'My brother of Gloucester will be Lord Protector, to care for our son and the realm until the boy is of an age to rule. I know you would have favoured...favoured your own Anthony, Lis, but this will be best. For everyone.'

'No, Edward, no. You cannot appoint Gloucester protector. My family—'

'Lis, please... Do not...not cause a struggle in this.'

Two days later, King Edward IV of England grows cold and stiff in death's embrace.

'Why is not Ed here, Lady Mother?' I dare to ask a few days later, as my sisters and I sit gathered in the Dowager Queen's chambers. She has often summoned us to sit with her on the pallets arranged by the fireplace, to read or converse or practice our needlework—I am impossible with embroidery, always pricking my fingertips bloody. This time, we have sat in silence so far, save for Kate's occasional little exclamations about this and that.

Mother appears captivated by the flames licking the logs, chinks of gold and russet red reflecting in her eyes. 'It will take a little while to bring him to London from Ludlow. My poor boy...

Your Uncle Anthony will take proper care of him till then, I daresay.'

Anne brushes a stray garland of ash blonde hair from her forehead. 'I read in a book once that King Richard II suffered a disastrous minority. What if that happens to Ed? And I read that—'

'Oh, Anne! Can't you see Mother is distressed? We must not bother her,' Elizabeth cuts off in a low voice, clutching the older woman's sinewy fingers.

'Apple of mine eye,' Mother says. It is the first time since Father died that I have seen a shadow of a smile on her lips. 'Anne is right. This is not an excuse to fade away into obscurity. We are Woodvilles, remember that; you are of my blood. Woodvilles find a way to win, and if not win then survive. Always.'

'*Always!*' Kate mimics, extracting a trickle of laughter from Anne and myself. Still, the shroud of graveness settles over us once more.

'But they don't approve of Woodvilles,' I say. 'The nobles. They never did, did they, Lady Mother?'

'It is true there is some resentment towards my own siblings and myself. It's different with you girls, for as much as you are of my blood, you are of your father's, too, and princesses.' Her words come slowly as if she is reluctant to admit this truth.

'Well, that was what I meant to say.'

For nearly two decades, the cream of English society has been split between Mother's myriad of hungry relatives and Father's age-old nobility, who have watched offices and lands customarily granted to them pass instead to one Woodville or another. Furthermore, the Woodvilles have snatched up numerous eligible heirs and heiresses for husbands and wives. It is only natural and quite expected that a king should lavish good graces upon his kindred by marriage, but these particular kinsmen and kinswomen are so many and have received so much. I prefer not to think about my maternal grandfather's humble origins, but it does doubtlessly play its part in the sore relationship between the two unofficial factions. Foremost among the old nobility is Uncle Richard, who is now to be Lord Protector—who else? He has firm beliefs as to how the government ought to operate, and is keener than any man to see his brother's dying wish fulfilled, yet Mother is wretched over the fact.

I pray I will not be forced to choose between my maternal and my paternal side of the family. There is nothing I should loathe more than to let Mother down, except to forsake the murrey and blue of York.

On the sixteenth day of April, we attend mass at Westminster Abbey for the late King's soul. Afterwards, the coffin—topped with a life-sized effigy that, to my disappointment, is a poor likeness—is hauled onto a carriage draped in black and brought towards Charing Cross, across the River Thames, to Saint George's Chapel. The chapel was Father's beloved building project, and there it stands, half-finished in all its Gothic glory. As we proceed inside, my clothes and hair are heavy with lukewarm rain, the kind that comes in invisibly small drops but nonetheless soaks one in a minute. At least my damp cheeks make it impossible to tell whether I shed tears, and I thank the Almighty, because my emotions have never been prone to follow my command. Just as I dive head-first into grief or anger or joy, just as easily do I lose myself in my inner fantasies and pay little heed to the world around me. Perhaps that is a less convenient trait that I have in common with Dickie.

The ceremony is the epitome of grandeur. I did not really notice the beauty of the glazed windows before, nor the carved stalls. The walls and floor are covered in black cloth, creating the illusion of standing in a gigantic swathe of quiescent shadow, illuminated only by quivering candlelight.

I raise my eyes to see Hastings and Dorset looking like a dog and a cat forced to behave together where they stand in the chapel. Next to them are a contingent of other great lords and nobles, such as the fickle Lord Stanley, and John Howard, whose comical moustache comes close to making me smile even now.

The lengthy last rites continue well into morning the following day. Through all the pomp and ceremony, the trembling tension in the air is so thick I could cut it with a knife and serve it on a platter.

We remain at the Palace of Westminster for almost another two weeks without word from Ed. The outward changes are few. People treasure stability; that is what they want and what they hope the new King, now styled Edward V, will bring them. Yet no one likes a regency, and plenty of irked whispers reach my ears. No one likes a regency, except the handful of relatives who hope to wield greater influence with a boy-king than with a more seasoned ruler.

I miss Father's roaring laughter and his strong arms. I miss his boasting about battles fought over a decade ago and the way he could suddenly have a fit of generosity and shower us girls with dresses made from the finest velvets and cloth of gold. I confess, however, that I no longer mourn *him* so much as I mourn the sense of security he imposed. True, he could change his mind easier than a weed bends in the wind, but one thing that never changed was his ambition to create a powerful dynasty. Who knows what my brother's minority government will decide regarding my future and my marriage? I still struggle to grasp the changes: I hate change and always have. Uncle Richard once suggested it might be a remnant from the turbulent years before and just after my birth—the betrayals of Warwick and Clarence and Father's struggle to retake the throne from Henry of Lancaster—just like Uncle Richard's own fear of turbulence.

Towards the end of April, I discover Mother standing with her oldest daughter in the gilded bedchamber of the queen's apartments. She is clasping Elizabeth's hands, looking as pale and pinched as when Father died. In that moment, they resemble two versions of the same woman: one young and blossoming, one aging though still a handsome figure, both exuding rigid elegance. The sole difference I can distinguish, apart from the years, is the resolute, ruthless glimmer in my mother's eyes, something Elizabeth's more demure character does not leave enough room for.

'What is it, Lady Mother?' I inquire, unable to hide the sparking curiosity in my voice.

Mother does not let go of Elizabeth's hands, nor does she turn her glance to me. When she speaks, the words come slowly, carefully, as if she is afraid of them. 'Your Uncle Anthony has been arrested on his way to London, my sweet. My son Richard, too. Ed has been taken care of.'

A thousand worms crawl under my skin; cold rat's feet skitter up my spine. *Impossible.* The King gives orders of arrest, and Ed would never give these orders. And if not Ed, then it must be a conspiracy of nobles, acting on pretend-authority, their hearts set on demolishing my mother's family. Unless, of course, Anthony Earl Rivers and Richard Grey are indeed guilty of some foul crime.

'On what charges?'

'On the charge of ruining your late father's health by encouraging his vices, and for plotting to kill the Duke of Gloucester, for plotting against the very government.'

'*Uncle Richard?*' My breath tangles in my throat. 'Is he unscathed?'

Finally, Mother averts her undivided attention from Elizabeth's lily-white hands and looks at me. 'He is the one who gave the orders of arrest. Buckingham is with him.'

My thoughts are spinning fervently to catch up with everything she tells me. 'But then...then it must be well, surely? The charges must have been a misunderstanding. Uncle Richard has ever been loyal to us, and a champion of justice.'

'He was ever loyal to his *brother.*'

'You cannot rely on one wolf to protect you from a pack,' Elizabeth says, her voice like a crystalline mountain brook.

Once upon a time, when we were younger, there was affection in that same voice when she spoke of that same man. Then, as the years wore on, Mother's influence begun to infiltrate every fibre of her beloved eldest daughter, and these days, I fear their views lack distinction more often than not.

The violent turmoil in my chest and the familiar heat in my eyes and nose erupt even before I open my mouth. 'Don't say things like that! Maybe you just say it because he likes *me* best, and you cannot bear the thought of anyone being my ally!'

Elizabeth gives me one of her long glances and smooths the non-existent creases on her pearl-stitched gown. 'Oh, Cecily, you're being ridiculous.'

Mother comes to her aid. 'Control your temper! Your sister is right. And, prithee, be careful when you speak of allies. We can trust the Woodvilles alone.'

'Well, *why?* Surely, we are as much royal as we are Woodvilles, no less so than Ed?'

'You do not understand. Mayhap you are too young yet,' Elizabeth says. 'Father's side of the family are greedy nobles...Nevilles, Gloucester, Hastings, all the rest. There will be factions in Ed's government just as there have been at court, and we can only belong to one: the Woodvilles.'

'The families you speak of are ancient, and deserving of more respect. You think you know everything—'

Mother's nails dig into my arm. 'Quiet, my sweet. You know what Clarence did to my father and my brother John. I *will not* risk putting my family in harm's way because of a son of York— not again.'

I swallow hard. I have crossed the line, the line that I so rarely spot until it is too late. 'Forgive me, Lady Mother...you will know what is best.' There is naught to gain by pointing out that if opposites exist in people, Uncle Richard is Clarence's.

'I do. And you will be safe with me, all of you, whatever the future holds.' She lets go of my arm and I resist the temptation to rub it. Cupping my face in her strong hands, she places a kiss on the tip of my nose. 'Be a good girl and leave us now. I need to speak with Beth.'

This time, I obey. Not until I have departed do I realise I forgot to ask whether there was indeed a plot and one she knew of.

Rivers and Grey are under lock and key in the north, in Uncle Richard's domain. Neither I nor my sisters are permitted at the meetings of the royal council, hence I know only what Mother tells us and what I interpret from the courtiers' chit chat.

While Anne sits in the window seat, immersed in her romantic manuscripts, and Kate plays rather roughly with her new doll in the nursery, I spend the afternoon flitting around in the palace between fur-clad ladies and their boisterous husbands. At first, I approach them directly, trying to steer the conversation towards politics. There is a tinge of reluctance in their faces, though, their words too delicately chosen to reveal much. I quickly grow

19

impatient and lose my tact, which hardly improves my chances, and retreat to listen from my place in the corner of the presence chamber, occasionally taking a sip of the wine in my jewel-studded cup.

John Howard is speaking to Henry Percy, Earl of Northumberland. They are standing close together, both in robes of dark velvet, eyes shifting from one side of the room to the other in an attempt to keep their peers under surveillance.

Howard scratches his curved moustache. 'I reckon my lord of Gloucester will be named protector when Parliament convenes. It must be so.'

'Ye-es. But protector in what sense? As a formal office only, or with all the authority due to a regent?' Northumberland says, licking a wine drop from his chapped lips. 'There are degrees as to how much one may exercise control over a boy-king.'

'Indeed. Let's hope Parliament understands that Gloucester is the only reasonable choice regardless. His late brother's choice.'

Margaret Beaufort—an overbearing, older woman with enviable cheekbones and equally enviable grit—has surrounded herself with a small cluster of heavily veiled ladies.

'Will you petition King Edward?' one of them asks in hushed tones.

Beaufort nods. 'I shall. Though he be a Yorkist, such an impressionable young mind ought to listen. My son's lands will be restored to him, finally.'

I shut my ears at that. All these people in whose presence I have come of age, all these people talking about who will and who will not influence their new monarch... Do they know the boy they are discussing? Because I do. My brother may be a couple of years short of his majority, but he has a mind of his own, and a sensible one at that. Must he be someone's puppet on the throne? If he must be, I still think the Duke of Gloucester—in partnership, of course, with Mother—will be the preferable choice. Woodvilles, Nevilles, other nobles... How are we to navigate?

Mother acts that same night. We are, she declares, to seek refuge in Westminster Abbey.

'Mama! Mama! *Why?*' Kate insists, pulling at the Dowager Queen's skirts with her plump hands.

'Because no one dares violate sanctuary. We will be safe there.'

I bite my tongue. I want to ask what exactly we will be safe from. The infighting must be worse than I first thought, wounds inflicted during more than two decades festering. Mother has her heart set on steering the government further to accommodate the Woodvilles, just as Uncle Richard and other nobles are striving to turn back the clock to England as it was before her family made their entrance. If only we stayed, and if Mother calmed the silent panic sprung from her ambitions being threatened, the panic that must be boiling underneath her cool surface... But no, she has already decided that this must be an open feud. Has she learnt nothing from the years of civil war? Yet she is my Lady Mother and it is her I must trust above all others, despite my doubts, since she will do what she deems best for us, her children.

Eight people leave the palace under darkness' cloak that night: Mother, Elizabeth, Dickie, Anne, Kate, Bridget, my half-brother Dorset, and myself. It feels rather silly that a grown man like Dorset should flee into sanctuary when no one has tried to so much as slap his fingers, but then I suppose it wrecks his nerves that his old adversary Hastings has allied himself with Uncle Richard, who has possession of the King's person. Lord knows that if anyone of us have anything to fear from Hastings, it is Dorset.

A humble barge carries us to where we may more easily walk the stone's throw to Westminster Abbey; our most prized belongings and furniture follow on carts accompanied by a handful of loyal guards. The Thames ripples as the boat cuts through the blank surface of the river, the reflection of the lanterns' warm light creating a patchwork of amber and yellow. I watch the colours and the shadows mingle, mesmerized, resisting the temptation to stretch out a hand and dip my fingers in them.

'I wish it wasn't so dark,' Anne says, shifting her weight next to me. 'I hate the dark.'

'I *know*.'

'I hope it shan't be like this in the abbey.'

'Well, you know what the abbey looks like. You don't have to be scared. Picture it in daytime.'

She bites her lip. 'I have tried that before but it never worked.'

21

Once we have dismounted the barge and arrived by the gates of our new home, Mother instructs the men in charge of our belongings to await her call while the rest of us continue inside.

There is the sound of seven pairs of shoes against the stone floor—Mother is carrying Bridget, having wrapped her in a cloak like a bundle of silk—as we scuttle past the colonnade of the south aisle, turn right, and continue down the vaulted north cloister. The windows are shuttered against the night chill but I am shivering nonetheless. I clutch Dickie's hand in mine so hard that I have to remind myself not to squash it. An expectant smile is playing on his lips and his glance flits from me to the ceiling to the ornaments on the wall.

'Exciting, is it not?' I press forth, stroking the back of his hand as we near the far end of the cloister.

Dickie bobs his head up and down, his locks a bouncing halo in the gloom of the abbey. 'Yes! Like an adventure.'

'Exactly.'

'Will Ed come and play, too, Cece?'

I quicken the pace and pull him with me so as to not fall behind the others. 'I do not think so, but it's not for long. We can see him again soon, I promise.'

'Even when he's crowned? He won't be too busy?' The sudden, keen anxiety in his voice makes my heart shrink.

'Not at all! No one could be too busy for you, Dickie.'

We have reached the deanery, where Abbot John Esteney resides. Mother gives Kate's hand to Dorset and shifts Bridget to her other hip, then pounds her fist against the door.

A moment of agony passes. The abbot has already agreed to shelter us, but if he has had a change of heart and we are locked out, we can hardly make an elegant return to the Palace of Westminster. Just imagining what Uncle Richard and the rest of the high-ranking nobles would think makes me squirm.

I have begun to despair when a brittle voice calls from within: 'Who goes yonder?'

'The Dowager Queen of England with her children, seeking your blessed aid, Father.'

A set of locks and chains rattle and the door is pushed open. An elderly man with oddly childlike, large eyes and a beard like swan's down greets us, surveying us. In his one hand he holds a cresset, shedding warm light on our strained faces.

'Come, come, Your Grace.' The abbot steps aside and we enter the college hall. The room is large and rectangular, hung with tapestries depicting biblical scenes. In the centre burns a fire in the circular hearth, the sheen from the flames penetrating corners otherwise hosting bottomless darkness. The room usually serves as the abbot's dining hall, but he has had the long tables hastily shoved to the sides to make space for our furniture. The men we brought have to knock a hole in the wall of the abbey, for the entrance is too small for Mother's clothing coffers, but they proceed to have the brilliant idea of turning the coffers over on the side to that they do not have to damage the walls of the college hall as well.

The lootings litter the floor, the men in a frenzy to push everything into place and fit as many valuables as possible inside. Mother has even ordered them to bring the vermilion wall hangings of her bedchamber, though that is far from what takes the prize. As it turns out, we have more money with us than I have ever seen before.

'You brought the royal treasury?' I ask Dorset, who controls said treasury as Constable of the Tower.

He shrugs. 'I gave some to Mother's brother Edward, and brought the rest for Mother and me.'

'But…but you had no right to dispose of it as you please, surely?'

'Too late.'

As the soldiers carry the last chest inside, the lid cracks open and I catch a glimpse of the Great Seal. The Dowager Queen has as little right to control the seal as she does the treasury. God keep us all from what might befall us, not to speak of England, for Mother's defiance of Father's dying wish.

Chapter III

THE FOLLOWING WEEK is an eternity to me. Living on charitable merchants' gifts of food and drink as well as the abbot's kindness, we do our best to adjust to our new living quarters in the college hall. Admittedly, some try more than others, but I cannot for the life of me think of it as *home*. It is absurd: here we are, *princesses*, huddled up in a secluded corner of the abbey where we have attended lavish ceremonies all our lives. What bothers me most is not the lack of fine dining or the dullness of having no chattering courtiers to listen to, not even the humiliation, no, what bothers me most is that every sweet breath of fresh air has been snatched from my lungs. How am I to live when I cannot feel the May sunshine bathing my skin? How am I to endure this peculiar situation when I am not allowed to stride over dew-drenched lawns and across wide-stretching courtyards?

Before, I would wander every castle we visited throughout the year—Westminster, Windsor, Eltham, Marguerite d'Anjou's Palace of Placentia—basking in the rich views and colours, the dulcet fumes of honeyed cakes from the kitchens and the fragrance from the gardens. My legs are accustomed to carrying me wherever I wish to go, at least when court courtesy and my curriculum do not require my presence, and now I am confined to the abbot's stale dining hall, restlessly pacing back and forth. The boredom is like a rash I cannot reach to scratch. I am not even allowed to dance the *saltarello*; it would be improper, Elizabeth says, an offence to the sombreness befitting God's house.

My one solace is Dickie, with whom I act out imagined tales of knights and damsels, dragons and beasts, often inspired by the

24

manuscripts Anne insisted on bringing to the abbey. I have not played thus since I was younger than he is now. A girl of fourteen ought never behave so childishly, yet this is different than when at court, because here, no eyes are upon me save for those of my closest kin.

However, our studies occupy much of the time, for the circumstances are apparently not outlandish enough to neglect practicing French and spelling. While Dorset sulks over the lack of 'sultry women and merriments', Mother acts tutor to Elizabeth, Anne, myself, and even Kate, who keeps bouncing in her seat and doodling in the margins.

'Kate, darling, please!' Mother exclaims.

'But *Mama*—'

'Just think, if you marry a French duke someday, then you would want to converse with him, would you not?' I say in an effort to help. Actually, Kate was intended for the son of Isabel de Castilla and Ferdinand de Aragón, although none of that matters to my little sister, who dips her feather pen in ink once more and starts to draw a cat with whiskers stretching across the paper.

We abandon our studies for the time being. I consider asking Dickie to play a clapping game with me, but he is preoccupied with watching Dorset polish a favourite gilded dagger. Dorset emits a sullen reply every time his royal half-brother inquirers about how to best use the weapon, still, Dickie is content, resting his chin in his cupped hands. I return to my mother, sitting by the table. Her mouth is contorted in a strange expression, a smile too taunt to leave any trace in her eyes or glow like only her smiles can. All of sudden, the lines in her face are deeper than before, mercilessly carved with a dagger rusty rather than gilded.

'Lady Mother?'

Her hand shoots up to her cheek, brushing the first tear that I can remember seeing her cry all my life.

I swallow, trying to remove the feeling of caked mud in my throat. 'Are you...is it Father?'

'Never take anything or anyone for granted, my sweet. I daresay I shan't make that mistake again.'

'But surely we should take *some* things for granted? The things that are rightfully ours by blood?'

25

'Not even that, which is all the more reason to fight for them.'

'I wanted to speak to you about another matter, Lady Mother.' I gaze at her through a shield of eyelashes before lowering my eyes like I have learned to do whenever there is something I want. 'I pray you send for my woman, Agnes, so that I may have a companion in these dire times.'

Mother squeezes my hand. 'You know it cannot be.'

'It can if you will it.' I hold my breath. Have I crossed the line again?

Fortunately, though, she licks her delicately sculpted lips, a sign of relenting. 'Very well. Agnes and one or two maids to tend to the rest of us. But she will conduct herself according to my wishes, is that understood? I'll have no talk of her wanton aunt.'

'Of course not, Lady Mother.' I turn on my heel before she can change her mind, my face cracking a grin she cannot see.

Mother need not worry. Agnes rarely so much as mentions Jane Shore, my late father's infamous mistress, who is rumoured to have shared a bed with both Dorset and Hastings as well. 'That woman' has been a forbidden topic to all of us for years, and still is. One small comfort is that Father did not have any children by her, as he did with other wenches. He never confessed to having sired all of the suspected offspring, but several girls and boys were brought up at court. Mother was diligent in keeping them separate from me and my siblings, ensuring that we did not play or converse together. There is no word of what has befallen that scatter of half-brothers and half-sisters, and, frankly, I am too concerned with our own situation to give it any considerable thought.

The wounds inflicted by Father's death are still fresh on all of us. While Kate and Bridget are too small to fully understand that he is gone forever, and while Dickie and I manage to distract ourselves from the grief with games and fairy tales, there are three members of our family who are not as fortunate. Mother, Elizabeth, and Anne are not prone to open lamenting, though they cannot be said to be of the same disposition. Nevertheless, there is no mistaking the irreversible impact that our loss has had on them. It shows in the smallest details, like the way Mother mends Father's shirts one evening, or the way my sisters sleep more than when they were infants. It is a pity we did not think to bring enough mourning garb to sustain us very long—presumably, the royal treasury was first priority.

The day after Agnes and the two maids arrive in the sanctuary, the fourth morning of May, there is upheaval on the streets outside. The noise trickles through slits and keyholes in the firmly shut doors, and the shouts are unmistakable: 'Give way for His Grace King Edward!'

'Papa?' Bridget asks where she sits on one of the maids' lap, a spark of recognition lighting in her grave, abysmal eyes.

'Not he. The new King Edward, your most revered brother,' the maid says.

The clamour escalates, and now the heralds extend their proclamations: 'The King has been preserved from the malicious plot hatched by the Earl Rivers and those his kinsmen who relate by blood to the former Queen, Elizabeth Woodville! The culprits have been disarmed and dealt with in the most deserving manner through the grace of His Lordship the Duke of Gloucester! God save King Edward!'

Mother looks as if someone smeared grey ash on her face. She still has not told us how much truth there is in the accusation.

Elizabeth, as rosy-cheeked as ever, takes her hand. 'Don't listen to them. They are fools if they believe such slander.'

'Agnes!' I grab my companion's thick wrist. 'Go to the nave, see if you can peer through a window or the hole in the wall! She can, Lady Mother, can't she? No one would recognise her.'

'Do it.'

A short while later, Agnes knocks on the door to the college hall again and slips inside as soon as Dorset creaks it open for her. Is she blushing from how his hand brushes against hers with indiscreet intent, or merely from running?

Mother stands up, the ash washed away. 'Did you see my son? Tell me, woman, did you see him?'

'You should 'ave seen the monks, Madam, when I passed through the North cloister! Eyes round as cups!'

'*Did you see my son?*'

Agnes crosses her arms over her chest, pushing her bosom up. 'I did, Madam. Lookin' fine and dandy to me. They passed right by, the three of 'em, all dressed up, the soldiers in murrey and with the boar badge. Buckingham, Gloucester, and His Grace on a horse between them.'

Relieved glances flash back and forth between the lot of us, including the old abbot, who has joined us in our commotion.

'Anything else?' Mother says.

'Hmm, yes, four cartloads of Woodville weapons. Confiscated from the plotters, I'll wager.'

I fear Mother will lash out at her for daring to presume the allegations true, but mayhap she knows as well as I do that Agnes' brazen tongue and inclination towards juicy gossip has nothing to do with any ill intent, because Elizabeth Woodville remains calm as a glacier. Calm enough to tempt me into asking what I have been yearning to find out since we left Westminster.

'Is it true, then? Was there a plot?'

'There was not!' she snaps at last. 'Anthony and I agreed he should collect any weapons required to muster more men if the need arose to...protect our influence. That was all.

'Some would say that was quite a bit, Lady Mother.'

Anne plays with the silver crucifix resting at the base of her throat. 'Does this mean we can leave sanctuary? It's so dark here sometimes.'

'Once Ed is crowned King, we may. You shall have to manage the dark a little longer, dear. As long as Gloucester and Buckingham and their power-hungry sycophants have possession of my boy, our position is no less precarious than before,' Mother says.

Dorset scoffs, tearing his eyes from Agnes' ample cleavage. 'Hastings, too, the villain.'

Dickie pokes my stomach, where I am the most ticklish. 'Cece, you promised he could play with me! Why can't I see him?'

'Because...because Mother says so.'

My reply far from satisfies him, yet I am rather pleased with being able to tell the truth without offending the woman who has gone to such great lengths to protect me and my siblings, while at the same time slipping in a subtle note of blame where I believe it belongs.

A week later, we receive word through a messenger boy that the royal council has discussed the issue of the King's minority

28

government. Like I suspected they would when Father was on his deathbed, all the nobles hankered after the role of Lord Protector—although few have a realistic chance of attaining the title. Uncle Richard officially claimed it as the council convened. I knew he would, we all did, because virtually no one is equal to him in wealth, vast landholdings, or experience in ruling those lands, not even men twice his age. Father's endorsement of him only elevated his claim, and the council agreed despite the envy brewing hot in several of its members.

Agnes still brushes out and braids my hair in the evenings; she performs the service for Anne and Elizabeth too, while the maids take care of the little ones and Mother insists on managing her own beauty routine, keeping her secrets to herself. Despite our baggage from Westminster, we only brought one mirror, a gift from a benefactor like so many of the trifles here, and I always wait until the others have gone to bed so that I might use it for as long as I please.

'I think I'm a pain in your Mother's bottom,' Agnes mutters one night.

I steady my head against the thorough brushstrokes pulling at my hair. 'She just does not want to think about, well, about *that woman*.'

'Hmm. I'm nothing like her, though, love.'

'I wish I could ease her mind. I wish I could make her see that she has nothing to fear now. My brother is safe and as befits his status—you said so yourself.'

'Like a stuffed duckling on a golden platter.'

'What?'

'Just an ol' saying, love. Give me a pin, will you?'

I reach for the silver hairpins scattered on the small table where the mirror leans against a ceramic vase. The candle has burnt down to the wick, the flame a single firefly in the gloom, the last drops of scorching wax landing on the back of my hand. I bite my lip to prevent a cry that might wake the others.

'Anyhow. He lodges in the Tower, a date has been agreed upon for his coronation, and Uncle Richard made everyone swear allegiance to him, or so the messenger boy said. Everything is precisely as it should be.'

29

'Maybe it's her nerves, then. Lord knows they're made of steel but this place could make anyone witless.'

'Agnes!'

'Pardon.' She grins.

I shrug. 'Mayhap you are right. I am certain being here reminds her of the last time, and then there really *was* something to fear.'

'You remember anything?'

'No. No, I was so little then, barely Bridget's age. But my mother survived that and she *will* survive this and see I was right all along.'

Agnes smacks a kiss on my temple and gives the thick braid a demonstrative tug. 'There. Goodnight.' She takes the taper in one hand and her skirts in the other to avoid tripping on the hem.

I frown. 'Where are you going?'

'None of your business.'

'*Yes*, it is.'

'I said goodnight, love.'

She slips out through the door, leaving me to curl up on my bed. The mattress is too hard; the blanket too coarse against my skin, my chemise providing only a flimsy sheath of comfort. The beds are gifts from the abbot, since our own were too unwieldy to bring.

Perchance Agnes has made one of the monks in the cloister complex her lover. I press my hand to my mouth, stifling a giggle.

My thoughts stray again to Mother. It cannot be easy to be of good cheer in a place one associates with rebellion, usurpation, and death. Elizabeth likely does remember the last time we were here, yet I would never dream of asking her. Much like Mistress Jane Shore, the events of 1470 and 1471 are subjects best kept behind firmly locked lips.

'Sir Thomas will see to it that your daily needs are met,' the abbot says, his babyish eyes twinkling. 'I fear I have grown too old and stiff to go hither and thither, and the lad has served me well.'

Mother nods. 'We thank you, Father, for all that you have done for us.'

Our new servant is a peculiar sight. The back of his nose is slightly curved, as if broken and never healed properly, and he stands wiggling up and down on his heels and toes. A little older than Elizabeth, I would say.

'Your Grace. Your Royal Highnesses,' he mumbles, tucking a coil the colour of ink behind his ear. The greeting is all we can expect, but he stands erect, and the abbot has to nudge him to provoke an awkward bow. Even I, with my fits of emotion, know better manners than that.

'We shall leave you, ladies, and pray send for the young man if there is anything you desire.' The abbot makes a clicking sound with his tongue, then departs with the servant at his heels like one of Father's greyhounds.

On his way out, Sir Thomas casts a glance over his shoulder. I look at Elizabeth, expecting to see her refuse meeting said glance, before realising it is not for her, not at all. It is for me. My cheeks heat. I could discern nothing amorous in it, indeed I hope there was not, yet I am conscious of my pulse quickening. He is lowly born and somewhat odd—but he chose to look at *me*.

We must have been in sanctuary for more than a month—I am beginning to lose track of the days—when Uncle Richard's wife, Anne Neville, arrives in London. The Kingmaker's daughter, Dowager Princess of Wales, Duchess of Gloucester. Such grand titles; were I not a princess myself, I would envy her.

Truthfully, I do. I always have, although it has very little to do with her history of titles. I recall a quaint, fragile beauty lodged in her heart-shaped face despite the prominent nose, a quiet intensity in her eyes that only her husband can compete with. A reserved spirit, stubborn, yet loving in nature. If I could pluck one of Anne Neville's qualities and make it my own, it would be her courage. At the Battle of Tewkesbury, where Father defeated the Lancastrian rebels once and for all, she chose to stay at the battlefield and face Father's enraged men rather than join her mother in sanctuary. While I cower in the college hall with my family like a caged rabbit, Anne Neville has lived a far more eventful life and never fled danger. The Duchess of Gloucester has endured not only a forced marriage to the venomous Lancastrian prince, a marriage that placed her at Tewkesbury to begin with, but also Clarence's wrath, and emerged from these

31

perils victorious. The more I think of it, the more I extend my envy to admiration.

'She rides through the streets like a *queen*, does she not?' Mother asks Agnes. 'She must think herself so noble, so… She should not be allowed to breathe the air in the Palace of Westminster!'

Agnes shrugs. 'In earnest, I didn't see her, Madam. Just her retinue—very fancy.'

'And she brings the bastards with her, does she? Gloucester's offspring. And only one of her own! What kind of woman begets a single son and then turns her attentions to caring for two *mistakes* from her husband's youth?'

To my own horror, I let the words pour out, failing once more to suppress my initial reaction. 'Not everyone has the Woodville hips for childbearing, Lady Mother. Perhaps it was brave to care for babes whom others might have feared to be rivals.'

'My sweet, you do not know what you speak of.' She strokes my cheek, her composure cooling. 'If you could remember her and her sister's betrayals of your father, you would understand.'

'Warwick's betrayal. He forced his daughters to obey and marry the men that fitted his interests, surely?'

Mother only sighs. To her, when one errs, all are to blame.

Elizabeth looks at me as if I was a stray dog lying coated in filth and scab by the roadside. With *pity*. 'I only wish you would cease making excuses for our enemies.' Her voice is barely audible.

Her—and my own—rescue appears blissfully unaware of the tension as he sticks his head into the room. Sir Thomas balances a refilled flagon of bitter wine and a dish of cheese, bread, and gleaming black olives. He is humming a tune I have never heard before, probably some indecent song that commoners sing when visiting a tavern, his unruly hair shielding his eyes.

'Here we are—' He trips over Kate's doll on the floor and regains his balance just in time to keep the flagon from falling. 'Dear me!'

The fire burning in my stomach is instantaneously extinguished, a smile tickling my lips instead. What a clumsy youth! Worse than me, which is a nice change from how things usually are.

32

Sir Thomas takes the last steps with utmost care, his jaw visibly clenched, then slides the dish and the flagon onto the safety of the table. He looks at us a little too long and a little to boldly, from the pigeon-chested Dorset and the ever-sombre Bridget to Anne with a vividly illustrated manuscript under her arm—and, at last, at me. He pushes back the hair from his face, and for the first time I notice his eyes: like moss and earth shovelled together.

Thomas clears his throat. 'Olives? Cheese?'

'Grammercy. We can see to it ourselves,' Mother says, her hands clasped. There is a note of forced patience in her voice, a note I am well acquainted with.

'Right. I'll leave you, Your Grace.'

'Prithee, do that.'

I daresay we would have a merrier supper if he were to stay, but naturally, such a thing is out of the question. I can afford to feel less alone in my flaws; I can even afford to grant him a capricious smile. I cannot afford to speak to a boy who I deem to be the son of an esquire or a merchant, if the 'Sir' is a mere courtesy, much less entertain the incredulous thought of being *friendly*. Princesses are not friendly to subjects, and I am still a princess of York in every respect, regardless of the fears Mother harbours regarding our future.

Chapter IV

J ANE SHORE IS a woman of unmatched, incandescent wit
and a renowned lack of scruples. She fades next to Mother
in terms of appearance, despite the years being to her
advantage, but *something* in her kindled Father's desire and
kept it burning longer any other mistress could. I resent her,
and I resent myself for forgetting it as soon as I do not see her
for more than a day or two. When she demands to see us in
sanctuary, I plead with Mother to comply.

'I have a message for you. From Lord Hastings,' she says and
sticks out a hand, waving the neatly folded piece of paper under
her former rival's nose.

Mother eyes her and slowly takes the letter, cracking the
crimson seal. We all—including the old abbot and Sir Thomas,
who were discussing practicalities with us when Mistress Shore
knocked on the door—watch as the dowager queen scans the
lines of ink.

Dickie tries to peer over her shoulder. 'What does it say, Lady
Mother?'

She strokes his arm. 'Lord Hastings wishes to reconcile. He
has realised that he was wrong to rally to Gloucester's side, and
says that he will help us bring about your brother's coronation.
There are others who are also willing to aid us in removing
Gloucester in return for the Woodvilles' favour. Bishop Morton,
for one, and old chancellor Rotherham, and Thomas Stanley.'

Her tone rather than her words tell me that she means
'removing Gloucester from the face of the earth'. The Woodvilles
would not feel secure in their positions unless their main
opponent had resigned his soul to God.

I cannot help myself, but at least I manage to sound composed. 'Why would we need Hastings, or any of those men? Uncle Richard will have him crowned soon enough, won't he? Must you dispute him so, Lady Mother?'

'Indeed, why do we need Hastings?' Dorset folds his arms over his chest, his glance flickering back and forth between Mistress Shore and Agnes like a skittish moth. 'That scoundrel has never been a friend of ours before. Not to me, at least. God's truth, we need neither Hastings nor Gloucester. We are important enough to make and enforce these decisions without their help.'

Jane Shore clears her throat with an impish look in her eye. 'As it happens, I know Will's mind. He believes Gloucester will try to postpone the coronation ceremony.'

'I know *that* much,' Mother says. 'He will wield power as protector for as long as he can, to keep my kindred from the government.'

'Then perchance you ought to ally with my lord Hastings. You hardly have any other alternatives, do you?'

'Unlike you. You have so *many* alternatives, don't you, Jane? Every bed you stumble across presents another one.'

'I did not risk coming here just so you can slander me.'

'No.' Mother wipes her face blank of emotion. 'I'll write a reply for your lord. You may deliver it with my gratitude.'

My eyes widen in awe as she scribbles a note, folds it over, and presses her seal to the steaming dollop of wax, her own seal, because chancellor Rotherham was made to fetch back the Great Seal from us.

Mistress Shore slips the letter in her bodice, gives Agnes and Dorset both a quick nod of recognition, and disappears as swiftly as she appeared.

Kate tilts her head. 'What did you write, Mama? What did you write?'

'That I intend to raise troops with his aid, and that I require him to swear by the sacrament not to betray us. The same stands true for Morton, Rotherham, and Stanley.'

Sir Thomas continues to assist us in our daily life. The maids are dismissed from sanctuary, as it is too crowded and we have little

35

need of them, hence he and Agnes become the entirety of our personnel.

One afternoon, in the midst of the simmering June heat, there is banging on the door, and Thomas bursts into the college hall when Dorset at last opens. His cheeks are flushed and he pants too heavily to say anything comprehensible. The alarm rings louder in my ears with every passing moment.

'Lord Hastings—' he begins.

Dorset scoffs. 'What of that rascal?'

'Dead!'

'*What?*'

'Dead. Executed. No longer among the living. Passed over to our Lord Jesus Christ—'

'Yes, yes, that's enough!'

'Why?' I manage. Cold sweat is breaking out under my chemise.

Sir Thomas stares at me as if he does not recognise me. 'On the charge of plotting to harm the Protector of the Realm, Richard of Gloucester. They say there was a council meeting, usual procedure, and the protector's men stormed the chamber and seized Hastings along with a few others. No trial, nothing except a priest to hear his last confession. Just straight to Tower Green and the axe.'

My tongue swells in my mouth, making it impossible to speak or breathe; my entrails turn over in my belly; my head is burning. Another plot? What about Uncle Richard? And then I understand: the letters.

'No…no trial?' Anne whispers.

'Only the protector's word, and the words of other councillors, I was told.'

Mother reaches for Elizabeth's hand. 'And what does London say to it?'

Thomas purses his lips, shaking his head. 'Some say aye, others nay. Some are outraged, but many believe the charges to have been genuine. Hearsay is he confessed. I can't tell for certs. Gloucester has given orders to bury the man in Windsor next to the late King Edward, and his family won't be attainted, won't suffer for his crimes.'

36

I know what the others must be thinking. If Hastings, who was one of Uncle Richard's closest friends and allies just as he was Father's, is not safe in his own council chamber, then who can truly feel secure? Certainly not magnates and royals. Not so long ago, people used to be put to death for treason against the King. Now, the arrests and executions are based on treason against the Lord Protector, and what the actual King thinks is steeped in mist.

There can be but two explanations to this reckless violence. Either Thomas is mistaken and there really *was* a proper trial and conviction based on the letters—or my uncle acted out of searing desperation. The only two things that he values above justice and the principles of the law is this: his own ambition and the stability in the country. If Hastings threatened that ambition, whatever it might consist of, or appeared to threaten the stability in England by forging an alliance with my mother... This is the result. We have all seen before what a trusted advisor and friend turned traitor can do if not dealt with at once, because Father pardoned Warwick one too many times. At least there was considerable mercy after the blow towards Hastings had indeed been dealt.

'Was that all? Hastings alone was accused of this?' Dorset scratches his nose. 'The rest of us—'

Thomas cuts him short. 'No. They say Hastings conspired with Mistress Jane Shore...and the Woodvilles. Sorry, my lord. The protector accuses your mother of trying to murder and utterly destroy him. As I said, other men were arrested, too, and put in prison. Bishop Morton, the old chancellor, Thomas Stanley.'

'This is madness! Madness! How could we have conspired any-damn-thing from *here*? Not with Anthony and my brother still under lock and key! It was just a silly letter, just a plan in its cradle. And Jane Shore! Her thighs are too big to make room for any malignant conspiracy—'

'*Thomas.*' Mother speaks the word through gritted teeth. Her oldest son seems to shrink several inches, his pigeon-chest flattened.

Kate's forehead is set in a deep frown, her rose-petal lips in a troubled pout. 'Why, Mama, why? Not nice!' She turns her back to us and buries her face in Mother's skirts.

'I do not know. Perhaps because Buckingham whispers in Gloucester's ear. And because they both fear my family would have ousted Gloucester from power together with Hastings.'

'Would you?' I ask. 'You said you wrote to Hastings about raising troops. Is that not treason? Don't you know there is naught Uncle Richard fears more than to see England plunged back into the chaos of civil war?'

I receive no answer.

The following Sunday, Jane Shore does penance at Saint Paul's Cross. I am told she walks through the streets barefoot, clad in a flimsy kirtle, convulsively clutching a taper in one hand. The punishment is one for adultery, not treason. Uncle Richard has been lenient; he did not put her on trial regarding her involvement in the Woodville plot but instead reached for the offense everyone already knows Jane to be guilty of, one with a far milder repercussion than high treason. I find it difficult to despise her now—she bore the punishment with great dignity, Thomas says—but no one utters a word of pity here in sanctuary. For once, Mother is well pleased with the Lord Protector's actions, though she might not have minded seeing Father's mistress face a grimmer end. Jane Shore could deliver a thousand messages, and Elizabeth Woodville would not look kindly upon her.

Our windows are heavily shuttered, as always, yet the shouts creep inside the room regardless. I cannot discern any words, but it sounds like a small army. There is the clatter of weapons and the trample of hundreds of pairs of boots, then the unmistakable creak of the great western door opening, robbing us of our most symbolic protection. No boots beat against the floor of the nave or the aisles, though.

I sit frozen on the bed I now share with Anne, clenching a handful of the covers until my knuckles shine white through my skin. Dickie is sitting on the other end of the bed—I was telling him the tale of Robin Hood—and for the first time since we settled in the abbey, I swear there is a shadow of panic lurking behind the mask of excited cheer.

'Don't worry. No one dares violate sanctuary. It would make God very vexed.' I am not so certain of it myself.

Three echoing bangs sound on the door. I flash Agnes a glance, but she is, to my agitation, looking at Dorset.

Mother lifts Bridget off her knee and stands up, stroking her gown with her palms to make it fall in even folds around her legs, then tips her chin skywards and takes four long strides to the door.

'Who are you, and what reason do you give for intruding in the house of God?' Her words are mere show; she possesses no real authority here.

A man's voice pierces the door. 'Thomas Bourchier, Archbishop of Canterbury, comes to speak with Lady Elizabeth Woodville, wife of the late King Edward IV.'

'You may present your query.'

'You will open the door, Madam, or I shall have it breached.'

Elizabeth has placed herself by our mother's side. 'Open. We want no brutality.'

Thus, we are faced with six men: four soldiers impeccably dressed in murrey and blue, with the badge of the White Boar staring back at us from their chests, headed by two men draped in clerical robes. One of the churchmen I do not recognise, but the other is the Archbishop. His skin is the colour of cream gone stale, his scalp bereft of a single hair. We watch him like mice watch a cat.

'The Lord Protector of the Realm, in unanimity with the royal council, hereby demands that you place Prince Richard, Duke of York, in his care. The young prince is to join his brother the King's Grace in the Tower for his own protection.'

Mother's cheeks flush yet her voice does not tremble the slightest. 'No. I will not. My children stay with me. I have not been blind to the actions taken by the protector these past two months.'

'The King wishes the company of his brother and heir. It's fitting that the young prince should play a central role in the coronation ceremony, after which he will be returned to your loving arms.' The Archbishop attempts a stiff smile.

'I said I *will not*.'

'Then, Madam, I have no choice but to allow the men who have surrounded the abbey to take the prince by force. Believe me when I say I have no desire to violate sanctuary, but such are the terms.'

A silent battle issues as the former queen and the churchman look one another in the eye long and hard.

At last, Mother buckles. 'Very well. No harm shall come to my daughters because of your soldiers' reckless conduct. And you will return my son to me the very minute the coronation has come to pass.'

'Indeed I will. I knew you would see reason, Madam.'

The cat has selected a mouse. Unbeknownst to the Archbishop, it is me rather than Dickie, because while he glows at the prospect of being reunited with the brother he adores, I can feel claws tearing my heart apart. If my angel is taken from me… Yet I must not let despair overwhelm me. If I am right, the coronation is a week away at most. In a week's time, then, Dickie will be returned to *my* loving arms, or all of us will have re-entered London to take our rightful place at the glorious court of Edward V. A coronation… What a splendid thing! I have never attended one before, and I will not now either, unless—

'Can I come?' I leap to my feet. 'Can I join my brothers?'

The Archbishop arcs his sprawling, white eyebrows. 'Why, ye-es, I presume you may. The Duke of Gloucester will undoubtedly accommodate the princess in great comfort.'

For a fracture of a moment, I dare hope. I can be with Dickie and confirm that Edward is well and I can attend the coronation! And I will finally escape from this drab hideaway.

'You stay here, my sweet. Gloucester has not commanded your presence, and I'll be damned if I give up more than I must under his threats.'

'But I want to go—'

It is futile. I should have known. I wrap my arms around Dickie as tight as I can without hurting him. He raises himself on his toes to place a smacking kiss on my cheek—it seems he grows taller every day—and then takes a hasty farewell of the others, even embracing Agnes.

The Archbishop puts a firm hand to the prince's back like a shepherd guiding a sheep, and the small entourage leaves us. Just before the door slams shut, Dickie turns and calls out to me.

'See you soon, Cece!'

For once, I manage to force my hot tears to sink back into my eyes instead of spilling over. He is right; I can have a thousand of those kisses and a million of those buoyant smiles if I just wait a while. After all, we have our whole lives ahead of us.

Something Mother *does* allow me to do is venture outside the college hall to pray for our safety in the age-old Chapel of the Pyx. At least that is my alibi—it makes me wonder how well she really knows me when she does not question it. However, the abbot must accompany me there and back again, in the event that all the soldiers have not yet dispersed, or that the guards now permanently placed around Westminster Abbey grow rash and unruly.

The chapel is situated in the eastern corner of the abbey, across from the cloisters. When the abbot, showing strength I had not expected in such a corpulent little man, opens the robust oak doors, I am enveloped in a gust of pungent air. It is a small room, smaller than the college hall, yet it gives the impression of a vast crypt. Thick columns curve to vaults melting into the low ceiling; dark brown tiles cover the floor; two lone candles animate the plain altar where a silver cross stands erect.

'Thank you, Father,' I say in my most reassuring tone. 'I can manage from here. I would like to pray in solitude.'

The abbot, who, not by any fault of his, knows me even worse than Mother, nods. 'Naturally, Your Royal Highness. I'll wait for you in the deanery.' He backs out of the room with his swan-down hair fluttering in the breeze from the cloisters, leaving the doors half- open. I am glad. I might not share Anne's fear of darkness and enclosed spaces, but I doubt I could push those doors open on my own.

Naturally, I do not pray. Not properly, at least. I know I should, I *really* should, for I have been negligent in my piety lately, but the moment is too precious to waste. I remove my slippers, placing them by the foot of by the altar, hitch up my skirts in one hand and send God a cautionary apology for exposing my ankles in this holiest of places.

I have to imagine the jolly tune in my head. The floor tiles are smooth and cool against my bare feet as I trip between the columns and make skipping steps before the cross. In one of my twists and turns, the sable fur lining on my sleeve is a finger's width away from catching fire from the candles. I squeeze my eyes shut until white spots flicker against the black of my eyelids. *Everything is the way it used to be. Father is healthy as a horse. The court is sparkling. No one is feuding. And I'm the golden yolk of it all—*

'By Saint Edward's toes, what *are* you doing?'

I falter in my step, stumbling, my head colliding with the wall with a *thump*. Pain shoots out from my forehead to my temples and neck. My eyes still closed, I reach up to feel for blood, but my fingers find nothing except a sore spot.

Slowly, slowly I squint at the young man by the oak doors. He stands wiggling on his feet, watching me through dark coils of hair.

'That's "Your Royal Highness" to you.' My face is burning, and it is not from the *saltarello*.

'Sorry. What are you doing, Lady?'

'Nothing for you to be concerned with.'

'But your head—'

'I said it is nothing.'

Thomas pulls at the hem of his doublet—a plain though well-tailored garment made from dark grey brocade—as if trying to correct some error I cannot see. Silence hangs dense in the air, worse than any ruckus.

'So,' I say at last, 'what was it you wanted?'

'Your sister sent me to tell you to come.'

'Which one, Sir?'

'The old one, with teeth like a hare. Lady Beth is her name, is it not?'

Laughter bubbles up and spills over my lips despite the throbbing ache in my head and the embarrassment still fresh in memory. I have never noticed any hare's teeth in Elizabeth, on the contrary, but the image is marvellous.

Thomas mirrors my smile. 'I'm only jesting, but it worked. I have not seen you smile at all since the prince, the little one, left for the Tower.'

The laughter dies down inside me at the thought of Dickie. I must keep in mind we will be reunited within days. 'Mayhap I have not, but I shall smile a whole lot soon. I know it.'

'Will you return to court then, Lady? Once the King is crowned? I'll miss you—and the others. Brings a bit of life to this old place,' Thomas says, finally standing still.

'You speak out of place.' I try my best to arrange my skirts smoothly, then drop to the floor and retrieve my slippers. They are stiff and warm after the stone tiles, like climbing back into a prison cell after a brief excursion outdoors.

'You often do that yourself, I've noticed.'

'Well, that is… That is different! I am not a servant like you. And I *try* not to, anyhow.'

Thomas raises one eyebrow, strolling further into the chapel. I count his steps: one, two, three, four, before he halts foolishly close to me.

'You have not answered my question.'

'I will be glad to leave this place as soon as Ed is crowned and Lady Mother can take her rightful place in the regency council.'

A shadow crosses his face. 'What about the allegations, what about the letter? If the Protector was willing to execute Hastings—'

'No!' I inch closer so that I can lock his gaze with mine. 'They *must* come to terms. My uncle will drop the accusation, and my mother will not attempt to diminish his influence in the north or anywhere else. That way, we can have unity, like Father wanted.'

'I don't care much about all that.' His hair hides his eyes from me once again. 'But I do know one thing: there isn't enough power to satisfy every greedy mouth in this land. Some will have to go hungry.'

I shove him aside, gathering my skirts in a knot in my fist to avoid stumbling on the hem as I race down the cloisters and through the Deanery, past the slack-faced abbot and back into the college hall. Stupid, stupid… And I thought there was nothing but awkward kindness in that peculiar commoner!

43

Everything happens horribly, ruthlessly quick. I could elaborate on every time we receive another blow, but I fear our misery—especially Mother's—would do little good to repeat. As misfortune hails down like nails pouring from the sky, stinging us bloody, I eventually grow numb. Thomas, Agnes, and the rare messenger boy do their best to bring us news, but said news is never joyous.

First, Ed's coronation is postponed until November. This is the second time Parliament sets a new date, and it is starting to appear as if they intend to wait forever.

Then, on the twenty-second day of June, Parliament declares that Father's marriage to Mother was invalid to begin with, claiming that he had already made a plight-troth to a Lady Eleanor Butler. The lady in question has been dead for years, and thus there is no way of proving the declaration false. His liaison surfaced when the Bishop of Bath and Wells came forth and confessed to having officiated the plight troth, just as a priest later officiated the wedding ceremony between Father and Mother, a wedding kept secret for months afterwards.

I press myself flat to the wall, as does Anne, while Elizabeth and Dorset try to console our mother with words soft and foul respectively. Dame Elizabeth Grey, as Parliament now refers to her, paces up and down the college hall for hours at length, teeth gritted, repeating that it is all a venomous lie. I want to believe her, of course I do, because I must. If the bishop is in earnest, every single one of my siblings and I are bastards. *Bastards.* The word tastes sour on my tongue. Some would say it contains an unspeakable shame, but that is a splinter in my finger compared to the loss of the title Princess of York. As if that is not enough, Father is also said to be born on the wrong side of the blanket, shedding light on the old rumours about his mother and a common archer. This part of the story, however, is easy to dismiss, at least if one knows my rigidly moral grandmother, Cecily Neville.

What follows trumps the declaration, though. My uncle Anthony and my half-brother Richard Grey are executed on the same charges that they were arrested: of plotting against Uncle Richard and the rightful government, among other things. I weep because I know I should; I weep with my eyes burning, curling

44

up in Agnes' strong arms, letting her stroke my dishevelled hair. Even Dorset sheds a tear for the two men closest to him all his life, before resorting to kicking the wall until his foot starts to bruise and swell.

Mother says nothing, nothing at all. She is motionless, a sculpture, as beauteous that day as she must have been at twenty. Looking at her from afar, one would assume her serene, even, but her eyes are often where her emotions lie. They are black as charcoal now, demanding divine retribution. This is the second time she has lost two of her dearest family members to a son of York, and I fear she will confuse recent events with those that took place more than a decade ago.

Is Uncle Richard responsible for all this? Buckingham and the other advisors—Catesby, Ratcliffe, Lovell—may have considerable influence, but my uncle is a man of his own mind. There are so many questions tumbling in my head, questions I want to ask to his face, if only I could. I want to scream and shout and stare him in the eye. If only I could. I am not merely thwarted with my uncle, though, but also with the world at large, with my father for his womanizing, and with my Woodville relatives for conspiring against better judgement. The follies of mankind will ruin us all.

The final blow is what truly strikes me. Parliament offers Uncle Richard kingship, since the boy-king Ed is baseborn and Clarence's only son is barred from the line of succession through the act of attainder passed after his father's treason. Naturally, the protector accepts the offer. Only a saint or a half-wit would not. *King Richard III.*

Thus it is that I become the daughter of a king, the sister of a second, and the niece of a third, all in less than three months.

Chapter V

I SQUINT IN the dark. Two smudged silhouettes stand by the open door. Chilly whiffs of air stream through the slit; I wrap my blanket tighter around my shoulders and press closer to Anne's warm little body next to me. Whispers under heavy breaths, a sheer chemise, boots tramping on the spot, impatient. A lingering kiss. Dorset's cloak flaps around his legs as he turns and slips out of the room, melting into the darkness. Agnes pinches the fabric of her chemise and pulls it up a hand's-width by the shoulders so as to raise the neckline, hiding a considerable patch of skin. I always wished I had skin like hers, soft like cream. When she turns around, I half-expect her to discover that my eyes are open and give me a scolding for spying on her, but the gloom is too heavy.

I should have known…I should have connected the dots long ago. I have watched Dorset drool after damsels—in distress after he finds them if not before—for well over ten years, and what better way to pass the time in this dreary den? Elizabeth, perhaps Anne also, would be in a state if they knew the woman who combs their hair at night is as chaste as a courtesan in a Southwark alehouse, but I am not. At least Agnes has found a way to cure boredom. There is only so much a woman of her status can do to further herself, and mistress to a high-ranking nobleman is not for shame.

What truly sparks my curiosity is the whereabouts of her lover. None of us are supposed to leave the safe harbour of sanctuary, least of all in the midst of night, least of all the man who has the most obvious prize on his head. Dorset is the only one of us who risks his life if he is caught, because the House of York does not wage bloody war on women and children. He *must* understand that, fool or not, when mere days have passed since Rivers and Grey's gore poured thick over the block. For all my uncle's startling actions the past month and his advisors' poisonous words, he loves us girls, and his attachment to chivalry is too deeply ingrained for him to execute a woman like Mother rather than imprison her—but Dorset? I admit I fear for him, or rather fear for Mother, who unlike myself loves him with ardour.

When dawn's soft light cracks through the blackness and morning arrives, he is still gone. No one dare speak a word of what our glances communicate. At last, Mother confirms to us what has happened.

'We discussed it, he and I. My son was never one to make sensible decisions or bide his time. Methinks he will join Ned.'

My uncle Ned left England with the fleet, which he commanded, before the better part of said fleet abandoned him and surrendered to Uncle Richard's authority. Having fled with two ships and the ten thousand pounds that Dorset doled out from the royal treasury, Ned is thought to be in exile in Brittany together with some upstart named Henry Tudor. I believe Tudor is Margaret Beaufort's son from her first marriage, a banished Lancastrian boy, but I have no memory of him, and I wager his name would not spark recognition with many Londoners. I shudder. Henry's fate is one I dread beyond most things: faded away into obscurity in exile, living day by day eating crumbs from the hand of the Duke of Brittany.

'Will he be back, Mama? Will he?' Kate cranes her neck, boggling her eyes at Mother.

'I do not know just when, darling.'

That same evening, when Agnes sees to my nightly routine after the others have dozed off, I subject her to my curiosity.

'Do you love him? And he you?'

Her face freezes in the mirror. 'What did you say?'

'Dorset. Thomas Grey. You know *him*, I'm sure.' I fail to disguise the smirk playing at the corner of my mouth.

Agnes gives my braid a firm tug. 'Never you mind that, love. Should 'ave shut your eyes and ears both.'

'It would be dreadfully romantic.'

'I never thought *you* cared 'bout romance.'

'Agnes! Of course I do!'

'Hmm. With all your talk of prosperous matches?'

I sigh, for it is a common enough misconception. 'That comes first hand, and then we have love. If one has to choose, one chooses the first—but if one can have both… Isn't that *delightful?*'

'You think that knave would marry the like of me?' Amusement glitters in her pale sage eyes, emblazoned in candlelight. 'Doubt it. For what it's worth I'd not wed the like of him, either.'

'He is a bit of a mediocrity,' I concede. 'And perhaps silly.'

'Silly and with a temper worse than yours. But there is so little else to do in this hellhole.'

I bite my lip. 'Are you not worried? What if—'

'I 'ave my secrets.' She winks at me in the mirror, the spotty silver blurring her features slightly. 'Nothing that I'll tell *you,* love.'

I cannot hide my flaring red cheeks, not even in the dim candlelight.

'Don't worry your pretty little head. You won't ever be preventing babes, just squeezing 'em out as often as you can.'

I want to laugh but it is impossible; the air knots in my throat and swells as if to choke me. Blood-soaked linen, cramps, skin transparently pale, a tiny heart beating too faintly to survive, like a sparrow with broken wings… The thought sends chills all the way to my fingertips. I have not kept record of the women—not to speak of all the infants—I know of who have languished in childbed. My second cousin Isabel, Clarence's wife, is the example that springs most readily to mind, as well as my aunt, the former Duchess of Exeter. Then there are those who keep their life and their health, but who are unfortunate in their fertility, like Uncle Richard's wife Anne and the Lancastrian Marguerite d'Anjou, both of whom have had only a single surviving child.

I should be reassured by the fact that my mother and my grandmothers have performed their wifely duties with admirable success. But no, I feel less reassured with every passing day, because each nightfall brings me closer to when I will find myself under the crushing pressure of childbearing, Woodville hips or not. It is the price I must pay for a high-ranking husband: the continuation of his dynasty.

I am grateful when Agnes diverts my thoughts.

'They'll start preparing the coronation soon, just you wait. Of course, we won't be able to see a thing, but maybe hear some of it. To think they'll be about in this very building!' she says, opening a small wooden tub and dipping her finger in the salve.

First, I think she is going to attack me with the rancid, milky-white substance, but then she starts massaging it into her own cheeks and forehead.

'What is that?' I crinkle my nose.

'Goat's fat and valerian. Keeps the skin young.'

There is no use in reminding her that she is far from old. Instead, I return to the subject of the impending coronation, for it has been on my mind the whole day.

'I hope Ed and Dickie will be there, so that Mother can feel reassured. We have not heard anything more of them. And how I wish I could attend, too! Just picture all the splendour—'

'Thought you hated the lot of 'em,' she says.

'I cannot, though I suppose I should. Part of me does, but not all, because I have been thinking properly about it, and I...I understand. My uncle holds land seized by the crown from George Neville, Agnes, and George died this May, meaning the lands can pass to his heirs rather than remain with my uncle. If Ed had been crowned, he would have listened solely to the Woodvilles, since he grew up with them, and all this might have left my uncle and his family with nothing all of a sudden. Add to that the fear of turmoil under a feuding regency council, and his own ambitions for England... I believe I would have done the same thing.' I draw a shaky breath. This is the first time I have dared voice my musings in their entirety, and guilt over my final conclusion stings.

Agnes throws up a hand in the air. 'I still don't see why you'd attend.'

'You don't see? Because I feel too many things to name— hate and fondness and... I used to sit on his lap sometimes when I was this small—' I put my hand at the seat of my chair to demonstrate. '—and wanted to play with his gold chains. He was awfully uncomfortable, I think, but never brushed me off, not like Father could when there was some prettier girl to occupy his attention.'

'Prattle, prattle.'

'Agnes, be serious. I know I have too much emotion, and sometimes it drives me mad, but if I can nurture the nice ones and not dwell on the rest… There are to be winners and losers in all this, and I do not want to lose. I *do not*.'

'Be glad I'm not telling your mother what you've been saying, love.'

I dig my nails into my palms, leaving bright red imprints. 'Mother thinks we can oppose this and be successful. I have no intention of waiting to see if she is right.'

To me, it is at once plain and simple: I am a daughter of York and we still have a Yorkist king. One cannot betray one's own kindred when the war is internal.

Come the morrow I deem Mother sufficiently recovered from the recent shocks for me to investigate further in the matter of Father's alleged connection to Eleanor Butler.

'Well, was he?'

'Cecily!' she snaps like a bowstring.

I was wrong regarding her recovery, it seems, but there is no turning back now. 'You have not denied it, Lady Mother. Please…please say something of it.'

'Your father had a dalliance with that Butler woman when he first became king, but he was wed to none but *me*.'

I hesitate. 'I know that. But I asked about a plight-troth, not a wedding ceremony—'

'Hush now! You shall have to take either my word, sweet, or the word of your wicked uncle. If your father was still with us, he would tell you himself.'

I frown but dare not insist she elaborate. To her, this last statement is apparently of obvious clarity; she does not seem to realise that I take a different meaning from it than she intended. Yes, I do have to trust either her or my uncle's word, but the choice is not all that obvious to me. Yes, if Father was still with us, he could tell, but what would he say, and would he not be inclined to lie? A consummated plight-troth may not be the same as a proper wedding ceremony, but it would have been as binding as one in cannon law.

I knew Father's character well enough. All the nights I have lain sleepless in the nursery, hoping he might come to kiss us goodnight, only to remember that he was surely with Jane Shore or another one of his strumpets. All the times I have watched Mother turn a blind eye to his scattered affections. That was his most charming and most agonizing quality: each of his affections was intense and indulgent by any man's standards, yet there were so many of them, too many. It sometimes felt as if he gave me the moon, until I discovered he gave Elizabeth the sun, and our brothers even brighter burning stars. It was thus with his amorous side, also, not just with us children. I doubt not he desired Mother above all others, at least when she was still budding beautiful, just as he desired Jane Shore ten years later. But there were so many others, so many... Some were his for a single night, others for a fortnight. Though I dare not say as much to Mother, I do not find it improbable that Father would have beguiled a lady with promises of marriage to get her in bed, nor is it difficult to fathom that Bishop Stillington did not want to come forward with this knowledge until Father could no longer give him a rough silencing.

Judging by the pinched look on Mother's face and the way her hands are trembling in the shadows of her voluminous sleeves, she knows precisely this. What she might not know is whether there was indeed a plight-troth—she simply wants to believe there was not, wants it desperately. A tinge of shame sweeps through me, for I share this wish. The more I think about the matter, the more the rational part of me is inclined to trust Uncle Richard in his discovery, and the more the rest of me screams no, no, I cannot be baseborn! I must not think about it, then. There *is* a possibility we are as legitimate as we were brought up to believe. If Mother can cling onto that possibility, then so can I, and spare myself suffering I know would take a toll on the little sanity I have managed to maintain in this prison of ours.

I have made the Chapel of Pyx my place of refuge. It is safe enough, close enough, and certainly holy enough that no one can object to my daily visits there. I do not dance the *saltarello*. Not even I can muster enough mirth to perform the steps at a time like this, at least not without music, and the nasty memory of last time I tried keeps picking at me like the sharp little beak of a blackbird.

51

One day, the first day of July, when the sweltering heat seeps through the abbey's thick stone walls and invades every room through the cloisters' open windows, I find an intruder in my place of refuge.

Sir Thomas is sitting on the upper of the two steps leading to the altar, legs pulled up to his chest, back hunched over a something resting on his knees. When I take a few steps into the room, treading carefully on my toes, I see it is a piece of paper, yellow with age. He moves a withered goose pen across it with utmost concentration, the scratching sounds like thunder in my ears. He is not supposed to be here. This is *my* place. I despised him for a good hour or two after the things he said to me about power-hungry nobles—after that, I became preoccupied with the hailstorm of news.

I quickly search through my emotions. No, no hatred there, unfortunately. He never said '*I told you so*' when he heard about the executions or about my uncle claiming the throne, which redeems him to me. Elizabeth did not either, but her face was shouting it from the spires of Westminster.

I decide to be as amiable to him as I can. 'What are *you* doing here?'

Thomas' head snaps up from the drawing at the sound of my voice, his hand jolting so that a plump ink stain bleeds over the paper. 'Sweet baby Jesus!' He composes himself and puts down the pen on the step. 'Drawing. Nothing special.'

'I can see that much. I just cannot see why you do not draw someplace else. The abbot has given you a chamber of your own, surely?'

'He did, but with all due respect, Lady, I have as much right to be here as yourself.'

He has not addressed any of us as 'Royal Highness' since we were declared illegitimate, and I would be furious, were it not for the fact that he barely used the title before the declaration either. This is not contempt for us as possible bastards but merely another aspect to his awkward nature.

I take another step towards him. 'Well, then. What are you drawing?'

'Promiscuous pictures of the Virgin Mary.'

My eyes widen in disbelief. 'Really?'

'No, but I made you smile again.'

My lips curve farther. It is as I suspected: I have found myself a person, apart from Agnes, whose bluntness surpasses my own. 'Can I see?'

The shadow of a blush grazes his cheeks. 'I guess. The paper is brittle—I borrowed it from one of the abbot's old scrolls.'

He hands me the sheet and I sink down on the step next to him, the stone pressing against my skin through my layers of skirts. The sketch is exceptional, although I only have Kate's hideous doodle-cats to compare it to. The ink is swept in light strokes, crafted in the black contours of a dramatic landscape. A grassy plain upon sharp-cropped rocks with waves crushing against the stone below; I can almost taste the sea salt on my tongue.

'I do not recognise it.'

'I would not expect you to, Lady. It's the Isle of Wight, where my father lives. We come from Friskney in Lincolnshire originally, but the isle is where I was born and raised.' He traces a line with a finger seeming to move at its own volition.

'You miss it?'

'Quite.'

I frown. 'Then why are you here? I cannot imagine anyone willingly spending their days shut up in Westminster Abbey, except mayhap for Margaret Beaufort.'

Thomas' moss-green eyes flash in brief recognition of the name before he snatches the drawing from me again. 'Because my father is a pious man, and his father knew the abbot when they were younger. He thought I could make something of myself in London. My family has a tad of noble blood, but you know what that's like. It won't bring any magic money just because you brag about it.'

I almost cannot believe it. Noble blood? *He?*

Thomas puts my mind at rest before I get a chance to answer. 'Only a drop, really. My father is an esquire; my grandfather was a knight during the reign of King Henry.'

'Henry of Lancaster was never the way a king ought to be.'

He shrugs. 'Hardly matters now, does it?'

We sit in torturous silence for one, two, seven eternal heartbeats, before I decide what to say. 'Pardon, but you should not become a cleric or a servant. I think you should become an artist. It sounds like something from an old fairy tale.'

'Maybe you can tell my father that.' He tucks his hair behind his ear and grins; I have struck the right chord.

'Why not? I think he might heed my command. Will you do something for me, then?'

'That sounds ominous.'

'I would very much like to have my portrait painted. Father said he'd commission it but he never had the chance.'

Thomas shakes his head. 'I don't have any paint or coal.'

'And I don't have my most precious gown or my favourite jewels. Mother was too caught up in bringing her own coffers. Ink and plain clothes will have to do.'

We remain in the chapel for almost two hours that afternoon. I am warm and stuffy in my many layers, the summer air tempting me to kick off my shoes and remove the two-parted caul that keeps my hair in place under the modest gauze veil. I strike one ridiculous pose after the other, until Thomas lashes out and begs me to 'Just sit still like a normal human being, by Saint Edward's toes!' However, he promises to continue with the portrait the following day, and somehow, it is never quite finished, hence we keep returning to the chapel. Mother must think I have a newfound piety—but she does not mention it.

My sisters and I sit huddled up around Mother like we used to do when she would summon us to her gilded chambers, except no one speaks. We listen instead, using every sound from the nave of the abbey to craft images in our minds of what it must be like. Is the coronation well-attended? It sounds like it. Are they being anointed with holy oil? Of course. Are they wearing imperial purple and ermine? We need no more than the common sense of hens to know this much.

Mother's face is a mask of granite, and though she clutches Elizabeth's and Anne's hands, one on each side, she does not move an inch. Elizabeth's mask is decidedly softer, docile, her gaze fixed on one of the candlesticks on the table. Anne is turning the rustling pages of a book with her free hand; Kate is wiggling on the spot with one thumb in her mouth; Bridget sits doe-eyed as usual. I swear we will never fully learn the machinations of her serious little head. Agnes has managed to fall asleep, staying true to her routine of naps.

At last, I fail to resist the urge of speaking. 'Do you think Ed and Dickie are there, Lady Mother?'

She draws a quivering breath at the mention of her youngest sons. 'I dearly hope so, my sweet. God only knows what will become of them—God and Gloucester, that is. It makes my heart quake with fear.'

'I wish you'd let me go with them. I could have kept an eye on them and—'

'And spend your days clapped in the Tower?' Elizabeth says. 'You are not talking sense, Cecily.'

'The Tower has rooms that are much fancier than *this*.'

I stay quiet after that. No one else appears to be in the mood to discuss who's carrying whose train on the other side of the two walls separating us from the ceremony, nor speculate in what the prominent Londoners and nobles are thinking.

Uncle Richard uses his increased authority to invest his friend, the insolent Duke of Buckingham, as Constable of England, and the new prince, my ten-year-old cousin Edward of Middleham, as Lieutenant of Ireland. Shortly thereafter, the new King and Queen—it is odd to refer to my uncle and second cousin as such, when I had barely grown accustomed to my brother holding the regal title and not my father—embark on their royal progress through England. The people will emerge from their houses in every town and village, flocking to the streets and roads to see their monarchs pass by. What will they think? The north will assuredly give a warmer welcome than the south, not only because of the northerners' adulation for their new liege lord, but because they once owed affinity to Queen Anne's father the Kingmaker.

While this is happening, no one hears a word from my brothers in the Tower—and a lack of words is as ill-boding as can be. We used to receive vague reports of how they practiced archery outside, or how they were spotted in the window, but as July wears on there is nothing. *Nothing.*

August fades into a mild, rusty-red September. Our life in sanctuary drags on: half-hearted studies, dining on Londoners' gifts of eatables, on occasion praying with the abbot, playing cards with Agnes or teaching Anne a rhyme, stealing away to the chapel to chat with Thomas. Despite the isolation from the lively world I so long to return to, it would be endurable but for one fact: *nothing*.

There are whispers on the street, Thomas tells us after venturing outside, whispers that the princes have been smothered in their sleep, starved to death, or the key to their room simply thrown down a well to rid the new King of his foremost rivals for the throne. Cold claws reach inside my chest, breaking my ribcage, closing around my heart. If the rumours hold even a grain of truth, if my Dickie has drawn his last breath without so much as letting me place a final kiss on his velvety forehead... I believe that is the one grievance I could never completely forget, the one sorrow I could barely survive, come hellfire. Uncle Richard would never harm them; this I know just as I know the sun will rise in the east, not merely because of his personal bond to them but because of the political disaster their deaths would assuredly bring on him. Still, others might act rashly, others in whose interest it is to remove them from the face of the earth.

I am more restless than ever, unable to focus on even the simplest thing without the image of my angel brother nudging me, urging me to *do something, help them, find out the truth*.

It is when I wake up sweating and kicking one night that Mother at last shares her secrets. She will not stand by idly and allow the suspect fate of her boys go unpunished. No, she has already taken action.

Chapter VI

*M*ARGARET BEAUFORT?'
I nod, livid. 'That's what she told me. They share a physician—that Welshman who has been coming and going, the tall one with the tawny beard and white hose.'

'But he started visiting...a month ago.' Thomas knits his brows, propping his chin in his palm and his elbows on his knees. We are sitting on the altar steps with two plain cups of cold wine between us.

'I know. I did not pay it much attention.' My cheeks heat. 'I would rather not pry in Mother's private health.'

'I see. You have not told me what this *plan* involves yet.'

I draw a deep breath, preparing to unleash the beast. 'To marry Elizabeth—or if she dies, to marry *me*—to Henry Tudor and assist him in an invasion. My uncle, Ned, will contribute ten thousand pounds, and they believe the Duke of Brittany is also willing to support the endeavour. Then, the throne will be returned to my brother, and Tudor will be returned his own lands as Earl of Richmond as repayment.'

'Who on earth is Henry Tudor?'

'Her son—Beaufort's son. But you are missing the important part. If...if my brothers are dead, though they cannot be, then Tudor may take the crown for himself. A *Lancastrian* with no credible claim!' I have to pinch myself at the thought.

Thomas shakes his head so that his hair swirls around his ears like a dark cloud. 'You're crazy, the whole lot of you. Sorry, but you really are, Lady. What does it matter who sits on that throne when ordinary people will not get a scrap more regardless?'

'It matters because the foremost enmity lies not between York and Woodville but between York and Lancaster, or so I have been taught my whole life. It matters because my Lady Mother and her family have turned in a direction I cannot follow, not truly.'

'And I thought you wanted your brother restored.'

'Of course I do. It is what I want most of all. But if he is already…you know, then I would much rather have Uncle Richard than a Lancastrian upstart without real blood royal in his veins. What do you take my loyalties for?'

'God save your sister then.' He raises his cup in a toast and drinks hungrily.

'What?'

'God save her, so *you* won't have to wed that Tudor lad.'

I pout. 'Don't give me nightmares.'

To tell the truth, I am a little embarrassed that I did not grasp what was in the making earlier. I have barely noticed the physician arriving more frequently than my mother's health could require. I have been too absorbed in lamenting my brothers' unknown fate, blind to Mother's revived determination now shining in her eyes as if she was a hungry cat on the hunt. Elizabeth and Anne both knew before I did, while Kate and Bridget are too young to be involved. I hope Agnes was oblivious, too, else she ought to have told me.

It is such a gamble—it gives me the chills. We might rise to our former fortune, providing Tudor succeeds and the princes are alive, or we might be plunged into an abyss if the invasion is crushed or if my brothers are dead and we are left under the rule of a Lancastrian king. My kinswomen act as though they would be perfectly happy with a minor nobleman on the throne and Elizabeth as the Queen. Elizabeth for Queen! The idea prompts a sour taste on my tongue. I always expected her to wed one of Europe's great princes, just like myself, but this is not the same thing as to have her presiding over a foreign court far away. I would have to dip into a curtsey before her every time she swept into a room; I would be forced to look upon her as she sits on the gilded throne once occupied by our mother. I would have to seek her permission to move my little finger, and I would be forced to watch her prance under a royal canopy to the accolades of the people. Then I would indeed have to marry abroad, to escape.

Do they not understand? We have everything to gain, yet we also have everything to lose. I shall rejoice if my brother is restored to the throne. I shall despair if a Lancastrian stranger with Elizabeth at his side takes it instead. And if the invasion fails altogether... Then I will curse Mother's endeavour, regardless of my love for her. Uncle Richard will still look kindly upon us, at least on me and my sisters, if we bide our time and blend into the new regime. He might not have the option to be lenient if we become rebels in the rawest sense of the word. I would not be if I were in his shoes.

And then there is Dickie. If he is dead, he ought to be avenged, the perpetrator slaughtered. Yet none of us can know whether Uncle Richard is the perpetrator—though I do not believe it—or if it is one of his nobles, or even one of Margaret Beaufort's men seeking to clear the path to the crown for her son. There are so many *ifs*. I hate this uncertainty, this mound of doubts and off-chances. Unfortunately, my proneness for hatred is part of the family flair, both on Mother's and Father's side.

Thomas quickly grows bored as I ramble about the matter. He tries to hide the yawn tugging at his face, and empties my cup as well as his own.

'You'll intoxicate yourself,' I say.

'Hardly. This is about as strong as milk.'

I tilt my head. 'It is? I did not think so.'

'That is because you're tiny.' He grins, giving me a light shove. 'I think Lady Anne is taller than you soon.'

I laugh. 'She is *not*. She is not yet eight years old.'

'Oh. I've never been drilled in the biographies of the House of York.'

'You have not told me your own age either. I cannot believe I have not asked before—'

'My father told me I was born in the year of our Lord 1466 for quite some time, before my cousin had to correct him and say 1465. He doesn't like to remember it too well.'

'Because you are at odds?' I can detect family feuds better than most.

Thomas' eyes have turned oddly pensive, languid, as if someone had smothered a spark with a wet blanket. 'Not over anything I did—only it was a tough birth. My mother became weaker after that, and did not last long. She was your age at the time.'

I shift my weight, plucking at a loose thread in my lavender damask gown until the pearl attached to it comes loose and rolls down on the floor. 'I see.'

To my relief and disappointment both, the conversation halts there, because Anne's pointy face has appeared in the crack of the door. Her skin is translucent in the crisp light flowing from the east cloister's windows, the crucifix on the chain around her throat catching chinks of sun.

'Cecily?' Her glance darts to Thomas, quizzical. 'Lady Mother bids you to come.'

When I return to the college hall, there lingers the stale aftertaste of a quarrel. Mother is pacing the room while Elizabeth is sitting on a stool, her shoulders sloping, eyelids puffed and the colour of bruises. I have rarely seen her in such a state.

'I *will* have one of my children crowned in this abbey, just as I was,' Mother says. 'You deserve no less, apple of mine eye.'

Elizabeth studies her palm, carving white patterns with one nail. 'Thank you, Lady Mother. I will wed him if you demand it.' She sounds…yes, defeated.

'I have no wish to force this upon you.' Mother sinks down on the stool next to Elizabeth. 'You were raised to wed your father's choice, and he entrusted me with that choice before he died. You can be *happy*, if you put your mind to it. You can influence your husband, should he gain the throne, and raise the Woodvilles to favour again.'

'I know.'

'Believe me, Beth, I find the situation as grim as you do. But we will do what we must, all of us, and be rewarded thousandfold.' She bends forward and kisses her eldest daughter's temple, then smiles, and her smile could melt the solid stone walls of our protective prison. I am reminded, once again, why Father gambled all he had to win her.

Elizabeth can be queen. She should be gloating and basking in that knowledge. Perhaps it is the Lancastrian husband that has shattered her spirits—yes, that must be it. I pity her, and the pity makes me soar, as cruel as I know this sentiment is, because it has been the reverse for as long as I can recall. Still, part of me genuincly wants to provide a sliver of comfort, though I do not know how.

'Poor you,' I say, placing a hand on the patch of bare skin in soft the curve between my sister's shoulder and neck in a half-hearted attempt to soothe. My hand is cold, I know. 'I would have thought you gleeful. Think of the...the bright side.'

'Oh, Cecily, you fool!' she bursts, shaking off my hand. 'I have never met the man!'

I take a step back, grappling for words. 'Just like you had never met the Dauphin, and yet you did not mind being betrothed to that frog!'

'Girls. Please.' Mother rubs her forehead. 'Beth, we have discussed this before, many times. You told me then you would be pleased to do your duty, and the daughter I love so dearly would stand by her word.' She turns to me. 'Cecily, why don't you go and dice with Agnes? Take Anne with you, too.'

I swallow the bile of words rising in my throat and force a nod. *Dicing.* How pleasant.

The Welsh physician, whose name I soon learn is Lewis Caerleon, continues to deliver Margaret Beaufort's secret messages. Henry Tudor is planning to launch his invasion in late October or early November with Ned Woodville's ten thousand pounds from the royal treasury to oil the wheels. When they land, they will be in dire need of support in the form of English soldiers as well as simultaneous revolts orchestrated within the land. My other maternal uncles are heavily involved in this aspect of the scheme, promising assistance.

We wait, limbs heavy with boredom, skin itching with nervousness. I would gladly fling the door open and bolt past the guards, out into the filthy streets of London, if Mother would let me. Reading and praying and playing stupid card games does little to ameliorate the distress.

During one of those card games, Agnes clasps a hand to her mouth, panic mounting in her eyes when she looks at me. She pushes back the chair with a screeching sound and turn from us, however, she does not get far, the doors being firmly shut. Vomit the colour of mustard spurts between her cramped fingers before she surrenders and empties her stomach in the bucket Thomas uses to fetch water.

I drop my cards on the table, spoiling the perfect fan, and scramble to her side while stopping at a safe distance. I do not wish to be contaminated with whatever illness ails her.

She wipes her mouth with the back of her hand and brushes a thick lock of hair from her cheek. 'It's nothing, love, nothing.'

Thomas, frozen with half-emptied dishes in a firm grip, stares at her. 'If you're sick, you will make all of us sick, too!' He puts the dishes down and crosses himself, something I have never seen him do before.

'I would be surprised if my condition transferred to *you*,' Agnes mutters. 'T'would be a first, that's for sure.'

I rub her back like I have seen Mother do on Bridget when she coughed up milk as a baby. 'Perchance you ate something bad.'

'Yes, yes, that must be it.'

'But we have all eaten of the same cheese and bread—' Thomas insists, his complexion drained of all colour.

'God's truth, you are driving me mad! Unless you've become a woman overnight, you've no business sticking your nose in this.'

'Agnes?' The implication dawns on me like a flood of ice water. 'You said you had your secrets.'

She crosses her arms. 'Hmm. I thought so, too.'

Mother has been watching in silence; now she strides forward, shoulders squared and mouth puckered like a drawstring purse. There is no fooling her. She has been with child twelve times herself, more if she has ever suffered a miscarriage.

My sisters cluster behind her and even Bridget watches from behind Elizabeth's skirts.

'If you are not ill, methinks I know your condition,' Mother says. 'And you—' She measures Thomas with her eyes. 'You ought to know better than to argue with a woman when the blame for this misfortune is as much yours as it is hers.'

It takes me a moment to grasp what she is insinuating. When I do, the ice water returns. 'It is not *his*, Lady Mother! It's not, is it?'

Thomas shakes his head frantically, his face shifting from marble-white to scarlet in a matter of seconds. 'I think the abbot asked me to attend on him once I was finished here.' He manages to open the door without putting the dishes down and scuttles past the guards like a stung hare.

'You are not four months gone. It would show more. I presume then, that this child was begotten here in sanctuary.' Mother lets out a heavy sigh. 'My boy will ruin himself one day with all these dalliances and escapades. He will not shoulder the responsibility, if that was what you thought.'

Agnes juts out her chin. 'I know. I did not think there'd be any blasted responsibility to shoul'er that's all.'

'You cannot give birth here, not in sanctuary. Believe me, it is no pleasant experience.'

'Pardon, Madam, but if you could, I can. I'm no frail wench.'

'I said no. There is no knowing whether a midwife will be allowed to visit, and we are cramped enough as it is. My daughter values your company—thus you may stay until your confinement begins.'

I reach for Agnes' hand. 'I do not think we will even be here at that point. So much can change before…April, is it?' I count the months on my fingers.

'Yes. Think so, love, or March. And what'll I do with the brat?'

Mother frowns. She is too attached to her own children to apprehend the term. 'We can concern ourselves with that once the time comes. Cecily is right: much may yet change. God willing, the court will once more be a friendly place, and if so, I shall see to it that my son gives you a small pension. You can live comfortably, if not virtuously.'

'Just cause not *everyone* can catch a king with their garters—'

'*Silence.* I will have silence.' Her voice cuts like a razor, clean and cool. She closes her eyes for what feels like forever, and when she speaks again, the edge is gone. 'My husband may have lusted at first, but he loved me in truth. He did.'

A week later, we receive another message from Margaret Beaufort. Mother and Elizabeth are both asleep when the physician arrives early one morning, and he places the intricately folded piece of paper in my outstretched palm.

'They let you pass as usual?' I say.

He scratches the wart on his sturdy chin. 'Else I wouldn't be here. Will the Dowager Queen write a reply?'

I throw a glance at the women lying like two spoons on one of the beds, seemingly comatose, and shake my head. 'I can write it.'

The excitement of intrigue ignited in me, I ignore the physician's raised eyebrows and sit down by the table, unfolding Beaufort's note.

Henry Stafford, Duke of Buckingham, has aligned with our intentions. He and the usurper Gloucester no longer share common interests, nor are they in personal accord. The Duke of Buckingham swears fealty to our cause.

M

I stare at the ink until the letters blur. Is this some cruel jest? No, it cannot be that. A full signature is indeed missing, but naturally, she would not want to spell out her name and title in the event that the note was intercepted. My thoughts rush to Buckingham. All I know of that toad is that Father never trusted him with significant tasks or offices, that his lineage consists of past Lancastrians, and that he scorned his wife—my mother's youngest sister, Catherine—on more than one occasion. He is the man who has benefited most from the new rule except Uncle Richard himself: he has been brought into the golden light at last, granted a massive portfolio of lands and honours. Would he truly betray his master?

Well, he might. The Duke of Clarence was equally lavished upon by my father, and still he rebelled openly not once but twice before meeting his fate in the barrel of malmsey wine after further indiscretions and galling behaviour.

I am uncertain as to whether we ought to embrace Buckingham's aid or reject it—and I have no time to consider it, for Mother rises from her bed quicker than a weasel and snatches the paper from me.

'Cecily!'

'I merely read it, Lady Mother—'

'That may be so, but the less you know, the safer you will be if this does not succeed.'

I glare at her. 'You involve Elizabeth in your plans.'

'Because I have to, because she plays a central part in all this.' Mother cups my chin in her hand and kisses my nose. 'You do not, and you should be grateful for it, my sweet.'

I compel the rumbling frustration to settle inside me before it breaks loose like a storm. Perhaps she is right; I *am* grateful it is not I who has been betrothed to a Lancastrian exile.

Mother does not show me the reply she scribbles, but she tells us in the evening that we cannot afford to be hostile towards Buckingham. Toad or not, he sits on a wealth of resources, and Tudor's army of exiles and mercenaries is not yet sufficient for dethroning an anointed monarch.

With each passing autumn day, the flourishing rumour of the princes' demise acquires another grain of credibility, if not necessarily truth. No one has seen so much as a tendril of their hair or the tip of their shoes for months, and rumour also has it that their servants were dismissed in the summer. My despair deepens, because while the pain should dull with time, it increases as it feels more legitimate. They are not *perhaps-dead-but-perhaps-just-kept-away-from-public-sight*; they are now plain likely dead. Hence, the scheme which Mother has thrown in our lot with turns more into a pursuit to place Henry Tudor and Elizabeth on the throne, and less a restoration of my brother Ed. I ache for Dickie far more than his older brother, for although I loved Ed as I was bound to do by nature and duty both, I only saw him on the rare occasions when he was brought to court from Ludlow. Now, it appears I will not see either of them ever again.

In the first week of October, the physician informs us that a brushfire of revolt is sweeping across Kent, instigated by the Duke of Buckingham, soon joined by further insurgencies in other areas. I still cannot for the life of me understand *why* he has abandoned his fierce allegiance to my uncle and instead decided to support Henry Tudor. Either there is something deeply personal to it, or he is simply a greedy rascal. Perhaps it is both. If Margaret Beaufort knows, she does not see fit to tell us.

The heart of the rebellion is a close-knit net of my father's old household knights and others who have been faithful servants for years, several Woodville-relatives among them. Dorset, who never arrived in Brittany, resurfaces and links his forces to the uprising. It is dawning on me how extensive the coup is: Mother, Beaufort, and Buckingham must have mustered every effort and exploited every source of acrimony towards the regime.

A month later, a panting, red-faced messenger boy is allowed to enter. I can sense we all hold our breaths, awaiting the conclusion.

The messenger speaks in a frail voice. 'The Duke of Buckingham was captured and, on All Souls' Day, beheaded. The other ringleaders have scattered. Some have fled southwest. Others are racing to join forces with Henry Tudor's five thousand troops.'

The fool Tudor is late in coming. He sailed from Brittany at the head of an invasion force, but his fleet has been torn apart by the stormy sea, and although he did arrive in Plymouth, he turned and sailed back again with his tail between his legs once he learned the rebellion was being stamped out like a trembling flame. We should never have entrusted him with our fate.

'Lady Beaufort assures me he will attempt it anew when the time is ripe. She is under house arrest, but writes her son's faction is already growing stronger with the disaffected rebel lords fleeing into exile to escape the block and gallows,' Mother tells Elizabeth and me one night in late November, before tossing the letter from our ally into the hearth to be consumed by the fire. Powdery ash is poor proof of a plot, should the guards search our living quarter.

Only the three of us are awake. Elizabeth sits shoulder to shoulder with Mother, her back erect, the warm light and shadows playing on her wistful face.

'Shall I still become his wife?' she asks.

'Yes. You or, if the worst happens, Cecily. We cannot abandon the possibility of Tudor's victory quite so swiftly.'

I bury my face in my hands. We are crushed rebels. Uncle Richard knows it, regardless of how many suspect notes Mother burns, and she still wants to push ahead! She is pushing in the wrong direction! As I rub my sore eyes and quench the panic within me, I thank the Holy Virgin that the King is a pious man, and one who loves his nieces, for else he might already have violated sanctuary and dragged the dowager queen out to face his justice.

Chapter VIII

C HRISTMAS THAT YEAR is, despite the odds, a gay
occasion. The college hall is still decked with valuables
from Westminster, but mother is hesitant to sell any of it,
and Dorset smuggled out the rest of the royal treasury when he
fled. Misery has saturated us, nearly paralyzed us, and so we grasp
for an excuse to indulge in life's pleasantries, putting our plethora
of concerns aside.

We break the fast with an improvised feast, marking the
beginning of the Twelve Days. The Londoners have been
particularly generous, providing us with roast veal, chestnuts
stewed in thick cream, spiced wine, and flaky pastries. Thomas
and the abbot join us at the table, since the social boundaries are
blurred by the festive atmosphere and Mother says it is only right
that they should dine with us. Even so, there is a gaping hole
where Dickie ought to sit. I push away the memories of how he
would bicker with Kate, how he never wanted to admit that the
roasted swan Father ordered for Christmas dinners frightened
him with its magnificent feathers and dead eyes like black beads.
I have to visit those memories another time, not now, not when
I have a blessed chance to make merry.

'Father, will you tell us of the nativity?' Mother says, granting
the abbot a precious smile. 'My daughters know it, naturally, but
it never hurt to be reminded.' My 'daughters'. Not 'my children'.

The abbot nods, wiping his stubby fingers on his trencher.
'With pleasure, Madam. The angel Gabriel was sent from God
unto a city of Galilee, named Nazareth, to a virgin espoused to a
man whose name was Joseph—'

Bridget and Elizabeth alone remain attentive, for we have
indeed heard the tale countless times, although the abbot takes

no notice. Even Mother, whose faith is as much a well-rehearsed farce as it is genuine, takes to examining her impeccably rounded nails.

I nudge Thomas with my elbow before I remember my manners. 'Pardon.'

'What?'

'Nothing. Is he like this often?' I throw a glance at the abbot, who has clasped his hands as if praying, and speaks with the zeal of a preacher.

'Always,' Thomas whispers back. 'I've heard enough sermons for a lifetime during these past six months. This dinner is grand enough to bear any sermon, though.'

'Well, it *is* an eminent change, but it is still a pauper's meal compared to last Christmas. We had glazed boars' heads then—four of them.'

Thomas cracks his knuckles; he knows I cannot stand the sound of it. 'Stop whining, will you?'

'You have no right to talk to me like that.'

'You say that most days.'

I glare at the plump chestnuts on my trencher, the pool of cream sauce spreading. I want to be furious with him, I really do, but it is impossible. I have too few friends to afford it.

'Are you vexed now?'

'Terribly,' I whisper. The abbot is still immersed in his beloved nativity tale, his baby-eyes even rounder, his hands wildly gesticulating. 'But I'll forgive you.'

'Sorry—again. You know you can be a whiner, though, do you not? Anyhow, I have a gift for you, if you come and *pray* with me in the chapel after dinner.'

I practically fizz with delight. 'But it is not yet New Year's Day!'

'I know, silly, otherwise it would spoil the surprise.' He blushes, dropping a slice of veal on the table just as he is about to transfer it to his trencher, and I have to stifle a giggle.

The guards have been reinforced ever since the failed rebellion. Six men stand tramping on the spot outside the door to the college hall, and I do not doubt there are some twenty or more of them by the main entrance to the building. Normally, only Thomas and the abbot are permitted to come and go as they please within the abbey, and they too face slight restrictions if they wish to venture outside. If I were my uncle, I would not want to risk another damned conspiracy.

However, the White-Boar-badged men are lenient this Christmas Day and none denies us to visit the Chapel of the Pyx. After a hesitant nod from Mother, Thomas and I embark through the cloisters, guided by the flitting flame of a candle. With combined force, we open the door and close it after us.

Thomas puts down the taper on the altar, where several other candles are already burning down to the wick, then rubs his arms in a futile attempt to keep warm. The lack of a fireplace is painfully obvious, the biting chill creeping under my clothes and into my marrow.

'So, where is my present?'

Thomas digs in his pocket and extracts a small package of folded linen. I remove the cloth with eager fingers. It has been so long since I had any gift at all, so many months without much new to call my own.

The caul I unpack is exquisite. The hairnet is made from delicate silver wire, like trickles of liquid moonlight, with pearls the size of cranberries fastened at each knot. The headband is of silver also, engraved with roses and with four miniscule hooks where one might fasten a veil.

I trace the rose pattern with my fingers and feel the smooth pearls against my skin. 'Thank you. So much—truly.' At Father's court I would have asked first whether the pearls were authentic, for anything else would have been unacceptable, but now I mean each word of gratitude. The headdress is gorgeous, it must have cost him every penny the abbot pays him, and deep down I know he is right to call me whiny.

'You're welcome.' Thomas' skin has turned to bronze in the blend of gloom and candlelight dappling his features. 'I thought your Lady Mother might disapprove.'

'She will. I shall wear it regardless.'

'I am glad.'

'But I have nothing for you yet—you have to wait until New Year's Day just like the others. Do not worry, for I shan't tell you what it is. I know how to keep a secret.'

I discard my hennin and undo the intricate braids that Agnes spent almost an hour pinning to my scalp, re-gathering my curls in my new caul and fastening the headband. Not until it is too late do I realise that I ought never, *never*, to let a man see my hair loose and unveiled unless he is my husband or a close blood relative. But no, it does not matter. Thomas is different…he must be, although the long glance he now gives me contradicts my conviction.

'I know you do,' he says. 'Though maybe you can give me something now, too?'

'What would that be?'

He draws a deep breath. 'Teach me that dance—the one you danced the first time I came here. It looked so jolly.'

'You are mad! Or far too clumsy, at least.'

'You're not exactly poise incarnate yourself, yet you performed it with more grace than I ever saw.'

'Because dancing is the one thing I can do without faltering.'

He arches an eyebrow. '*Please*. It will be a merry-go-round, that I do promise.'

And it is. He proves every bit as gawky as I predicted, and the *saltarello* quickly turns into an incongruous craze of improvised movements. Had there been minstrels to play for us, we could have continued forever.

When I return to the college hall, breathless and flushed, Mother takes me aside to a corner.

'My sweet, you must not let the festive spirit overwhelm you so utterly. Where is your hennin and veil? You cannot fool me. You would not look thus if you had been praying all this time.'

My cheeks burn. 'Mayhap. But it was nothing indecent, nothing like *that*, at least.'

'It matters not.' She sighs, stroking my hair. 'What matters is that the guards see you in this state, not to speak of your impressionable little sisters, and the last thing we need is a rumour of misconduct to spread in London.'

She does not allow me to visit the chapel after that evening, even at the rare times when the guards would have permitted it. She only has my best interests at that scorching heart of hers, yet to add another restriction to the ones I already live under is like pouring salt in an open wound.

With the new year comes a glint of hope, the hope of being released from our invisible chains after all this time. Despite our plotting, the King must be inclined towards reconciliation, because he starts to negotiate with Mother anew. He has begged her to come out from the abbey before, but her terms have been beyond reason. Now, Uncle Richard presents yet another offer.

He swears an oath on the gospels, with London's mayor and aldermen among the witnesses. He guarantees that, were we to emerge from sanctuary, we would be in surety of our lives, we girls soon wed to gentlemen, and furthermore, he claims he will provide for our livelihood, giving Mother a quarterly pension.

I soar at the news. Finally, *finally* I will be released from this cursed dungeon. I will be able to tread barefoot through swathes of lush grass and run up staircases and dance freely, at least when no one is scrutinizing my behaviour. I will dine on food of my own choosing instead of what the Londoners grants us. I will sleep in a *proper* bed, commission new clothes to replace the garments I have grown out of, and I will converse with people other than the little circle of personages who reside here with me. And if I am allowed to visit court, I can fight to rise above my current station, fight to ensure my future husband is more than a gentleman.

'The snake makes no mention of my boys. He only spoke of you girls,' Mother says, interrupting my enraptured musings. 'If that is not a confession of the vile deed—'

I shake my head. 'It is not, Lady Mother, not necessarily. If they are...gone to God, of course he cannot speak of their safety, but it is not the same as taking the blame upon himself. The formulation could be because Dorset is a rebel on the run, or even because of Richard Grey. And that is in the past if we let it be.'

The last words are words I am ashamed to speak, but I am desperate. We have to accept this offer, because another one is not going to come, and it is no paltry offer either. Besides, I believe I am right. The oath does not include Richard Grey or Dorset, since one was executed in the summer of 1483 and the other fled abroad after the failed rebellion, denounced as a traitor. The princes might be part of it also, but how can we ever find out if we tarry in here?

To my astonishment, Elizabeth is my ally in this, as is Kate—Agnes would be, I am sure, but she has recently left sanctuary for her confinement at one of Dorset's houses in the outskirts of London—and together we manage to sway our mother's iron will.

'Very well,' she says. 'We will be in a position more advantageous to craft a new plan once we join the rest of the world.'

It is not exactly what I meant myself, but I hold my tongue this time. Let her use her freedom to try and change the rules of the game, and I shall use mine to master the present rules. We will all have our comfort returned to us whichever way we chose.

It is decided that we will leave on the first day of March.

We dress in our finest clothes—that is, in the clothes we have worn the least and which fit the best, although Mother now finds use for the extensive wardrobe she brought, and Elizabeth is tall enough to borrow one of Mother's gowns—and I help my sisters arrange their hair like I have seen Agnes do. I study my reflection in the mirror. My gown is the colour of a dove, too pale for my taste, with a deep, square neckline revealing my white kirtle. The billowing sleeves are lined with ermine fur, covering half my hands. I fasten the silver buckle on my braided belt and reach up to smooth the veil over my hair, which I have gathered at the nape of my neck in the pearl-caul Thomas gave me at Christmas.

He stands wiggling on his feet, waiting for me to finish. I wish we could say our goodbyes in private, but there is nothing to be done about it; we have not enjoyed a moment alone together for months.

I cast a glance over my shoulder to ensure the others are preoccupied with their own preparations to take notice of us. 'How do I look?'

Thomas' grin does not touch his eyes. 'Splendid. Older.'

'Grammercy. Not too old?'

'Not at all.'

'Good.' I gnaw on my lip, fervently rummaging through my mind for the right words. Our eyes are locked, and perchance they speak more than either of us has the oratory capacity to.

The silence is absolute for what must be well over a minute before I press forth. 'I'll miss you a whole great deal.'

Thomas reaches for my hand. 'No, you won't. You will make other friends, if they can stand you.'

'Only suitable ones—not the same thing.'

'Goodbye, silly. Do not let them flatten you out.'

'You think they could?'

'Never.'

I fling my arms around his neck and after the initial surprise he lifts me off my feet for a wonderful moment.

'Cecily!' Mother's voice slices through the sound of blood rushing in my ears and I break loose from the embrace. I will not cry. I *refuse* to cry. It turns out I am no better at mastering my emotions than I ever was, though, and as I follow the small train of women and girls out of the college hall, my cheeks are cold and clammy with tears.

Four guards escort us the stone's throw to Westminster Palace, not bothering to use a barge. They then lead us through a series of passages and rooms as if they have forgotten we know this building better than anyone. One can never be too careful, I suppose.

It is outlandish to be back in the place where I spent much of my childhood, a time which in itself feels as distant now as a previous life. Hardly anything has changed here. The clock has stopped, smashed at my father's last breath, leaving the palace the same while the world has changed around it. The grandeur is a sight for sore eyes after our year in sanctuary, or rather, in self-inflicted prison.

The presence chamber lies open to us. My heart hammers against my lungs, bruising.

I spot Howard, who I hear has recently been re-invested as Duke of Norfolk and thus will not waver from his benevolent liege lord's side, standing next to the wrought wooden thrones, scratching his moustache. At his right, Henry Percy, Earl of Northumberland, lounges in his jewel-encrusted doublet, flashing the blue ribbon marking him as a Knight of the Garter. I have one of those myself, forgotten somewhere in my old chamber, though naturally, I am not 'knight' but 'lady'.

74

There are others, almost all of whom I recognise from Father's court, such as the slippery Stanley, who is the husband of Margaret Beaufort and charged with keeping her under house arrest, having recovered from his own fall from grace last summer thanks to his great value as an ally. There are the new men, also, like Uncle Richard's three closest confidants: Lovell, Ratcliffe, and Catesby, all prospering under the new rule.

And there, at the far back of the hall, they sit. Regal in their dress, dignified in their expressions, yet I spot a shadow of insecurity crossing their faces as Mother strides towards them with my sisters and I in tow. We stop at the proper distance, just like I have seen hundreds if not thousands of people do before my parents in the past. When Mother curtsies, it is the slightest of movements, and her chin remains stubbornly raised. I believe it is the first time she performs the act since before her marriage nigh on twenty years since. Even Kate's bubbly manners are humble in comparison.

Queen Anne's eyes are bright and hard like steel when she looks at her sister-in-law, hair brushed glossy and tucked safely under the coronet. Here is the woman she has grown up envying, tried to replace, feared, flattened herself under, and finally defeated. Except my mother is never truly defeated, and the new queen ought to know that. Anne says nothing, though, but simply spreads the rich folds of her ivy-green brocade gown so that it falls more evenly over her slippers. I wonder what it is like to have such a precarious position, before I recall that none of us has been secure in our fortunes for almost a year, except the common servants, who have very little to begin with.

The King sits silent for a good while, then gestures for us to rise, and speaks. 'Dame Elizabeth Grey. It pleases me to see you have come to your senses and chosen the path of conciliation.'

'Yes. Misunderstandings within the family can be so unfortunate.'

'Indeed—we are in accord, then. You are to live at Sheriff Hutton. Your eldest daughter is welcome at court, and your other children may be called upon on certain occasions.'

'Yes, Your Grace.' The words come slow and pained, as if pulled from her throat with a barbed thread, yet she retains her perfect posture.

Elizabeth... Of course *she* is welcome. However, it must be obvious to everyone present that 'welcome' is a code word for 'kept under close surveillance', now that she is presumably Tudor's linchpin to the throne. My thoughts are cut short as Uncle Richard turns his attention to me.

'Cecily.' His voice is soft and low as always but betrays no emotion. 'Come hither.'

I hold my breath as I dip into another curtsey, deeper this time, my eyes glued to the floor at his feet. My mouth is dry as a cracker. Never before have I shown myself to be beneath him and his statuesque queen or indeed anyone other than Father and Mother; I never will be, but the court demands this spectacle. Both he and I know it.

'How old are you now?'

I straighten up and meet his gaze. To my triumph, I can compete with it. 'Fifteen in little more than a fortnight, Your Grace.'

'Then I have an early gift for you.' A gesture with his slender fingers calls forth a servant boy holding a velvet-clad pillow. Upon it rests an exquisite broach composed of a multitude of miniscule diamonds set on an octagonal base of mother-of-pearl.

Uncle Richard props his elbow on the armrest and his chin on his fist. 'You care little for rubies, if I recall correctly. And a broach is so much better than a casket.'

I fill my lungs with the scent of the courtiers' perfumes of orange blossoms, hiding a tremble. 'I do. It is. Thank you, Your Grace. Thank you.'

Perhaps it is shallow of me that the gift goes such a long way in easing my twinge of hostility—but it is not just diamonds. It is not even just diamonds like the ones Elizabeth received when she turned fifteen years of age. It is a symbol of what might come, a gesture, this I am certain of.

The servant boy transfers the broach to my eager hands and is dismissed.

My uncle and aunt exchange a lengthy glance before granting Elizabeth a few words, and we are seen out of the chamber by the guards.

Mother, Anne, Kate, Bridget, and I are due to leave court for the countryside and Sheriff Hutton the following morning. Our belongings from the abbey are being loaded on carriages, and our new household has already been set up with a sufficient staff.

Until our departure, we are kept under close watch, but we are by no means explicitly prisoners, and may roam the palace as we please. I find myself drawn to Saint Stephen's chapel, for it was not only the place were Father lay in state awaiting his burial, but also the place where Dickie was wed to little Anne Mowbray six years ago, the child bride who died not long after. If we had known on that day what heaven had in store for those poor children... I dismiss the aching memory as I take a step into the gothic chapel, striding through a mist of incense.

Two figures are already standing not far from the entrance. I instinctively come to a halt and slip behind one of the pillars.

Queen Anne has removed her coronet and allowed her hair to drape her shoulders in light chestnut waves. Uncle Richard casts a long glance at her, absorbing the view. At once, I come to think of the times they visited Father's court during my childhood—it happened less frequently as the years went by, but I remember it well. There was one occasion in particular, a jousting tournament that Father hosted, where his youngest brother competed against William Hastings like a model of chivalry. The look that I see passing between the King and Queen now is the very same as in that moment, when she tied her ruffled token handkerchief to his lance a decade ago.

The Queen makes a show to leave but my uncle catches her hand. 'Anne?'

'It is no good, Rich.'

'I know. By God, I know, I—' He draws a hand over his face as if to pull a veil of composure of over his bewildered eyes.

The Queen cups her husband's face in her hands. They are small and dainty, like those of the child she once was, and her short stature does little to dissuade the youthful impression. 'Together we are strong. Together, we can weather this storm.'

He remains motionless for a moment before giving a nod. 'Yes. Together. What have I dragged you into, *ma belle?*'

'I believe I did my fair share of the dragging. You're the *King* now, yes? Kings do not weep.' She brushes away the single tear that has spilled over and is trailing a path down his cheek, her own eyes glistening wet.

When their lips meet, I avert my eyes and retreat on light feet. As I escape the chapel, something nasty stirs in my stomach. I know Mother is right, I know Elizabeth and Anne speak the truth: my brothers, my angels, are with all likelihood lost to us, vanished or dead, and I ought to hate the man who was responsible for their safety, regardless of who ordered their removal. I want to, I do, but I cannot. In this, the Woodville flair fails me.

It is peculiar how the things one sees can play with one's heartstrings until one feels as though they might snap.

Chapter VIIII

SHERIFF HUTTON IS a place of marvel, or it is to me, after nearly a year in the college hall. Although the Yorkshire castle cannot compete with any of the palaces that I am more familiar with, and although it is far too distant from London for my liking, I thank my lucky star upon arriving.

The castle is a rustic, quadrangular building, its four ranges connected by one square tower in each corner, framing an open courtyard. I count the oblong windows and conclude there are five stories in the main buildings, while the towers poke the sky above that. The walls are made of brick and mortar, thick as Dorset's head in late evenings. With the rolling green hills and fields stretching as far as the eye can see, our new home resembles a jointure of fortress and country retreat.

'It looks very much like the castle from an old legend,' Anne says, clapping her hands.

I ruffle her hair. 'You say that about anything. But it *is* lovely at least if one does not lament over Westminster or Windsor.'

Mother takes Kate in one hand and Bridget in the other as we enter the open courtyard through the arched gateway, and says, 'Gloucester wants to keep us at safe distance. He knows full well you girls have royal blood in your veins.'

'He'd be a fool not to. But he could have placed us somewhere far worse, and he did not. Besides, we shall be in good company.'

I am gratified as soon as we enter the castle. The painted plaster walls are coated in thick tapestries to keep out the chill of winter storms; the furniture is only a notch below that of our old chambers; every room is redolent with the scent of lavender and leather and cedarwood. I believe I can be comfortable here,

79

especially when spring buds in earnest and we can stroll through the picturesque landscape.

The company, on the other hand, turns out to be quite the disappointment. There are three other noteworthy occupants at Sheriff Hutton, all of whom are our cousins, and none of whom we know particularly well. The head of the household is John de la Pole, my father's sister's son, a strapping young man with wily eyes and a pointy beard the colour of a fox. He is rarely here, his duties as Earl of Lincoln requiring him to be at court or at Sandal Castle, a fact which does wonders in making me find him agreeable. When he *is* here, he frequently stands too close to me, brushing a hand against my back when passing by or touching my foot with his under the dinner table, but he is a staunch Yorkist and adroit, too. Nasty or not, he is a possible future husband, at least if Uncle Richard continues to lavish favours upon him, and if our consanguinity is overlooked as it so frequently is.

My two other cousins are much younger than Lincoln: Edward, Earl of Warwick, is nine years of age and his sister Meg eleven. They are Clarence's offspring and as such I have always found it difficult to befriend them. Their own attitude towards us is suspicious, also, because since they were orphaned, they have been Dorset's wards, and learnt to associate the name Woodville with their tactless guardian, though there must be more to it than that. We have spent limited time together as children, and I do not know them well enough to tell.

Young Warwick is a provocatively pretty child with an equally pretty singing voice and, I believe, a heart free from malice—buts that is where the praise ends. Days on end, he rambles and shouts about how this castle belongs to him simply because he is Warwick the Kingmaker's grandson, going as far as to say *he* should be king. It must have escaped him that he lost his right to inherit *anything* the moment his father was convicted of high treason and attainted, and his title as Earl is only a courtesy from my father. Mayhap he will turn to the Lancastrians just like Clarence did. When he does not rail over all he thinks he is entitled to, he causes havoc with his rough games and pranks. If only he was as sweet as Dickie, I might have taken to transferring my affections to him, but no, comparing the two of them is like comparing a badger to a puppy. I know he means no harm, he never does, but he also does not know better.

Meg is a tougher nut to crack, or at least understand. Despite the age gap between her and her brother being narrow, she has taken on the role of his adoptive mother, scolding and protecting. I never once hear her encourage his illusions, though, in fact she barely mentions court at all. They are nothing alike in looks, either, because where Young Warwick is soft-cheeked and rosy, Meg reminds me of a haggard old woman with her long, bony face and sickly complexion. Her small mouth puckers whenever she looks at us—except for Anne, whom she occasionally sits and reads with in silence. In spite of all this, I cannot deny there is sharp intelligence flickering in her eyes, and I can imagine her thoughts darting between observations and conclusions, clicking like an abacus.

'Why is she so…strange, Lady Mother? She cannot believe I'll soften towards her if she looks at me like *that*,' I say one day in late March as Mother and I walk along the outside of the south range, plucking wildflowers.

My gown and hands are stained with grass and we have only found enough daisies for a meagre bouquet. The sun is hard and bright like a chip of white gold in the sky; it is growing warmer by the day. I relish in the crispness of the fresh air and the open landscape, still starved on such simple things after our confinement to the abbey.

Mother tilts her head back, bathing her features in splashes of sunlight. 'The girl is infested with her late parents' superstitions towards me and, hence, you. She has not accepted the natural causes of her mother's death, just like so many of her kin. I believe you remember that Clarence had two innocent servants executed for the murder of Isabel Neville when he found he could not crush *me*.'

'I thought they had forgotten that…that nonsense. Surely, everyone knows it was naught but childbed fever?'

'Rumours are not so easily extinguished, my sweet. My mother, too, suffered under their yoke, as did her mother.'

'But there's no truth in them. Is there?'

She studies me a moment in silence, her hooded dragon eyes burning on mine. 'If I could indeed wield magic, your father would never have died, and we would not be here.'

'Will you not tell Meg that?'

'You are mistaken if you expect the girl will listen to reason. A vice inherited from both her parents, I daresay.'

'Yet she is no dimwit at all—I do dislike her less than her brother. I thought...I thought perhaps he'd be like our Dickie. They are almost the same age.' I clench the bouquet to keep my hands from shaking.

Mother's granite silence reigns for a moment before she at last replies in an oddly recoiling voice. 'Do you blame me for your brothers' disappearances, my sweet?'

The words she uses are painfully clear to me. 'Are', not 'were'. 'Disappearances', not 'deaths'. At times, they live in our speech, if nowhere else.

'You thought the soldiers would storm the abbey and take him by force if you did not, Lady Mother.'

'I wonder if the common people will remember that. My boys...' She wrings her hands until I fear the rings will cut into her skin. 'I thank the Almighty every night I still have my eldest, but he may yet be taken from me.'

'He should not have participated in the rebellion.'

'We had to try.'

I squat to the ground and pluck another daisy. 'You still have us girls and your grandchildren. And soon you will have another one!'

'Agnes Lambert's babe? If I involved myself in all the results of my Thomas' foolishness, I would not know where to start.'

'Agnes is different, Lady Mother. She's lowly born, but I do care for her.'

'It is not her lack of lineage that concerns me, but rather her conduct and influence on you in thought as well as in action.'

I kick my heels against the ground as we continue our walk. I suspect she is referring to my dishevelled appearance that Christmas Day. She is right, although I hate to admit it. I miss my sketching friend more with each passing day, and it physically hurts. I often catch myself rushing to tell him how one of the cats caught the fattest rat thus far or how I heard a servant tell a bawdy joke, before realising he is three hundred miles south.

At least Mother can tick my inconvenient friendship off her tally of anxieties.

I break the seal with curiosity simmering in my stomach. Few people correspond directly with me apart from a relative here or there, and I have never been a skilled letter-writer. Elizabeth has called my handwriting 'a thorough travesty' ever since we were little, and unfortunately, she is right.

The message consists of four lines. Four ink-smeared, fatal lines. I crumple the paper in my fist, my vision blurring. I am alone, not just in my bedchamber, but in my grief. No other living soul will mourn the death of Agnes Lambert. Perhaps Dorset would drink himself into a stupor if he knew—if not for her sake then for the baby following her into the grave—but attempting to contact him in Brittany would be perceived as treason regardless of one's reason, and not worth the peril.

I topple down on the thick coverlets of my bed, pull my knees up to my chin, and draw the bed hangings around me. Is there no end to the searing pain of death? My sister Mary, Father, Rivers and Grey, presumably my brothers, and now Agnes… Whenever I regain my spirits a little, someone else is stricken down. Let the sky cave in and crush the earth for all I care.

I do my best to smooth out the letter, then read it three more times, still lying on my side, the embroidered cover damp under my eye. The steward of the household offers no details, not even the sex of the baby, yet the images flash in my mind. Rumpled sheets drenched in blood, screams tearing the air in invisible shreds, the midwife's red hands, a fleshy lump swathed in linen without the chance of being christened, a miscoloured little foot sticking out from underneath the cloth. Agnes' unseeing eyes, never to soak up the sun again.

I scan the lines one last time. No, the steward says nothing of the funeral. No doubt it was a humble ceremony performed in haste for a 'fallen woman'. How did they know whom to address the letter to? She must have spoken of us, mentioned my name. I make a mental note to pray for her soul. Perchance it will ease the impending nightmares.

I refuse to leave my bedchamber. Mother pleads and commands; Kate pulls my arm, her pointy nails digging at my sleeve, but to no avail. I am weary of life.

To my astonishment, Elizabeth comes to Sheriff Hutton around noon the following day. She says she is here to comfort me. However, I figure she must have left court—which is currently at Nottingham Castle, since the royal couple are on a northern progress—several days ago and only learned of my loss upon her arrival. Knowing Elizabeth, she likely begged Uncle Richard to send her away awhile, seeking refuge from the nobles' scheming circles.

I am woken by my oldest sister's cool, clear voice. 'It hurts Mother to see you so desolate, Cecily.'

When I raise my raw face from the pillow, she is standing in the doorway. 'Do you not think *I* am hurting?' I mumble.

'I know you are. Please, Cecily, come out. You only add to her misery.'

'It is the last thing I want. But do you ever *feel?* You never show anything. I do not think you understand.'

The mattress squeaks as Elizabeth sits down by my feet. 'I feel every bit as much as you do. I keep it inside for all our weal.'

'I could never do that! I try, I do, but—'

'Yes, you can, Cecily… Where's your sense of duty? Women cannot heed impulses, least of all we.'

'It's not *fair.*'

'You want so many things, but you *have* to acquire more decorum.'

'Like you? All the decorum in the world does not change that you are willing to remain betrothed to Henry Tudor! A Lancastrian king, I might almost have fathomed it, but now he is a mere Lancastrian exile, and I confess I do not think he will ever be more than that.' I regret my words the minute they bounce off my lips, because now I am the one to be unfair.

'I keep my promise to Tudor for Mother's sake, for our family's sake!'

'Truly?'

'I dislike it as much as you do, but I know my place in this world. If Tudor prevails, your fortune depends on my marriage to him. We cannot discard that possibility, and *someone* has to

84

serve as his reason to look kindly upon us. Mother has not gambled me without good cause. We mustn't be ungrateful for her love and guidance.' Elizabeth spreads her hands on her lap in a solicitous gesture. Her slender fingers lack ornaments and rings, more beautiful in their simplicity than any I have seen. The one deficiency is her nails, which she has chewed down to the skin, as she tends to do when distressed.

'Well. I am not so very good at displaying gratitude.'

'But you feel it, surely, Cecily?'

I nod.

'Here. Dry your eyes and dab your face with cold water. You have to come out sooner or later, and we all prefer sooner.'

I obey, and after another hour, I have re-emerged into the world of the living. Later, we sup together. I am ravenous, having eaten nothing the past twenty-four hours, and I take secret pleasure in watching the colour return to my mother's cheeks when she sees me delve into a butter-crust pie. This time, Elizabeth is in the right. I shall do my utmost to mourn alone, and shelve my loss at the back of my mind.

The news spread like a wildfire in the castle in early April. The Prince of Wales is dead, leaving his father and mother grief-stricken and out of their wits. The life of their one son, their one hope of securing their branch of the Plantagenet dynasty through direct descent, has been snuffed out like the flickering candle it always was. A single child is never enough; it would have been a stroke of luck if he had survived every hazard. My mother was a wonder: though God snatches an ever-increasing number of her children, she gave birth to enough of us to afford it. Of course, her heart never afforded it, but that is a different matter.

I pray for the dead prince and above all his parents, who must be utterly desolate, and I pray that my credit with the Lord is not entirely non-existent.

The afternoon after we receive the message, we gather in a comfortable chamber situated in the east tower: my three younger sisters, Meg, Young Warwick, and myself. Anne and Meg are huddled up on the plush pillows in the window seat with books on their laps, Bridget is sat between them like a doll, and I am trying to concentrate on my lute over the noise of Warwick and

Kate chattering. Two servant boys stand poised by the wall, holding platters of sweetmeats. They are, to the delight of us all, our sole supervisors for a brief while.

'He has no heir! He has no heir!' Young Warwick bellows. 'I'll be on the throne soon, as soon as Uncle Richard dies!'

Meg leaps to her feet and clasps her knobby hand over his mouth. 'Eddie! Hush!'

Insinuating the death of the King is treason, no matter how innocently it is spoken, and people have been executed for less, although I highly doubt Uncle Richard would harm a hair on the boy's head. After all, the Warwick-children are the Queen's nephew and niece as well as his own.

'You are *not* the heir,' I say, putting down the lute and crossing my arms. 'The Earl of Lincoln is older, and you are the son of a Lancaster-traitor!'

Young Warwick sticks out his tongue at me and rushes from the room, feet banging against the floor.

'Cece!' Kate exclaims, pouting. 'That's not nice!'

'It's *true*.'

To replace one young Edward, Prince of Wales, with an even younger one makes little sense to me, especially when an act of attainder has to be reversed by Parliament to permit the inheritance. No, it will be Lincoln for certs, who has already proven himself capable and loyal. The prospect of wedding him at once becomes a hundred times more appealing: I could be queen. Fancy that! But Elizabeth would be his first pick, if he even cast a glance on our bastardized lot, and I am not so sure he would. In a single moment, my hopes are both ignited and dashed.

I turn to Anne. 'How did he die?'

'I do not know. He was always sickly. Lady Mother says it is divine retribution.'

'She told you that?'

'Yes.' Her voice is a mere whisper. 'Do you think so, too?'

I pace the room with my arms still crossed, kicking my skirts in order to not trip on the hem. 'How would I know? But it grieves me, it does. I think Queen Anne loved him terribly much—her only child. He fell and scraped his knee once, if you recall that one time when we met him at Eltham, and the Queen was like a wounded bear with her only cub.'

Anne turns the page in her book, refusing to meet my eyes. 'You ought not to call her that, Cecily. She is not rightfully queen.'

'She has been crowned and anointed, and the Earl of Lincoln would be displeased to hear us deny it.'

'Ye-es, yes I suppose so.'

'I hope Uncle Richard knows he has an assemblage of children to love, and I hope he loves *us* the most. Having cousins can be so complicated.'

Divine retribution or not, the significance of Edward of Middleham's death date does not bypass me. The ninth day of April was the one-year-anniversary of Father's demise.

Elizabeth treats me like a glass figurine. I am ashamed over the way I behaved in front of her, however, she has planted a peculiar seed of respect in me regarding her sense of duty. I could never mask my own desires and fears like she does; I could never squeeze myself into the ready-made mould of the perfect eldest daughter. Is it her own instinct, or rather our mother's unyielding affection and influence?

She knocks on the door to my bedchamber one evening, clearing her throat to announce herself. I reach for my sable plaid and sweep the fur around my shoulders to cover my thin chemise. Then, I hurry on my toes across the cool stone floor, careful not to wake the maid who sleeps on a pallet by the foot of the bed, and open the door enough to peer out at Elizabeth. She is still in her peachy gown and horned headdress, having stayed up uncharacteristically long.

'Cecily,' she says. 'I wish you to come with me to Nottingham in two days' time—or, rather, our uncle wishes it.'

I suppress a laugher of pure exaltation, the first laugher I have felt tickling me since Agnes died. 'Truly? You are not merely mocking me?' I squint at her.

Elizabeth presses her lips to a thin line. 'I would not mock you, dear sister. Before I left, Gloucester asked me to bring you back with me, so that he might have a word with you. It will not be for long, only a week, I should think. Then, the court will be traveling again.'

My heart sinks the slightest, but I recover in a matter of seconds. 'A week. Sublime.'

'You have to be on you guard.' She sighs and raises her glance from the floor to meet mine. 'I know not what they wish to discuss with you, but please, be careful.'

'I am always careful.'

'Don't be ridiculous. Oh, and Cecily? Bring that broach—the one he gave you.'

We travel with a small entourage of two carriages, one for us and one for our luggage of clothes as well as two maids, fifteen mounted soldiers riding alongside for our protection and safekeeping. The journey from Sheriff Hutton to Nottingham, where the King and Queen are residing at the moment, is less than half as lengthy as it would have been to London. I am yearning to see the bustling city by the Thames again, but I count myself lucky to only have to spend eight days confined with my sister, the carriage jolting whenever the wheels hit a protruding stone in the road. I doubt I could endure any longer without throwing open the door and escaping into the woods in a particularly unfortunate impulse.

When we arrive at Nottingham Castle, I thrill at the sight of this legendary stronghold: built by William the Conqueror, and the very place where my father proclaimed himself King. I have visited the castle before but only spent a fragment of time here compared to Westminster, Windsor, or Eltham, and the colossal grey towers dazzle me anew.

'Anne would say it resembles a place from the legends of King Arthur,' I tell Elizabeth as our carriage crosses the stone bridge leading up to the vaulted entrance. 'I wish Agnes could have come.'

A weary look has settled on my sister's face, making her appear older than her eighteen years. 'I would gladly have switched places with her.'

I cannot tell whether she means it.

Chapter IX

THE CHAMBER IS steeped in gloom, a few tapers providing the only light except for the crackling hearth where several logs have already turned to ash and grime. I have to round a robust table covered in silver dishes—grapes, honeyed walnuts, bread, glazed sparrows, gleaming oysters, all untouched—to reach the man standing by the fire. He is clad in mourning garb, his head bereft of both hat and crown. Facing the flames, he waits while I curtsey, but appears to take no notice.

When he finally speaks, his voice bears the tell-tale strain which follows tears. 'You will have heard of my boy. My heir.'

I keep my eyes fixed on his back, studying the writhing patterns in the black velvet. 'I did, Your Grace. It saddened me to hear about the Prince of Wales.' All three of them: Dickie, my Edward, and his. One dead, the other two almost certainly so. None of them deserved it; such innocent souls, necessary linchpins of their parents' dynastic hopes.

'Where are my brothers?' The words break out from behind my teeth before I realise their magnitude. All I can think of is Dickie's golden locks smeared with blood, Ed's eyes glassy…

The King raises his head but remains with his back to me. 'In the Tower, as you well know.'

I will not succeed in pushing the matter any further, hence I turn to another, equally bold question. 'Why?'

He knows what I mean; he must know. 'Your father named me.'

'He named you as Lord Protector, not king. Are we truly bastards?

'"Woe to thee, Oh land, when thy king is a child", says the scripture. A boy king is no recipe for stability, and whose council do you think he would have taken? The Woodvilles' alone. You saw the vices and debauchery at your father's court, and you saw how your mother's kinsmen encouraged his indulgent decline. You know how he demanded benevolence from subjects who could not afford it, who trudged in the gutters so that he could waste even more money. Jesus, I loved my brother, but... I have tried to cleanse his court, and you have my word I shall try to cleanse England.'

I ponder this for a moment. It sounds a trifle dull to me, for as much as I disliked Father's knot of mistresses, I enjoyed the merrymaking and excess in spite of my better judgement. However, I can imagine Uncle Richard with his staunch morality and idealism did not, and he certainly has displayed less waste of the royal coffers than Father ever did.

'And are you king in the eyes of God? You must tell me, Uncle, because he does not speak to me the way he apparently speaks to so many others.'

'Cecily. You know I did my utmost to govern the north with a hand of justice and precision.'

'I do.'

'You care not for disorder.' Uncle Richard finally turns from the fire to face me. Despite the obscurity in the room, his face is still young, even remarkably handsome in an unconventional way, and, I confess, in not cruel in the least. Yet that is the same well-proportioned mouth that ordered the executions of Hastings and Rivers and Grey—though not without cause.

'It frightens me, yes, but you have brought on the greatest disorder yourself.'

'Only because my foes swarmed around my head. Hasn't your mother confessed to the schemes to you? Once they align with my reign or are otherwise dealt with, England shall prosper, that I can promise you.'

I bite my lip, hard, a fat drop of blood melting on my tongue. 'And me? My sisters? Are we foes?'

'Not if you do not view yourself as such. Not if you follow your senses, dear niece. If you remain true to the House of York and your family—*this* family—all will be well. I have no desire to harm women or children, especially not those of my own blood.'

'I knew you would say that, Sire. And you know I am no fool, at least not when I have time to consider.'

The King arches an eyebrow, plucking a plump grape from the platter on the table. 'Mind you, you are not yet trusted. Not with that mother of yours whispering in your ear and your own ambition soaring. Once I can be sure of where your loyalties lie, you may be wed. My hopes are high that you will still be young and fresh as a budding white rose by the time I can offer your hand to a lord of significant rank.'

'Thank you.' I could dance to a cheery tune in that moment. The princes in the Tower and my maternal uncle and half-brother upon the blood-soaked block are as if lost in the mists of memory. They will resurface soon, naturally, but as for now, I am jubilant at the chance he has granted me, the chance of rehabilitation and restoration.

'Come, prithee. Let me give you a kiss on the cheek,' he says. I comply, and he continues: 'My dear wife wants to see you in her chambers anon. I believe she wants to have a Woodville girl on her side to protect her against the spells of the rest.'

I gape at him. 'I know nothing of spells and neither do my sisters!'

'And your mother?'

Of course, I know what commoners and lords alike whisper about Mother. That she is a witch, like my grandmother, that the two of them snared Father with spells and later used their dark magic to bring about the death of Clarence and his wife, the Queen's sister. I have never believed it, for the accusation of witchcraft is too dangerous to give credence. No, Clarence only met the end he deserved, and his wife died in childbed fever, just as Mother reminded me not long ago. And still, I cannot be certain beyond the shadow of a doubt that the superstitions do not carry an inkling of truth.

'Humour her, Cecily. The death of her sister is still a splinter in her mind. And now our son.' His voice cracks.

'The coronet looks fine upon her head, Sire. Glimmering.' The guilt stings me, but I mean every word. My mother was superior in beauty and charm when she sat on the throne, but Anne Neville possesses the greater ancestry by far, and I see more of myself in her.

Uncle Richard's sad smile reflects in his pebble-grey eyes. 'She always wanted to be queen, see. Ever since we were children. She is, after all, the Kingmaker's daughter.'

I march directly to Queen Anne's chambers as soon as her husband has dismissed me. A page announces my presence, to my surprise allowing me entrance into the bedchamber itself, and my hostess dismisses her ladies for the night. The room is bright in spite of the late hour, furnished with bleached birchwood, the canopied bed with covers of silvery blue. Three little bottles with beauty concoctions stand on the edge of the curtained marble bathtub, a tenth of the amount Mother brought with her into sanctuary.

Having exchanged the necessary pleasantries, the Queen sinks down on a pallet, gesturing for me to follow her example.

'Four children, Cousin Cecily. God has taken four children from me: three before they drew their first breath, and now my Edward. How can I have angered the Lord thus?' she says, her voice hollower and wearier than I remembered.

I wrap my arms around myself. 'My mother said it was divine retribution for…for…'

'For her own boys?'

'Yes, Your Grace.'

'Your mother is to blame, then, for I cannot believe the Lord would take my son from me. She has used her witchcraft again, yes?' Queen Anne crosses herself, the chain of her crucifix wound tight enough around her fingers to stop the blood flow.

'I don't think she has any such powers, Madam.'

'I *know* she does. And do you?'

'No, no. I swear I do not!' Panic bubbles inside me. Come anything, I *cannot* afford to be more associated with sorcery than I already am through my maternal inheritance. Treason and murder notwithstanding, it is the most dangerous thing a woman can be accused of.

The Queen shakes her head, slowly. 'Tell Dame Elizabeth she has misdirected her malicious punishment.'

'My mother never thought you to be the culprit, Madam. At least she never told me so.'

'No. Alas, she blames the King. I know she does.'

'So it is not true, then?' I hold my breath, but my inquiry is in vain. She would hardly reveal this innermost of secrets to me.

'The King's Grace will have spoken to you about your future, that you must earn your match with loyalty.'

'Yes. You can trust me, that I swear!'

'Trust is a grand word in times like these. If you abandon the Woodvilles, you could easily abandon us, too.'

My cheeks are damp, my nose runny. How I envy her now more than ever before, how I wish she would put her faith in me. Would she be right to do so? Could I truly forsake my mother and sisters in favour of those who have taken so much from us? I do not know, and it only adds to my tears. In the battle between my love for my closest kin and my desire to once more be a part of that glittering world of royalty, I am torn and beaten bloody. There is only one key to solving this conundrum: my loyalty to York must take precedence over both love and desire. Loyalty binds me—that is the motto Uncle Richard chose for himself many years ago, and it will suit me no worse.

'Madam, I abandon no one. Sometimes I think people forget I am Woodville and Plantagenet both, and I can play both cards. If forced to choose one or the other, my affinity will lie with the latter. I love my lady Mother and my sisters more than I love you, as is natural, but they cannot give me much, and my mother has turned her back on the House of York, which I will never do.' I decide to aim one last shot at what I think is my second cousin's sorest spot: her memories. 'You know what it is to be refused what is rightfully yours merely for being on the wrong side through the actions of others. Lancaster's heir was never *your* choice, was he?'

'No.' Her eyes have hardened again, though she is not looking at me, but appears lost in the haze of the past. 'It was my father's. I rejoiced when Edward of Lancaster was slain at Tewkesbury, for I knew then that he would not give me any further nightmares. Alas, I was mistaken. The difference between you and me, Cousin, is that when Rich—I mean the King's Grace—took me for his wife, I was alone in this world. I had very few scheming relatives who could pose a threat to your father.'

I clench my fists between the rich folds of my gown, defeated. 'I thought my lady Mother was lucky when she won Father's heart, but mayhap you were luckier still.'

She takes my hand, her own being as cold as ice-melted water, and caresses it, the grief chiselled in her face. 'The luckiest girl in the world, I used to tell myself. Security and status, even love. I thought I'd be happy.'

I shake my head, a tear smudging on my cheek. 'And you are not?'

'Youth fades. Security abandons you. Children die. Love wears on the soul. It grows tainted. Not weaker, but tainted.'

While my uncle filled me with hope, this woman renders me utterly hopeless.

Two days later, the King and his nobles embark on a hart hunt. The array of favoured nobles—Howard, Northumberland, Catesby, Ratcliffe, Lovell—ride at the front with Uncle Richard, all mounted on the finest horses in England. The creatures' hair shine in the sun, their hooves clopping as we cross the bridge from Nottingham Castle. Irish wolfhounds swarm around the horses' legs, tails wagging, noses already grazing the ground. Farther back ride lesser nobles and servants, as well as a small group of women headed by Queen Anne. It is not customary for the women of the court to accompany the hart hunt and I have not been before myself, but it does happen occasionally, and the Queen appears in dire need of fresh air and exercise. Her other ladies have whispered in my ear that she has grown more pallid and secluded each day since the news of her son's death reached her.

The Sherwood Forest has an air of mystique. The oaks stretch their knobbly branches skywards, their thick trunks coarse after centuries of wind and weather, their leaves budding this time of year. I almost manage to forget the constant itch of fear in my throat that comes from riding even the idlest mare. The hunt in itself is a nasty business in my opinion, since I never saw the pleasure in slaughter, yet the forest allows me to be oblivious of such gruesome matters.

Elizabeth turns her head like an owl, absorbing the view of the trees surrounding us. 'Have you heard the ballad of a man called Robin Hood, Cecily?'

I smile. 'I recognise the name. Dickie liked that story a great deal.'

The thought of my brother wipes the smile from my face in an instant. It brings to mind my secret mission, as I have begun referring to it in my head: to carry out my investigations.

When the opportunity arises, I fall behind the hunting party with Queen Anne.

I brace myself. 'I must know, Madam, what became of my brothers.'

Queen Anne reins in her horse further and tilts her head. 'Everyone believes His Grace did away with them, no? Isn't that what they say?'

'Yes—but that is not the same as *knowing*.'

'Your affinity is precious to him, and to me. I need to know first what *you* think, Cousin, and what your mother thinks.'

I search every corner of my mind for an answer, because all the sleepless nights I have spent wondering have only resulted in only the vaguest theory. 'I…I think there are too many who would benefit from the princes' removal to be certain. But His Grace is no fool, and he must know they are more dangerous to him dead—or thought to be dead—than alive and safely locked up.'

'Clever girl. You are right, naturally. Now, the rebels fight for Henry Tudor, who is both free and a man grown, and use my husband's nephews for martyr logs to fuel the flames.'

'That is what I thought, Madam. My mother…well, I believe she blames the King. It is easiest that way. She and my sister Elizabeth have a rather different perception of his character than I do.'

'Because of Rivers and Grey?' Their names sound stilted coming from her, as if she must force herself to speak them.

'Yes, largely. Because they are Woodvilles above anything, and because they confuse him with Clarence at times.'

'Rivers and Grey were a threat. They and Dorset would have pushed their own agenda too far with young Ed, used him as the pawn he already was, banishing us to the periphery, taking our

95

lands and estates. His Grace arrested them for our protection, fearing their plot.'

I clutch my reins tighter, as always fearing my mare might throw me. 'It is true there was much talk of raising troops. Still, could they not have been acquitted?'

'It is difficult to defect from a path once you have trapped yourself on it; to release Rivers and Grey and retreat from the stance he had taken against the Woodville threat would have been synonymous with political suicide, perhaps suicide in the most galling sense also, for the Woodvilles would have convinced young Ed to... There was no turning back.'

'I can see that.'

'Then there was Bishop Stillington and his confession about your father's plight-troth to Lady Butler. The more we thought about it, the more obvious the solution appeared. Why not avoid the instability of a boy-king with competing councillors? Why not steer England to its former virtue and prosperity?' She meets my gaze and holds it for several seconds, an eternity then and there, and I can spot the dwindling hope so clearly in her face it makes me ache.

'You, too, believed the bishop? I do not know what to believe myself, only what I want to believe.'

'I trusted him, yes. Truth is, we will never know with absolute certainty whether he is an honest man, but he was bound to come forth with his confession, and you know well enough the unrest a disputed ruler can cause.'

'I fear we have a disputed ruler regardless.' I sigh, the turmoil in my chest threatening to break my ribcage. 'You still have not told me what happened to my poor brothers, Madam.'

Queen Anne bends forward to stroke her horse's neck, her doll-like hand gloved and perfumed with honeysuckle. 'With their illegitimacy proclaimed, we thought they could be kept away from the public until the storm had settled, and then brought back to a quiet life away from court. You remember your late father's children by his mistresses? We thought your brothers could take a similar position, dangerous to no one, since they were illegitimate, but it was not to be. We talked about it, late one June eve, one of those eves with birds still chirping long after dusk. My husband said—' She breaks off and takes a deep breath, closing

96

her eyes for a moment before resuming. '—he said it would be easier if they had never been born, and, of course, he was right. I told him so. We were not as alone in that moment as we thought. The walls have ears.'

'Who heard you? Pray tell,' I hiss.

'The Duke of Buckingham. I knew he was a troublesome man when I first laid eyes on him. His Grace did not see it until it was too late. The Duke thought to curry favour by ridding his King of rivals, not pausing to give it further thought. He was greedy, always drooling after more than he had already been given, and there would have come a time when he might have asked for the crown itself.'

A cold wave washes over me, freezing the blood in my veins. *Buckingham.* I should have guessed. Mayhap I did. 'He had them murdered? Did he?'

'He ordered his brutes to perform the deed. When we returned to London after our progress and found out, His Grace was in a fury. I never saw him so outraged, except once, when his brother of Clarence tried to hide me from him to prevent our marriage.' A stroke of nostalgia colours her voice before she clears her throat and continues. 'I know not what befell their bodies.'

I frown, numb. 'Why did you not announce what had happened and rid yourself of Buckingham in the process?'

'Who would have believed it? That the King's most trusted man had acted without his knowledge, or even that they had both died of natural causes at the same time, and yet the bodies were already buried without proper ceremony? You know what the public was like, dear, already turned firmly against him. No matter what we said or did, they would have thought the same. So we said nothing, but prayed some would assume they had merely been tucked away in the north.'

'And Buckingham?'

'He was afraid after their quarrel. He thought he would be in higher graces with Henry Tudor on the throne.'

'Well, he was right. Tudor would be nothing without the princes removed to put him forth as their avenger and heir of their claim.' I have not spoken truer words in a long time.

'You see then, that we are doomed unless the people learn to love their true King and Tudor's opposition is rooted out. The princes must be forgotten altogether.'

I shake my head in disbelief. 'I wouldn't want my brothers forgotten.'

We are interrupted by Uncle Richard himself, as if summoned by our stealthy conversation. He has turned his horse around, allowing his arsenal of magnates to ride ahead, and now sides with the Queen and myself. There are smudged shadows under his eyes; his face does not bear witness of any joy in the hunt.

'Are you tired, *ma belle*?' he asks his wife.

She ignores the question, holding the reins in one hand while placing the other on his arm. 'She knows.'

'Anne?' Guarded, sharp.

'Yes. She needed to hear the truth.'

Uncle Richard turns to me, speaking with a clamped jaw. 'You must swear not to breathe a single word of what you have learnt. It *cannot* be known that they are dead for certs—they are still within the walls of the Tower, understand?'

'Yes, Sire. Though I do not think many will believe it.'

'It is too late to go back, Cecily. Much too late.'

'My mother deserves to know.'

'I very much doubt you can convince her, dear niece, when her heart is already carved with hatred. I bear her no tender affection, but she has the right to lay the blame fully on me, should it ease her pain in any manner.'

My vision blurs with tears. 'Yes, she does. They were in your care, Uncle. You may not have ordered their deaths, but you isolated them to begin with. And why my youngest brother? Why him?' I know the answer already, but I need to hear it from him.

He rides in silence a moment before speaking, his voice strained. 'I am aware of the part I played. Do not make the mistake to think I have not lain sleepless over what happened to those innocent souls. As for the younger boy, I believe you know why he had to be placed with his brother. Your mother would have tried to smuggle him out of the abbey otherwise, to be used as a figurehead for a rebellion.'

'We would not have talked about it had we known the Duke would be so rash in action,' Queen Anne adds, as if trying to build a defensive wall with her words.

Her husband continues, 'If you find this knowledge too difficult to reconcile with, you may return to Sheriff Hutton at noon. I won't force you to associate with me—'

'No!' I blink the tears away, shaking my head. 'I will stay the week, as was your invitation. I shan't abandon my York blood.'

'Good. My queen was right in trusting you with this innermost secret. Remember what you have sworn.'

'I will. And do you swear that what you have told me is indeed the truth?'

'I swear it on the sacraments.'

The three of us part ways as the royal couple spur their horses to the front of the hunting party and I remain back, lacking the confidence to let my horse gallop. The forest does not feel so enchanting anymore.

Am I a wicked soul? Would God—or worse, Mother—frown upon my decision to take the party of a man who played a significant part in the death of my brothers, whether he intended it or not? I cannot tell. The portion of his and his wife's blame is so much smaller than a tiny piece of me once feared, thus my relief is as pronounced as my wrath. I have to believe what they have told me, because I have very little else to believe that feels plausible. We all make mistakes, some of them fatal, and as I lament what happened, one thing becomes clear. Uncle Richard could not have put the princes anywhere but the Tower, not solely because it was expected that Ed should reside there till his coronation, but because their isolation was crucial. My uncle did what he had to do to protect his lands and realise his ambitions for England. Mother would indeed have turned Dickie into a figurehead, and more violence would have ensued.

And Buckingham…Buckingham is the true perpetrator. If he was still alive and stood before me now, I would not hesitate to trample him with my horse. His henchmen's hands squeezing my brothers' throats…or was the deed done with daggers? A dull blow to the head? Blood rushes in my ears; the trees swoon around me; my head spins. I have to lie flat against my mare's muscular neck to prevent myself from either falling off or vomiting.

The incident calls to mind the case of Thomas Becket. Some three hundred years ago, King Henry II, in conflict with his archbishop Becket, spoke a few thoughtless words in affect, which his knights interpreted as their cue to murder the archbishop and thereby increase their own favour. Naturally, the King was infuriated, for if it was thought he had ordered the murder, he risked being excommunicated by His Holiness the Pope. Rash sycophants for subjects can be a perilous thing.

I have at least learnt the truth, or so I believe. Even I know that breaking an oath taken upon the sacraments, or lying under said oath, is an offence one burns in hell for—that is why I myself have been careful never to swear such an oath.

If only I could declare what happened to all of England, all the world, not just to my mother, who I know will never accept the truth... Perhaps if she did, she would then be more lenient towards Uncle Richard and less so towards Margaret Beaufort, who must have known they were dead long before we realised if not accepted it. After all, she was in close communication with Buckingham before and during the rebellion last autumn; it was through her we received the wealth of information. How long did she know the fight to restore Ed to the throne was already lost, and that her own son had won his conditional claim? Was she perhaps even involved in the deaths?

But no, the King and Queen are right. No one except their closest confidants would believe Buckingham did it on his own behest, especially not now, when they have already darkened the crime for many months. The only outcome would be the public concluding once and for all that my brothers died by my uncle's hand, which would further strengthen Tudor's own claim. And the commotion over the lack of bodies or proper burial... I shudder, my horse's fur warm and thoroughly brushed against my cheek. If there is one thing that repulses me, it is maltreatment of corpses, the ultimate humiliation and dishonour of the dead.

None of us are exempt from loss. My cousin Edward of Middleham was no older than my brothers when he succumbed to disease. Indeed, boys are more precious than jewels, yet they die like flies.

Chapter X

THEIR SCREAMS HAUNT me that night. Elizabeth lies snoring next to me in our shared chamber—the night is the one time she lacks grace—while I curl up with my knees touching my chin and shut my eyes until I see bright spots dancing. I wish my sister would snore louder so as to drown my brothers' chilling cries for help. I imagine them smothered with pillows, kicking the mattress furiously. I imagine golden locks marinating in blood long after their throats have been slit, never to be washed clean again. There is nothing new to me about these visions, except they are clearer and more intense now that I know who was responsible but still not the details of the deed or what happened afterwards. Until I do know the full story, I fear I shall never be entirely free from their ghosts.

Nonetheless, my investigation will have to rest awhile. I have extracted more knowledge than I dared hope, and what else can I do at this moment? I can hardly embark on a search for Buckingham's men and kindly inquire if anyone is feeling inclined to shoulder the title of boy-butcher. All Soul's Day was the day when Henry Stafford, Duke of Buckingham, went to the block. How queer, to think it would also have been Ed's thirteenth birthday, had he lived.

I turn on my other side to look at Elizabeth. In the dark, her lips are the colour of slate, the oval of her face even softer than in harsh daylight. Had it been Anne sharing the bed with me, I might have woken her for comfort, but Elizabeth… I am not so certain she would refrain from chiding me for my meddling in these dangerous affairs, or for my trust in the King's oath. No, let her sleep and snore as long as she likes.

After supper the following evening, the King and Queen summon me to sit with them in the grand solar. I flush with pleasure, for it is a more intimate gathering than I anticipated: only four other lords and two ladies, presumably wives, are present, chatting idly by the end of the long table. I recognise three of the men as Francis Lovell, Richard Ratcliffe, and William Catesby, all sunburnt and smiling. The fourth I do not know, but I recall that his name is Sir James Tyrell.

The vaulted ceiling casts shadows across the room, streaking the warm glow from the crackling fireplace and the candles burning low. The walls are covered with Flemish tapestries depicting the Arthurian legends, serving not merely as decoration but as a shield against the chill that tends to lodge in stone castles in the Midlands. My slippers click against the floor, then sink into the thick carpet as I approach the pallets by the fireplace, where the King and Queen are sitting ensconced in a cloud of her honeysuckle perfume.

I catch a stray word or two on my way, enough for me to know what they are speaking of. The dead prince who was their sole hope and joy, the single fruit of twelve years of marriage. The little lives snuffed out in the womb or in childbed. The wretched unfairness of Mother Nature.

I shudder. I have no desire to hear about dead children, much less speak about them, not when my own loss is still so fresh to me. Nonetheless, as I sink down on one of the pallets, the topic is heavy in the air.

'When you spoke of my brothers, Your Grace, you said you had never seen the King's Grace so furious since the Duke of Clarence tried to keep you from marrying.' I edge forward on the pallet, hoping they might indulge me and distract me from the ghosts raging in my head, howling for my attention.

The King gives one of his intense, small smiles. 'Do call me Uncle tonight, Cecily. We so rarely used titles in previous years, did we? Yes, Anne spoke truth. But you know this story already, surely?'

'It was long since I heard it—I forget too easily for my own good, sometimes. Did Clarence really hide you away as a kitchen maid...Cousin Anne?' I decide that if this evening is private enough to dispense of one person's title, it is private enough to do without them altogether.

A shadow crosses Anne's face. 'Alas, he did, though he lacked the wits to remove me from his household at the Herber. The wits and the courage, yes?'

'Yes, *ma belle*. Brother George always did lack that.' Uncle Richard turns to me. 'First, he refused to let me see my intended bride, claiming a fever tormented her, then a cold, then an upset stomach. As the months passed, he ran out of excuses, hence dressing her in a kitchen maid's rags, thinking I would not recognise her.'

The lords and ladies at the other end of the solar are still talking in low voices among themselves, and to my relief, I find myself at ease with them. As I watch the pools of golden light from the hearth illuminating Queen Anne's translucent skin, and as I sip on my cloyingly sweet wine, the soft atmosphere of a springtime evening starts to chase away my anxiety. At least for now.

'Was he so eager for land and money?'

'Indeed. Your father had already granted him plenty, considering his defections from his house of descent. But George became obsessed with the Beauchamp lands, thought he could lay claim to them as long as he was married to one heiress and controlled the other with an iron first.' The resentment is clear as a in Uncle Richard's voice.

'But you proved him wrong, didn't you, Uncle—you got Middleham Castle? I remember how he looked whenever someone mentioned Middleham, as if he was choking on his own tooth!' A smirk jumps to my lips at the thought, though I am unable to lure either of my companions to smile. It is not unkindness on their part, but simply the aftermath of death.

'And still your father gave him nearly everything else in exchange for his begrudging consent to our marriage. Not that I disputed him further. I had what mattered most.'

'My father did not mind, did he? I never heard him say so.'

I realise my blunder too late; Queen Anne is at once defensive. 'How could he mind, when Elizabeth Woodville was no less the Lancastrian widow than I was? At least, *I* had the noblest of blood in my veins.'

103

'I hope you know, Cousin, that I think of my late father's blood as what flows strongest in my own veins,' I assure her with more fervour than I first intended, then turn to the King with what I reckon to be the most daring question I have asked him in my life. 'Were you pleased when Clarence met his end?'

'Pleased? No. There was a time when I could have killed him with my own hands for the things he did, but no, I was not pleased, unlike your mother. It was so odd, see. He crossed every boundary during a decade, yet the punishment did not come until…until it did. I always wondered if there was something more, something your father preferred to keep even from me. Edward was dearer to me than my own life, God rest his soul, but no man is without fault. You recall the French campaign?'

'I was so very young, Uncle, but I do recall Elizabeth becoming the Dauphine overnight. She was certain to remind me of it personally every day for a fortnight, if not more.'

'Ah, yes. A generous pension from the French King and his eldest daughter betrothed to the *Dauphin*, in exchange for turning back home without waging proper war. I believe he forgot honour on that day when he signed the Treaty of Picquigny, along with the taxes he had collected from the commoners with a promise to use the funds to reclaim French soil.'

The other men in the solar have grown silent. Even at this distance, I can trace the bitterness suddenly engraved in their faces. No doubt they, too, remember the failure of the French campaign.

I do my best to hide the blush that must be flaring on my cheeks on behalf of my father. 'I wish he had not turned back so easily. A glorious England and France under a single crown… And then Elizabeth would not be queen of either.'

'She cannot be now. She has too much of Dame Elizabeth Grey in her.' Anne presses a palm against her bodice as if to calm herself.

'Perhaps. At the very least, that is where her heart lies.'

'And promised to Tudor, that most foul of rebels.'

I hold my breath. How I agree with them! Only I still dare not fully say it outright. Mother is a spectacular woman, and none can deny that, but it is true her family was never as strong-willed or as beauteous, with the exception of my grandmother Jacquetta and my aunt Catherine. Their star rose high thanks to my father's generosity; it was not a rise based on merit. Of course, merit is rarely the sole reason for any courtier's success, and I have no grievances with this, but Mother's kinsmen did much to alienate the rest of the peerage, too much. Whatever my opinions of the Woodvilles and the Tudors, though, I am not accustomed to voicing them so freely, and my skin prickles.

'What is that scar on your hand?' I say, swiftly switching the topic.

'You were always curious about battle marks, dear niece, even as a small child. As it happens, this particular mark is no more heroic than the bite of a wolfhound cub. Isolde is breeding again.'

Even Queen Anne smiles at that, and I thank Our Lady for the turn of the conversation. Hearing her name, Isolde trots up to Uncle Richard and nuzzles her wet nose against her master's knee, before tramping on the spot and settling by the hearth, head resting on outstretched pawns.

We pass the rest of the evening speaking of literature rather than death, music rather than the French or my mother's family. I savour every moment, dreading the day I will have to return to Sheriff Hutton. I even manage to exchange a few genuine pleasantries with the other lords and ladies after Nan Lovell lures me to laugh at a comment about her terse relationship with her husband Francis, who drains his cup in response and calls for another flagon of wine.

When the hour grows later than prudence advises, I withdraw to the chamber I share with Elizabeth. Slipping between the silky sheets, I believe her to be sound asleep, until she speaks in a detached voice.

'Did you enjoy yourself?'

'I did.' I plump up my pillows, then let my head hit the feather-stuffed softness.

'I do not understand you sometimes, Cecily.'

'You have too much of Mother in you.' The echo of Queen Anne's words is deliberate. 'You are hostile to the wrong people.'

My sister says nothing more that night.

In contrast to the glamour of court life, which I had so sorely missed, Sheriff Hutton feels like a cave in the wilderness. No glittering dances, no hunting parties, and very little gossip. The most exciting turn of events during the week after I return is when one of the kitchen maids tries to smuggle away a couple of lamb chops under her apron and is duly dismissed from the household. If I were her, I would have made sure not to get caught, since that is half the crime.

Despite my grumblings, I quickly adapt to life in the countryside again. Spring is in full bloom, ripening into summer. The sky blazes blue, a thin veneer of clouds surrendering to rays of blinding sunlight beating down on our scalps, turning our hair to white gold. The trees sway in the faint breeze, their lace-pattern of leaves rustling, sending my spirits soaring. I always preferred this time of year to any other—except the Twelve Days of Christmas—and last time, I was unable to enjoy nature's beauty as I huddled up in the heat-baked abbey. Every morrow and afternoon, I venture outside the brick walls of Sheriff Hutton to promenade or rather, when the two guards accompanying me turn their attention elsewhere, dash through the fields. My gowns are perpetually wet with dew and covered in grass stains, but that is the bright side of Sheriff Hutton's reclusiveness: no one is watching, at least no one who matters. As much as I yearn to return to the knot of power and politics, I secretly treasure these moments of shelter from the public gaze.

I try not to think about Elizabeth prancing at court. Summer will soon wane and die, and when it does, I will once more wish to swap places with her. However, I discover a new advantage to her absence, for someone must fill the gap she leaves in our mother's love. Anne is too immersed in her new friendship with Meg and the texts they study together, Kate spends her days either doodling ugly fantasy creatures or trailing after Young Warwick, and Bridget—though she is a gem, promising to become the most beautiful of my sisters—remains quiet as a church mouse. I am only too happy to shoulder the role of Mother's main focus, temporary though it might be. Who would have thought it possible two years ago, when Elizabeth, Ed, and Dickie took precedence in the queue, let alone when poor Mary was still alive? I would willingly chop off my right hand to bring either of my dead siblings back to us, but I have wondered for a long time how it feels to be a favourite child, not just *another girl*.

Mother sometimes said she loved all of us equally. I think she meant it, believed it even, yet she had to say it to remind us as well as herself. That I should still be so eager for her affection puzzles me at first, considering my mild betrayal of her family, but I conclude it is only natural, when she is the sole parent of mine still living. My love for her as such is entirely separate from what I think of her politics. I do make an attempt at revealing the story of Buckingham to her, but she is hell-bent on not believing me, seeing as I have no evidence, and I refrain from quarrelling over it. I find it improbable that it would change her attitude towards Uncle Richard significantly, since, I have to admit, she has plenty cause to hate him regardless.

What my uncle said about her being pleased at Clarence's death... I remember it well myself, though I was barely nine years old at the time. Her smile could have melted men and marble alike the day the death sentence was carried out. Some might call it macabre, but the memory does not repulse me, for I shared her relief if not her glee, even at my young age. Yes, we do have quite a bit in common, she and I, not to be discounted simply because of our equally vast differences.

This summer, Mother spends hours teaching me to play the lute more skilfully than I have done thus far, since my fingers tend to tangle with the strings.

'There,' she says one mild August evening. 'You improve every passing day. Methinks you can play for all the princes in Christendom soon.'

I clutch the instrument to my chest. 'Thank you, Lady Mother. And dance with them, too?'

'That also, if the scoundrel Gloucester finds the time to arrange it.'

I put the lute down on the table, loud enough to provoke a glare, and at once regret it. 'I thought he was planning to invade Scotland. Perhaps it could succeed this time, without Father holding him back.'

'It seems not. Other threats demand his military power.'

'Henry Tudor?'

She does not need to reply; her pinched mouth is enough to confirm my fears. Yes, fears. Tudor has already failed once and put us in considerable danger. Uncle Richard forgave my mother

107

her involvement in the rebellion last autumn, at least publicly, but if Tudor made a second attempt to launch an invasion? We remain inextricably linked to him and his cause through Elizabeth's betrothal whether my oldest sister likes it or not, for the Lancastrian took an oath last Christmas to wed her when he becomes king. *When,* not *if.* Such folly! Of course, his aim is no longer to restore my dead brother the throne and merely reclaim the lands associated with the title Earl of Richmond for himself. His Yorkist supporters, largely Woodvilles and Father's old household knights, are no longer loyal to Edward V—they are loyal to his memory. They believe Tudor to be their only alternative, aligning with the Lancastrian rebel camp.

I often listen as the servants whisper among themselves, speculating just as we do about what the outcome might be, and through them I access information before the official letters reach the household.

The Duke of Brittany's backing is floundering. I hear he is old and grey, and with only a young daughter to inherit him, he is desperate to secure his duchy's independence from France's looming pawns. Uncle Richard vows to send six thousand English archers to aid Brittany if they hand over Henry Tudor, and the duke agrees. The French have not been particularly keen to face English archers since the battle of Agincourt almost seventy years ago, and little wonder at that.

The tension building on my shoulders eases when I am told of this deal struck between England and Brittany If my uncle can haul in Tudor before he tries to invade again, those of my relatives who might aid him, indeed my closest family, can be viewed in a much more lenient light, and both sides of the conflict can avoid a bloody confrontation.

I have just returned from a walk, my cloak soaked in autumn rain, when Meg unwillingly smashes my hopes to the muddy ground. Tudor and his closest men have bolted over the border to France, escaping by the skin of their teeth. The French regency council and its boy-king Charles VIII will likely hold onto him like a toddler with a new toy, latching at the opportunity to stir up yet more trouble in our country. The raw November winds sweep in from the coast, and while they chill me to the bone, the ominous political quagmire does the same with my blood.

Lincoln keeps us in fresh supply of news. 'That knave the Earl of Oxford has escaped his cell in Calais, defecting to Tudor's band,' he informs us during one of his visits to Sheriff Hutton, visits occurring more frequently now since he has been named head of the Council of the North which oftentimes holds its meetings here. We are crossing the inner courtyard, and I have taken his arm, allowing him to hold me a little too close and a little too hard, so that I can coax the details out of him.

'Can he defect when he was already a Lancastrian?' He does not answer. 'How did he escape?'

Lincoln scratches his fox-coloured beard. 'He ran off with his jailor. Should be a clue.'

'Oh. Cousin, I would have thought a man in his position should be more reliable.'

'Yes. Cannot trust anyone these days.'

Mother rejoices, because Oxford is a seasoned military strategic, and his allegiance increases Tudor's chances markedly.

'Did you know all this before we did?' I ask after my stroll with Lincoln.

She puts down her embroidery, a composition of daisies and cornflowers. 'I did not…Margaret Beaufort no longer corresponds with me. The risk is too great.'

'But you still hope her son will succeed?'

'I still hope to see my Beth on the throne.'

'And ruin my chances of prospering?' I cross my arms.

'You would prosper more under her rule.'

'But *she* would not rule, Lady Mother! Her husband would! And even if she did, I can prosper without her.'

Our sweet months of harmony have gone by quickly.

Mother sighs and picks up her needle and thread, making immaculate stitches. 'There is something else which I daresay will be more to your liking. Gloucester has sent an invite to join court for the Christmas celebrations. We leave for their nest towards the end of Advent.'

'Westminster?' I cannot disguise the elation instantly bubbling to the surface. *Finally.*

'Yes, Westminster. My sweet.'

Chapter XI

'ISN'T IT WONDERFUL?' I exclaim as we step inside the great hall at the Palace of Westminster. 'Every bit as wonderful as it used to be!'

'Your father would have enjoyed the decorations and the eatables,' Mother says, holding Kate by the hand to prevent her from scuttling ahead. 'If only he were here.'

The hall is swarming with clusters of nobles in their finery, trimmed in precious metals to their teeth. Holly and ivy line the walls and the rows of tables, their glossy leaves reflecting light from a thousand blazing candles, intertwined with garlands of silver and gold. The air is thick with the blend of courtiers' chit-chat and minstrels plucking on instruments, the smell of sweat and perfume and boots made of Italian or Spanish leather creeping up my nostrils.

I press my palm against my stomach to curb a growl. Advent fast is my least favourite time of year—so dreary, so dull. Why should we suffer thus? I hold firm in my belief that Jesus would rather we enjoyed the food and entertainment at our disposal, even if he could not do so himself.

'Their Graces, the King and Queen!' a man in livery declares.

Uncle Richard enters the great hall, nodding and smiling at his magnates, his wife on his arm. The Queen has donned a gown of olive-green silk, intricately embroidered with golden thread, its sleeves lined with ermine. Her hair is gathered in a two-parted caul underneath the coronet. At the base of her throat rests an obsidian-coloured jewel the size of a strawberry—I cannot tell what kind—and on her finger she flaunts a single ornament: the plain gold of her wedding band. From afar, she enchants, but when they pass us, her taunt cheeks and the shadows dappling her hollowed eyes are screamingly obvious, her delicate neck threatening to snap like a chicken bone under the weight of the coronet.

I force myself to give a small bow of my head and bend my knee—it still feels like such an absurd practice—and every guest lowers themselves likewise.

Once the King and Queen are seated on the dais by the high table, I claim my own seat next to Mother. We have been designated places at the end of the same table, with Elizabeth's empty chair closest to our hosts, as custom requires.

'A gay occasion. Methinks the vipers will attract the displeasure of clerics and monks,' Mother says, as if she herself was not once infamous for the luxury she rightfully gorged in before Father died.

Anne looks up from her empty trencher. 'Perhaps it would look worse if he *didn't* have a proper celebration, as if he were not king.'

'My wise little girl.' Mother strokes her cheek. 'I hope you prefer this to last year.'

Anne nods. I agree wholeheartedly, for although last year's Christmas Day seemed a true blessing under the circumstances, this is how it *should* be. One thing alone is amiss: Thomas. I reach up to touch the plump pearls sprinkled on my caul, recalling his embarrassed face when he presented me with the gift. No, I must not lend it a thought.

Servant boys enter the hall, balancing gigantic silver platters heaped with exquisitely decorated dishes. The glazed boar heads and the swan with its ivory-white feathers put back after the roasting immediately become the centre of attention and praise, though I confess I find their dead eyes as repulsive as Dickie once did.

We have been given personal knives, yet another sign of favour. I carve my roasted duckling, grease coating my fingers, desperate to satisfy my hunger.

'Remember your manners, my sweet,' Mother says. 'You do not want stains on your new gown.'

I force myself to slow down, sit back and square my shoulders. In particular, I do not wish to display any indecorous behaviour at this hour, when our moments of public glory are few.

The spices—cinnamon, nutmeg, cloves, saffron—intoxicate me. I sprinkle the stews and meats on my trencher with a hefty dash of salt, relishing in the knowledge that these luxuries belong to me for life. I cannot count the different dishes, but there must be thirty in the least. The banquet will last for hours, naturally followed by dancing.

I wash my hands in the silver basin I share with Anne before I stand and slip out between the chairs. Smoothing my gown, I round the table and curtsey before the King and Queen.

Uncle Richard gestures for me to rise, elevating his gold-embossed cup in a small toast as I do so.

Forgetting my new station for the briefest moment, I speak before spoken to. 'Merry Christmas, Your Grace.'

'And to you, dear niece. You enjoy the feast? I find it too extravagant myself.'

The nobles laugh as if at a bad joke, but I believe he is in earnest.

'I enjoy it immensely.' I turn to my second cousin. 'Madam, I do find your necklace most rapturing.'

'It pleases me to see you,' she says. 'Prithee, stay awhile.'

'Yes, Your Grace. My lady Mother says we may remain at court until after Epiphany, mayhap longer.'

The lines around Queen Anne's mouth harden at the mention of Elizabeth Woodville. 'You may remain for as long as I say so—you enjoy staying at court, yes?' The hopeful note in her voice is subtle but genuine. 'I would like a companion. You won't abandon me, Cecily?'

I can almost taste warm drops of pleasure on my tongue, for it is the first time she uses my Christian name in front of all the court. 'Never, Your Grace! I shall stay as long as you let me.'

'You are a sweet girl.' She smiles sadly before she transfers her attention to John Howard, who is sitting at her right fiddling with the table cloth with hands calloused from wielding a sword for the better part of his nigh on sixty years.

I recognise my cue to withdraw and return to my spot further down the table.

Mother eyes me. 'You are quick to discard my council.'

'I cannot argue with the Queen, Lady Mother.'

'Nor did you want to.' She sighs, patting Kate's hair.

'No, I did not want to,' I say. 'Well, why should I?'

'I know you do not like bowing your head to them any more than we do. You never will.'

I shrug. 'Of course not, but they are showering us with grace at last. Before, it was just a trickle.'

'We shall have to wait and see.'

The meal passes, my belly hurting by the time I have tried every delicacy. Mother often advises me to eat some bread and cheese before dining in public, so as to avoid gorging in front of others, but I was too excited to remember this in time.

As the eve wears on the courtiers flit around like sprightly butterflies, a few of them dancing already.

I knit my brows. 'Where is Elizabeth? It is frightfully unlike her to be so late.'

I receive no reply, but I need none, for my sister emerges into the great hall from a side door, at the heels of Queen Anne, who must have gone to fetch her. At first, I think my eyes are playing me a cruel trick. Then, murmurs spread through the thicket of courtiers along with a wave of raised eyebrows and long glances.

Elizabeth is clad in an exact replica of the Queen's lovely attire, and has even clasped the other woman's obsidian necklace around her swan-like throat. It is in truth an odd occurrence, because no other person save the King himself should ever be perceived as equal to the supposedly untouchable spouse of a sovereign.

To my puzzlement, Mother is nodding to herself. 'You were right. They shower us with favour, and disarm the rebel lords at the same time.'

'Lady Mother?'

'Is there any way Gloucester could demonstrate the Woodville girls' integration into his regime more clearly? I think not. I daresay he hopes the exiles will return begging for pardon if they hear what grace awaits former enemies.'

A familiar, nasty feeling brews in the pit of my stomach, a feeling I hoped had begun to subside while my oldest sister was away. 'But why *Elizabeth*? I thought there was little affection left between them and her.'

'This has nothing to do with affection. This is mere strategy.'

Very well. Let Elizabeth be their tool of conciliating the rebels, let her parade as a part of their frontline rather than act as Tudor's linchpin to the throne. It is only right the House of York stand united…as long as I am not neglected for the sake of it.

I turn my gaze on my sister, and my jealousy swiftly fades to sympathy of sorts. Queen Anne's health may be in grave decline, but she looks positively thriving next to Elizabeth, whose complexion is poorly suited for the olive-green costume she now wears. She omits no sound, but when I narrow my eyes, I spot her full lower lip quivering. Because she is so often on the main stage, I tend to forget she never asked to be, especially not on *this* stage.

The Queen strides forth and reclaims her seat at her husband's side. They speak in low voices, thus I inch closer as inconspicuously as I can.

'Will you grant me a dance, *ma belle?*'

'Not tonight, Rich. Dance with her.' The Queen nods towards Elizabeth, who is still standing in the middle of the hall making eyes at our mother. 'They will know she is one of us now.'

Uncle Richard frowns. 'One dance. You must try to eat some more, and give the herbal remedy the physician brought yesterday a chance.'

'I will. Pray do not concern yourself for me.' She manages a smile as he stands and kisses her hand before gesturing to the musicians to play.

How odd to think that it was less than three years since he danced with me on my birthday. His natural skill has, unfortunately, not improved. His technique is faultless, yet he is stiff and inexpressive, doubtlessly agonized by his back.

I am itching to join even in this *basse dance*, but the conversation between two minor nobles a few feet behind me captures my attention.

'As if she sought to replace Her Grace!' the lady closest to me hisses. 'Is this His Grace's doing?'

The man blows his nose like a trumpet. 'I bet the girl will have more than the Queen's dress ere long! His Grace needs a new son, healthy this time, and those Woodvilles are naught if not fine breeding stock!'

114

My insides turn as the full significance of the exchange of garments dawns upon me, for this is a double-edged sword, and a fickle one. If the King and Queen sought to set tongues wagging, they have certainly succeeded, just not in the intended manner. Not at all. It is one thing to display their newfound unity with the Woodville branch of the family—a splendid unity—but *this?* A rumour about wedding his niece could ruin my uncle quicker than Dorset could ruin a woman's chastity. The general public would frown and the north would renounce his authority for love of Anne Neville and her late father, the Kingmaker. I dare not think what Henry Tudor would do—move on to his second pick, *me?* Oh Lord, let the fool have forgotten I exist.

My head spins. If such rumours are already flourishing… Does Elizabeth have any notion about what she has partaken in? Do any of them understand the mistake they have made?

The dance comes to an end. My sister turns left and right, feet paralyzed, before retreating out through the side door.

I dart after her and find myself in the obscure passage where I used to hide from our governess. 'Elizabeth!' I grab her arm. 'I have to tell you what I heard—'

A strangled sob escapes her. She clasps a hand to her mouth, closing her eyes for a second, and is composed once more.

'You think I have not heard, too?'

'It's not true, is it?' I have to ask, if only to soothe myself.

'How can you think that of me?'

'I never said I did.'

'I ought not to have agreed to put on a gown like hers. It is even too short—look.' She spreads her skirts, nodding at her exposed ankles.

I clear my parched throat. 'And your hair is too…too blonde.' It feels easier to dwell upon these trivialities than the underlying issue. 'Did she say why?'

'To show me off, almost like a trophy. I liked it not then, but this is so much worse.'

'Mother guessed it. Though if I had been you, I'd have sung a merry little tune.'

She eyes me up and down in silence for a moment. 'And if you were me now?'

I grapple for the right words, any words, but find none. Never before have I seen her look like a trembling baby deer lost in the dark woods, and it baffles me. No one is more surprised than I when I wrap my arms around her in a crush of mutual despair, awkwardly patting her back.

'Oh, Cecily…' she whispers.

Indeed, how far would I be prepared to go to become queen? To wed a Lancastrian is on the verge, but I doubt I would. To wed an uncle and spoil something as rare as royal love… Well, that is definitely a step too far even in my universe.

I send God a genuine prayer to spare Queen Anne the dirty rumours about her husband and my sister. Naturally, God does not heed me, but perhaps He has little chance against the gossip-crazed mash of courtiers and servants who take such raw delight in their obnoxiously loud tittering and tattering, a delight I would have shared had it not been for the fact that the titter-tatter concerns those closest to my heart.

A week after New Year's Day, my mistress summons me to her chambers. I walk with brisk steps, my knuckles white as I pinch the folds of my skirts in an attempt to remain calm and elegant. The last thing she needs at this point is a frenzied girl bolstering her own concern.

Upon entering her bedchamber, I find her slumped against a stack of pillows on her bed. I neglect curtseying and drop down on the bedside, the heavy curtains brushing against my cheek. To my relief and, frankly, astonishment, she does not protest.

'Are you well, Your Grace?'

'Do I look well?'

I have to bite my tongue. 'No. No, you look exhausted.'

'You should tell me I am beautiful. That is what flattering ladies do, no?'

'Pardon, Madam. I thought you wanted my opinion.'

The Queen lifts a hand, slowly, touching her lips. The cold, crisp light trickling through the window shines through her chemise, revealing the silhouette of her arm and the bone jutting out at her elbow, specks of dust dancing between us.

'Your sister Elizabeth is beautiful. Everyone thinks so.'

I swallow. 'Yes, they do. She is.'

116

'They offend me. They dare offend me, and the King! They spin horrible lies, just like they've always done, and they do not know their own good!'

'No, Madam, Cousin Anne, they do not know their own good.'

She sinks back into the pillows, fading against the sheets. The outburst has drained her further. 'Richard would never. *Never.* I took his bastards into my care because I knew…because I knew I would always be foremost in his affections.'

The sight of her brings tears to my eyes. It terrifies me what misery can do to a person. 'It might not be a comfort, but my sister is as appalled as you and His Grace. This was not her scheme.'

'Then it was your mother's. The witch.'

I shake my head. 'I swear it was not, at least not to my knowledge. You mustn't fret so. The north is loyal to *you*, and besides, my sisters and I are still…illegitimate, or at least thought to be so.'

'Does it matter?' A fit of coughs ride her frail frame and she buries her face in the crook of her elbow, muffling her voice. 'They offend us with slander. They…'

'Your Grace…Cousin Anne? Your chemise—' My breath twists in my throat.

She follows my stare. Her sleeve is spattered with blood, as are her lips.

I remain at court during the first months of the year of our Lord 1485 according to Queen Anne's wishes. I am like a fish in water here, a fully integrated part of high society once more, yet my joy is dimmed.

Despite my prayers, my mistress does not recuperate. She has been shattered since her only son died, and the whispers about her replacement make the shards clearer for all to see. Uncle Richard banishes Elizabeth to Sheriff Hutton to stem the rumours. He sits by his wife's bedside, reading to her for hours on end, watching her flit in and out of sleep, holding her close when the coughs rack her fragile body, his face etched with helplessness. It is not long, however, before both the Queen and the physicians forbid him to visit her at length or at a close

117

distance. They have discovered she suffers from more than grief: a contagious illness, consumption. If the King catches it and dies without an heir… England is turbulent enough as it is.

The Queen cannot be abandoned entirely, though, hence I take it upon myself to assist the group of fretting maids who see to her daily needs, from washing and gently scrubbing to entertaining with soft music and ensuring she takes her prescribed medicaments. Her face is taunt, her cheekbones too prominent to be natural, her eyes feverish when open and like the veined petals of a rose when closed. She is a bird with broken wings and broken lungs, not to mention broken heart, and I wish more than anything that I could make her fly again.

During that eerie stretch of time, an inevitable bond forms between us through the intimacy of our daily routine, in spite of her dislike for lack of privacy. I find little time to think about my own health, but I have been persistent against disease since I was an infant, and the consumption does not touch me.

Four days before my sixteenth birthday, in the middle of March, a shadow passes over the sun. Londoners close their shutters and doors; I watch from a window as they make the sign of the cross to ward off this evil omen. On the same day, Queen Anne dies, left alone in her bedchamber on the physicians' command for fear of the disease in her lungs. I cannot think of any reason that the sun would go black other than to mark her passing.

I knew the end was near, we all did, but I fail to suppress my tears nonetheless. I am plunged back to the day I received word of Agnes' passing. Are all my friends doomed to die? I do believe the Queen was my friend, or at least I would like to believe it. However much she feared and loathed my mother, I thought I had found a companion.

She is embalmed in preparation for the sumptuous burial, laid out on a solid marble slab in one of the rooms in the palace, silver cressets lining the walls to envelop her in light. I cannot resist the temptation to visit her one final time.

Stiff and pale like a snuffed-out candle, her hands together in prayer, the change since the last time I saw her alive is marginal. Her gown is of thick, black velvet, her chest sprinkled with pearls and sapphires sewn into the fabric, the skirt long enough to cover her tiny feet poking up. She always had such lovely feet and hands. Her hair is gathered in intricate braids pinned to her head, the black gauze veil fastened on her coronet cascading down on her shoulders in delicate layers.

When I take a step closer, the chain with her finest crucifix wound around her fingers catches the light, the golden cross dangling against her wrist. Her wedding band and coronation ring compete in splendour on the other hand. What truly strikes me, though, is the Queen's face. Her granite-grey lips are slightly parted, as if trying to pronounce a final wish, the fringe of eyelashes prominent against her cheek. I count on my fingers. Twenty-eight, if I know my family's history. In death, she looks my age, the grief over her son and the tribulation of rumours erased from her face.

Without a thought, I reach out to let my fingers brush against her coronet, to touch this most glorious of symbols.

'Do not. You'll wreck her halo.' The King's voice cuts through the incense-saturated air.

I withdraw my hand and take a step back, heart thudding. 'You frightened me, Your Grace.'

'I frighten you?' He rounds the marble slab, facing me. The years erased from his wife's features have been added to his, and there is a certain hollowness to his voice, on the verge of bitterness, a sentiment rarely found there before.

I shake my head. 'I just did not hear you come in. I know I ought not be here—'

'No matter, dear niece. And do the rumours frighten you?'

'Which ones?' I know which ones, of course, but cannot bring myself to admit it.

'The story goes,' he says, running a trembling finger along the marble, 'that I poisoned my Anne in order to wed your sister and beget more sons.'

I want to vomit. 'Do people never tire of impish gossip? Have they no shame?'

'They will say anything to defile my honour. They will say I am a monster.'

What does one reply to such a statement? I know it to be true, yes, people can be wicked, cruel.

119

Uncle Richard at last turns his glance on me. 'The invasion is coming this summer, my councillors tell me. Let Tudor have my crown and my life—it matters not, not now. Not without...' He fills his lungs with air, pausing as if to regain composure. 'You are to be married, to Baron Scrope of Masham's brother.'

'*What?*' Panic bubbles in my chest. No, *no!* 'I don't even recognise his name, Sire! Does he have a title? You promised—'

'I know what I promised! You are missing the point. I will not risk you falling into the hands of a Lancastrian nobleman, not now nor if Tudor defeats me in battle.' He clenches his jaw.

I gape at him. I have barely begun to consider how I would act with an age-old enemy line on the throne, let alone at my table and in my bed. 'You think I'd do such a thing?' You think I would give myself to one of their lot?

'I think your mother would do it for you. Scrope's son is lowly enough not to attract Tudor's attention. If I married you to one of my magnates at this hour and you were widowed during the battle, the risk is greater he would maltreat you to demonstrate authority.'

'But...but you will *win*. You have to.'

'I might. I have the upper hand. If I do, your marriage will be annulled immediately. There will be no papal dispensation, nor consummation, and you can have a prince if you so like. If I lose, you can decide for yourself whether you wish to annul the union and seek your fortune elsewhere or not. You shan't be your mother's pawn.' He pins me down with his gaze, demanding to be obeyed.

Mayhap his words carry reason, but my instincts prompt me to protest. 'But I will be my husband's pawn.'

'The man is utterly witless. I have spoken to him myself— more compliant than a dog, the poor wretch.'

'A dog without a title.'

'Cecily. Your prospects will be no worse. If I win, a princess or duchess. If I lose, a woman with a choice rather than a scrap of meat thrown to Lancastrian wolves.'

I draw a shaky breath. Should I surrender? There is no credible alternative. I must trust in my uncle's judgement. 'Will you give me your blessing?' I kneel on the floor, the cold stone pressing hard through my silk gown and kirtle.

120

Uncle Richard's hand is warm on my head. 'Now go. Please. I wish to be alone with my wife.'

I rise, my knees sore, my tongue a lump of clay in my mouth. In the doorway, I turn only to see the King kneel himself and place a kiss on the Queen's pasty lips. I avert my eyes as I depart at last. When Richard II's wife, Anne of Bohemia, died, her husband tore the palace where it happened down to the ground. It is good fortune that Westminster is too precious to suffer a similar fate.

Dear God, let Anne Neville be remembered, and not just remembered as a victim of an unkind life, for she was so much more than that.

Chapter XII

AFTER QUEEN ANNE'S burial, I return to Sheriff Hutton to prepare for my impending wedding. Anne and Kate fawn over me, while Elizabeth and Mother sit tight-lipped. I am not certain what to feel myself: relief that Uncle Richard has a fairly sensible plan for me, or despair that it might not work? What if my husband decides to claim his rights and consummate the marriage in defiance of his instructions? I have not so much as seen him yet, and have only my uncle's word on his character.

'You mustn't let him,' Mother says during the fitting of my wedding gown.

I hold up my arms to survey the pinned-on sleeves in the mirror one of the maids presents us with. 'That is not exactly my choice, though, is it?'

'I warded off your father with a knife once, before he chose me for his wife.'

'You did?' I stare at her.

Elizabeth puts a hand to her lips to hide a sudden smile. Presumably, she already knows the story.

'It is far simpler than it might have been if you had gone to live with him at Upsall,' Mother resumes. 'I think I shall post a guard by your door.'

Anne stands on her toes and gather my hair behind my shoulders. 'Perchance it will be romantic. It *can* be romantic even if he does not have a title of his own, especially then.'

'You are too young to understand, but anyhow, I will not remain with him.'

'Really?'

'Really. This is just for now. When Uncle Richard returns in victorious glory, I shall have someone of higher standing.' I repeat this in my head like a mantra.

Mother strokes Bridget's hair, her youngest daughter sitting on her lap. 'It was devious of him to arrange this.'

I look at her in the mirror as the maids remove the pins in my sleeves. 'He thought you would betroth me to one of Tudor's henchmen to strengthen their claim as the invasion draws nearer. Would you have?'

She does not get the chance to reply, because Kate tugs at my hand, a grin on her cherub face. 'Cece! You'll be stuck with a commoner!'

'Hush! I shan't! Marriages are annulled all the time.'

'And when Beth wears the crown, you *will* have a Lancastrian husband. I refuse to see my lovely daughter live in squalor in Upsall,' Mother says.

'*If* Elizabeth is ever queen, I will marry the man it takes to advance my station, Lady Mother, but at least I will do it knowing I played no part in this…treachery!'

Elizabeth gives me a long glance. 'You mustn't say such things. Mother only wants what is best for us.'

'I know—forgive me.'

My wedding dress will be a waste: luxurious indigo, my favourite colour, embroidered with garlands of silver thread, the square neckline flashing a teal-coloured kirtle. This is the kind of dress I would have wanted the whole world to see.

Sir Ralph Scrope, third son of the 5th Baron Scrope and brother to the 6th, arrive a fortnight later. He has a small entourage in tow, consisting of two servants, a chaplain to conduct the service, and his younger brother Geoffrey.

I have not spent much time looking at muddied hay in my life, yet I dare wager Sir Ralph's hair is a perfect resemblance. His face is practically shapeless, blending with his throat in a fold of stubby skin, and his hands are the size of dinner platters. The contrast to my friend Thomas' nimble fingers, always sketching, is alarming to me. My fiancé has likely not held a pen more than a few times in all his life. His are hands fit for smashing men's skulls, and he walks with the audacity of a warrior, though lacking the finesse required to wield a sword rather than a club or axe.

We stand face to face in the great hall, me flanked by Mother and Elizabeth, he by young Geoffrey. I measure him up and down, trying to estimate his age, but it is difficult. Twenty? Thirty at most. I suppose I ought to be grateful he is not an old man with a cane.

'Lady Cecily,' he mumbles. 'An honour.'

I raise my chin half an inch. 'You are pleased at our union?'

Sir Ralph's glance darts around the room and Geoffrey has to clear his throat to bring forth a reply. 'Mm. Very.'

I turn and arch my eyebrows at Mother. The chagrin in her eyes is clear as day. Although Ralph Scrope is close to my father's height and equally broad-shouldered, my husband-to-be appears very far indeed from what hers was like.

The chaplain conducts the ceremony in the chapel situated in the north range, with Mother, Elizabeth, and Geoffrey serving as witnesses to give this sham an illusion of credibility. When the chaplain asks whether anyone knows of any reason we ought not to be wed, the silence is thicker than duck's fat. Of course, we will not remain silent hereafter, as soon as the lack of a papal dispensation becomes advantageous.

The groom stands with his feet wide apart. 'I, Ralph…take thee Cecily to my wedded wife and thereto plight my troth, endowing you all my…worldly goods.'

'I, Cecily take thee Ralph to my wedded husband and thereto I plight my troth and obedience.'

I feel sick when he puts the ring on, his thick fingers brushing against mine. All his 'worldly goods'? Meaning, what, an average horse and lodgings in his brother's modest manor house?

The ceremony is followed by a feast, or rather a dinner with two additional guests. Ralph and Geoffrey sit side by side, with me on my new husband's left and the rest of the miniature royal household—Mother, my sisters, and the Warwick siblings— spread out as usual around the long table. Lincoln is far too busy at court, helping our uncle prepare for the coming invasion, to visit us, which I am glad for, because I have a feeling it would cause a spat. Lincoln is the most possessive man I know, and the looks he grants me grow slyer the older I get.

In this moment, though, I would happily entertain him hours on end if I could only escape the slobbering noises of Ralph's gluttony. I used to think *my* appetite was hearty, but I lose it watching him gobble down three honey-roasted quails, half a pie, two bowls of leek stew, a small loaf of bread with cheese, and more cups of wine than I can count. When I think he has finally finished, he attacks the sweetmeats.

Geoffrey is an amiable little mouse in comparison to his brother the rat. He accepts no more food than the handful of dishes my mother recommends him, washing his hands between each. His physique is as barrel-like as Ralph's and, I suspect, that of their two other brothers, but his manners belong to a different world. Could I not have wed him instead? We soon learn, however, that he has already taken a wife.

'She's the fairest girl you can imagine. Her father is a miller.'

'A miller's daughter?' Elizabeth says. 'Lucky her.'

'How so, my lady?'

'She does not have to worry about anything except…except flour. And she chose you, too?'

'She did.' Geoffrey glows with pride. 'Imagine that: the fairest girl in Upsall chose me!' He dips his fingers in the water basin again.

I exchange a glance with Mother. If the fairest girl is a miller's daughter, she would have been a peculiar one if she had chosen anyone else; as it is, she has ensured a life well above her station. And I am now sister-in-law with a commoner… At times, I fear I am being unfair to those I have been taught are inferior to me, but this is the way my life is built, the way it has always been.

Elizabeth grants Geoffrey her undivided attention. 'Are you happy together?'

'Indeed, indeed.'

She says nothing more during the rest of the meal, picking at the fruit on her trencher. I wish she would give voice to her troubles—her own betrothal—but she says nothing of it.

My wedding night is as far from what I expected when I was a little girl as it could be. I lie awake, clutching the sheets to my chest, listening to my own deafening heartbeat and the fire dying in the hearth. This is one of the first times I have slept without one or two other girls in the chamber to preserve warmth.

Mother fulfilled her promise and a guard has been posted outside my door, which is locked as always, but the suspense is agonising nonetheless. I half-expect my husband to burst inside, blubbering incoherently, yet he never does. For all his rough appearance and manners, he has not said or done anything contrary to his instructions, nor shown a speck of cruelty. In fact, the one time during dinner when I remarked on the hem of my dress getting caught under the leg of his chair, he hung his head and mumbled an apology. Perhaps he is the compliant dog Uncle Richard promised me—I almost feel sorry for him. Regardless, he will not bother me for some time once he returns to Upsall, leaving me to live with my sisters as agreed.

Two days later, my husband and his brother are prepared to return to their little hamlet. Elizabeth and I see them off in the great hall, since Mother has taken to her bed with a headache, and Ralph manages a few muddled words before stalking out of the room.

Geoffrey clasps his hands behind his back with a grimace. 'My apologies for my brother, and my condolences for your betrothal, Lady Elizabeth. If it displeases you, that is.'

'Sir?'

'Fret not, for the pope surely won't allow it to pass. The consanguinity is simply too great.' He pats her hand.

Elizabeth purses her lips, her cheeks flushing peach. 'You are mistaken, Sir Geoffrey. If you are referring to my uncle, I must ask you to forget what you might have heard.'

I hook my arm with Elizabeth's in a rare fit of compassion for her. 'I like you, Sir Geoffrey. Please do not spoil that with slander.'

'But I—'

I pin down his eyes with mine. 'His Grace the King made a declaration to parliament a while ago to banish every trace of rumour, and moreover, Parliament has passed the act of *Titulus Regius* to confirm his right to rule. Surely you know that?'

'I heard something of it, Sister.'

'Then you know also that there is no truth in said rumours.'

'Pardon me for assuming…people say all kinds of things these days.' He wrings his hands.

126

'Yes, I've noticed. But you would never think ill of my family, would you? They are your family, too, now. Your allegiance is to the King.'

Geoffrey flashes me a nervous smile. 'Naturally. I'm a Yorkshire-man, if nothing else.'

'It pleases me that you are. Prithee remember it next time.'

'We ought to be on the road. My dear wife is awaiting my return.'

I nod. 'The groom will see to it that your horses are saddled and fed.'

Geoffrey gives a quick bow and turns on his heel. At the door, he halts and faces us again, running a hand through his hair. 'Never doubt my allegiance, Sister. We shan't tarry in Upsall long, for your husband and I have been tasked to muster fifty men and join His Grace's forces once he summons them.'

'You're a good man, Sir Geoffrey. Fight bravely—and return unscathed,' I say, my moment of aversion forgotten. He will aid Uncle Richard against Tudor's band of cutthroats, as will my husband, and this goes a long way in redeeming them both to me.

'Thank you. Farewell for now to you and your beauteous sisters. Farewell, Lady Elizabeth.'

My sister raises a hand, her fingers curling in a wave. 'Farewell.'

Once Geoffrey has left, I turn to her. 'Are you sweet on him?'

'What?'

'You almost seemed to envy that miller's daughter.'

Elizabeth sighs and draws me closer by the arm. 'Only because she cannot fail. Think about it, Cecily. If I become Henry Tudor's wife, and queen, I have to be *perfect*. What if I speak out of turn? What if I cannot have healthy sons? I would rather be the carefree wife of a lesser man than constantly fearing failure.'

'Well, you will not become queen, and even if you do, I know you will not fail. You never speak out of turn, and you have the Woodville hips for sons.'

I can count on one hand the times we have been this intimate, but the glimpses of helplessness endear her to me in brief moments. I fear the same failure myself, and am a hundred times likelier than her to commit it, though I would not switch places with the miller's daughter for all the joviality and ease in the world.

We watch from the window as the Scrope brothers depart, ambivalence stirring in my mind. I meant what I told Geoffrey: I do like him and his courteous manners. Still, I look forward to forgetting all about my wedding and returning to our comfortable existence without upheaval for a while.

Spring blossoms into summer, the sky stark blue and clearer than crystal, yet the weather is the last thing on my mind.

We welcome a new arrival in the household: the King's sixteen-year-old bastard son. His sister Katheryn would have come also, but she was recently married and now resides with her husband the Earl of Huntington.

Uncle Richard has scraped together quite the assemblage at Sheriff Hutton. We are now eight cousins with potential claims to the throne gathered under one roof, Lincoln notwithstanding. If one wonders how England was plunged into the past thirty years of disputes, one only has to look at our bickering. However, it is a logical arrangement, since our uncle can keep us both safe and harmless here, putting his mind and energy to repelling the invasion.

John of Gloucester is a grave but, as I discover, sweet boy, who likes to keep to himself—much like his father when he was younger, I believe. Like Edward of Middleham, I have met John and his sister once before that I can remember, but John made himself scarce behind Anne Neville's skirts that day. I secretly add him to my tally of possible future husbands, because sons have been legitimised before, just as my own supposed bastardy can be reversed through Parliament. Anything can happen.

Mother has been writing to Dorset since Christmas, pleading for him to return home from exile and reconcile with Uncle Richard. That last bit would be a farce, of course, but she wants her last living son safely in England, since she cannot know with certainty that Tudor will succeed this time. Dorset made a half-hearted attempt to heed her, but was intercepted at Compiègne, and let himself be convinced to remain with the rebels. I pity his wife, Hasting's step-daughter, at this time more than ever before, alone in England with the numerous children she has borne him. If I were her, I would be out of my wits.

Mother does resume her correspondence with Margaret Beaufort, who writes that her son is massing his army in France, having obtained a significant loan from the French King and his regency council. With this money added to the Earl of Oxford's military prowess, his uncle Jasper Tudor's advice, the exiles' support, and Margaret Beaufort's contacts in England, Henry Tudor's prospects grow more daunting by the hour. Uncle Richard may have the advantage in numbers and experience in battle—he was often the hero along Father in the stories I soaked up during my childhood—but his funds are tight after Father's unbridled spending. So-called benevolences present no solution since he has made these ruthlessly coerced monetary gifts illegal. Having left Westminster for Nottingham Castle, he is assembling his lords and their men, preparing to continue from there. Rumour reaches us that Howard and Northumberland among others have answered his call to arms most diligently; Stanley, meanwhile, refuses to declare himself on either side.

I would bleed for the House of York, my mother would do the same for the Woodvilles, and Stanley would sell his liver for the Stanleys. In that regard, we are alike. The difference is that the rest of us pick a side and stick to it as long as we have a choice, while he and his fickle brother flit from faction to faction like fleas on rats. Thus, they tip the scales like no other. What is mayhap most frustrating is that they *always* get away with it, and this is the thought that keeps prickling me as I sit bent over my needlework in the solar at Sheriff Hutton

In early August, the news reaches us that Tudor has landed in Milford Haven, Wales, with roughly four thousand men-at-arms consisting mainly of French mercenaries and exiles. With him is the stalwart Lancastrians Oxford and Jasper Tudor, as is Edward Woodville. Dorset, however, has been left at the French court as a guarantee for the loan, no doubt relieved he will not have to get dirt under his fingernails in battle, and sparing Mother the burden of more fretting.

I can practically taste the tense atmosphere as we wait…and wait. We become a divided household, praying for vastly different outcomes.

I have ventured outside to the courtyard for a pause from the bustle inside the castle one August morning, when I discover the courier.

The horse is gleaming with sweat, nostrils flaring, scraping the courtyard with its hooves. A corpulent man dressed in a murrey doublet and brown hose dismounts and strides forward when he catches sight of me. His face is ruddy where the blood vessels have bursts, his lips fleshy.

I wait on the spot, stomach fluttering.

'A letter for you, my lady,' the man says. He hands me the folded paper and mounts his horse again, kicking his heels until the animal turns around and carries him away.

I cast a glance at the red wax: Uncle Richard's royal seal depicting a knight on a destrier. My mouth is dry as I press the letter to my hip so that my gown hides the seal; it feels like a secret. I march across the courtyard, gravel crackling under my slippers, and continue through the east range. Speeding up the steps of the tower, my lungs and legs hurting, I break the seal and fumble to unfold the paper. The moment I reach the empty, square room at the top of the tower, I devour the words.

Ricardius Rex, by Grace of God King of England and Lord of Ireland, greets the virtuous Lady Cecily Plantagenet

I recommend myself unto you and pray you are well, and that your husband has not crossed the boundaries of your temporary union or in any way caused you discomfort. I am aware yours is a most unusual situation, though I found no alternative which could have served us both better.

If I merely gambled my life, I would be high in spirit facing this woeful battle, for it is a necessary confrontation, and I am eager to meet my Anne and our son in the Afterlife. Yet, as I am confident you will comprehend, it is the matter of my legacy which haunts me. If I slay the rebel Tudor and my reign is thereby given the chance to thrive, I hope to be remembered for my diligent enforcement of justice, God willing. Kingship is a lonesome burden, yet one I willingly shouldered, just as I willingly shouldered the burdensome titles and offices your most revered father bestowed upon me when I was little older than you are now. You know I have long strived to further England's weal, and would seek to mend the rift in our family were it in my power.

If I am defeated, the chroniclers will not write in my favour, for they shall be under the thumb of the victors. I dread the culprit they might well make of me.

The Duke of Norfolk will command my vanguard. My trust is utterly with him in this nest of traitors, and you may rely on his fealty should I die.

Prithee, give my affection to your sisters and your cousins of Warwick, and see to your own health always. I have written to my John also, but my nobles are in constant pursuit of my attentions regarding the invasion, and I have not as much time as would please me.

I beseech you to remember me in your prayers and to be faithful to the house of your descent. Loyalty binds us.

God be with ye

Written in my hand on the twentieth day of August in the second year of my reign, in the town of Leicester

I clench the letter in my hand. It was written two days ago; for all I know, the battle could be raging this very moment. It had not occurred to me that his legacy depends so greatly on who is hacked down into limbs and dirt. Until now, my concerns have been personal, but of course, this is as much a question of England's future as it is a question of individual futures. My uncle is right: with Tudor on the throne, learned men would write his predecessor into history as the man who murdered two innocent boys and poisoned his wife to wed his niece. The chroniclers would have little choice but to flatter their Lancastrian king, whether he proved an able ruler or not. I shudder at the thought. Another *Lancastrian king?* My grandfather and father would turn in their graves. Regardless of what they might think of Uncle Richard's actions, they fought too hard and bled too profusely for this to be the end of the rightful branch of the Plantagenet dynasty's reign. Saint Albans, Towton, Barnet, Tewkesbury… I can hardly remember all the gory battles. I had another uncle, too, named Edmund, Earl of Rutland. Edmund was seventeen years of age, wounded, and unarmed when a favoured Lancastrian lord gave the order to sever his head from his body and thrust it down

131

on a pike at York's Mickelgatebar beside that of my grandfather, some eight years before I was born. Will now the last York brother follow Edmund, George, and Edward into the grave?

I put the letter aside and my hands on the windowsill, leaning forward with my whole weight, the rough edges of bricks and mortar carving into my palms. The warm breeze caresses my skin, softer than silk. I breathe the fragrance of fresh grass. The tower's five stories place me wonderfully high above the ground, allowing me to gaze out over the hills. I squeeze my eyes shut, for I do not want to see all this cursed beauty, not today. My fingers trace the tiny diamonds on my broach, which is pinned to my bodice as always, feeling the familiar curves and edges.

England has only had two other kings named Richard, and both met premature, gruesome deaths. This time, it will be different. All will be well. It *must* be.

At dawn three days later, a blood-spattered and battered Geoffrey arrives from Redemore Plain and pronounces the sentence.

The King is dead. Long live the King.

Chapter XIII

G EOFFREY HAS TO empty three cups of our strongest wine before he can compose himself enough to give us an account of the battle. He has ridden for days on end, nearly spurring his horse to its death, and is as exhausted as he is splotched with red. Mother, Elizabeth, John of Gloucester, the Warwick siblings, and I swarm around him as he collapses on a stool in the solar. Mother shuts the door and turns the key before my younger sisters can slip inside, the story we are about to be told promising to be too horrid for their tender ears.

I cannot bring myself to sit down, because my instincts scream at me to run, run far away from this misfortune. My eyes hurt from crying and my breath comes in shallow gasps. The world is breaking into a thousand sharp pieces, piercing my skin.

Through a haze of tears, I glimpse the others' faces. Meg, too, is weeping, while her brother sits wide-eyed and unusually quiet. John of Gloucester is paler than eggshells, almost transparent, and perchance just as fragile. In a matter of hours, he has transformed from Captain of Calais and the acknowledged son of a king, albeit baseborn, to the offspring of a so-called tyrant.

Elizabeth sits square-shouldered and still as a statue, though I spot not only muted relief but flickers of genuine grief in her face. In Mother, the former sentiment is painfully obvious, dominant.

Geoffrey wipes blood from his cuticles with a damp rag and fills his strained lungs with air. 'Oxford…the man crushed Howard's vanguard. Howard was struck down…panic spread among the men.'

'What about Northumberland? He should have come to the rescue, surely?' I clench my fists, pacing along the table.

133

'Indeed. No one yet knows why he did not. Perhaps the terrain did not allow it. I'm sure there is a perfectly honourable explanation. Though some say…no, it is of little importance now.'

'And…and then?'

'I was mounted on my horse. King Richard caught sight of Tudor and his red dragon standard, and ordered a cavalry charge. I believe he rolled the dice, so to speak. We skirted the shattered vanguard and—'

John shakes his head in disbelief, his hands trembling. 'A cavalry charge? My father would have seen the danger he exposed himself to.'

'Yes, my lord. Still, the battle would have been won in an instant with Tudor dead, and I do believe his honour did not permit him to let another man do the hazardous task in his stead.'

Mother calls for a servant to bring Geoffrey a platter with refreshments, always the masterful hostess. 'Continue, Sir Geoffrey. Methinks we all want to hear the ending to this tale.'

'I've never seen anyone fight so ferociously. He killed many an opponent before a man gutted his horse and he was forced to continue on foot. He was close—Tudor had taken shelter behind his body guard but I could see him clearly, and the King struck down his standard bearer.'

'How did my uncle die?' I force the words from behind my teeth. *Die.* It feels surreal to pronounce it.

'They attacked *en masse*. They battered and sliced at his head, knocking his crown and helmet off. When he eventually sunk to his knees and folded over, a man swung his halberd at the back of his skull. The carnage was…' He runs a hand through his hair. 'It was a morbid sight. When they were certain of his death, they stripped him of his armour and continued to beat him. I only caught a glimpse of his body before spurring my horse to retreat, but I could no longer recognise his face for all the blood gushing down from his scalp. We fled, the rest of us. Tudor's men slaughtered many as we did so.'

I swallow. 'His…his body? Are they going to bury it?'

'I know not, Sister. There was no time to tarry and find out.'

I turn to Mother, and at this point there is no restraining my boiling tantrum. 'Well, it seems you've made a deal not only with

134

a usurper but with a coward who has no shame! Is that the way to treat a king, to treat the dead?'

'You both need to cease calling him *king*. Richard was the usurper in all this.'

'Who *hasn't* been said to usurp the throne? Henry Bolingbroke, Father, Uncle Richard, and now Tudor!'

She catches my arm, forcing me to be still. 'My sweet, your uncle brought on the downfall of the House of York.'

'No, Lady Mother. My brothers were lost on his watch and I shall never forget that, but the downfall of York was yours and Margaret Beaufort's doing.'

Elizabeth snaps awake from her trance. 'Cecily!'

'My father's magnates?' John asks poor Geoffrey, who is picking at a piece of cheese.

'Slain or captured, my lord. Though I am afraid some never came to his aid.'

I coax my arm from Mother's grip, a nasty premonition nagging me. 'Stanley?'

'I…yes, him, foremost. He and his brother intervened on Tudor's side towards the end of the battle.'

My stomach twists at this revelation. Damnation upon that whoreson Stanley! May he perish in hellfire-everlasting, because that is where he and his brood belong. Northumberland might have ignored his king's summons, but Stanley… Tudor himself is an angel next to Stanley, because at least Tudor has been honest in his aims if nothing else.

Young Warwick bounces from his seat, returning to his old self. 'The traitor Stanley made us lose! But *I* should be king now!'

Meg pulls him down and wraps her arms around him. The new usurper will want to rid himself of every male Yorkist claimant, including Warwick, John, Lincoln and his brothers. All but Lincoln and John are yet too young to challenge Tudor on their own but that is no guarantee for their safety. Boys grow, and until they do, others will fight using them as figureheads. Lincoln… Might he have survived?

Mother fills Geoffrey's cup a fourth time. 'Hush, both of you. I will say this once and for all: Henry Tudor is our new liege lord whether we wish it or not. What matters is that my Beth is as good as queen now, and our fortunes depend on this union.

Remember, children, the new dynasty will be as much ours as it is Lancastrian.'

I want to argue with her; I want to ask whether Elizabeth can have any real influence or if her betrothed will forget his promises now that he has achieved his goal. However, I am too exhausted to speak another word.

I have *not* lost. I have not won either—merely survived. I swear I am going to win, because this is far from the end.

My husband, Ralph, is alive and well, but fortunately I do not get the chance to meet with him before Henry Tudor's soldiers arrive at Sheriff Hutton to escort us to London. Geoffrey and the servants wave us off. John rides on his favourite stallion while the rest of us cram into two carriages, and embark on the tedious journey.

Several of the soldiers speak Welsh with one another, others French, and all wear the red dragon badge of their master. I catch a word here and a phrase there through the carriage windows, piecing together English and French like a puzzle. What I learn is gut-wrenching. The late King, God save his soul, was slung semi-naked over the back of a horse, his ebony hair tied under his chin. Once the drunken troops reached Leicester and had finished using his corpse as a plaything to stab at, they buried him without ceremony, in a too-small grave, his hands still tied.

I cover Bridget's ears for she is still too young to hear these nasty details.

'Why would they do such a thing?' Anne asks, clutching *Morte d'Arthur* to her chest.

I grit my teeth. 'Because they hated him very much. And because Tudor is a dishonourable man—remember how he took shelter behind his bodyguards while our uncle fought heroically?'

'I wish Beth could marry a handsome knight instead.'

'Me too, or a handsome duke. No one should be treated like that in death, not even a Lancastrian rebel.'

I lose count of the days we travel. I wish I could ride like John, but it would be unseemly for me to do so in the midst of the bawdy soldiers, and I would end up skittish that the horse might throw me, hence I remain in the carriage. When we at last reach London, I am as stiff as a broom, though the city revives me. The stench of the Thames and the filth on the streets are dearer to me than most of my jewels; the noise of merchants shouting and children running after hens fill my ears like sweet music.

The escort halts at the Palace of Westminster, the golden yolk of London and the place I have longed for most. There, an esquire duly leads us through the galleries and chambers to our new lodgings. The procedure reminds me of when we first emerged from sanctuary—what is it with new kings thinking we cannot see our own way through our own palace? Perhaps Tudor fears my mother will change her mind and run off with his treasury at the head of another rebellion.

John of Gloucester and the Warwick siblings are separated from us and taken to rooms of their own. I have no doubt we shall meet again once Tudor musters the grace to summon us.

Kate bolts between the corners of our shared bedchamber. 'Is this where we're going to live, Mama? I want to go home to Sheriff Hutton!'

'This *is* home, Kate darling. You know that.'

'But I like Sheriff Hutton—'

I catch her in my arms, holding her still. 'We'll tell Tudor to give us better rooms. He has to, does he not?'

To my dismay, no one confirms my hopes. It seems we are to live crammed in a set of two bedchambers and one small antechamber, all six of us, until Henry Tudor is in the mood to grant us something more suitable.

We do not have to wait long for his call. That same evening, after supping on pork and vegetable stew, the esquire reappears.

'His Grace will receive you now.'

Elizabeth straightens her posture further, if such a thing is possible. 'He does not wish to see me in private?'

'No, Lady Elizabeth. The King is a diligent man and does not like to waste his time.'

The man is not exaggerating. When we enter the presence chamber, we find John and the Warwick siblings waiting for us so that Tudor can tick all of us off his list in one sharp stroke of his quill.

By the throne stands Margaret Beaufort, draped in a shapeless, high-necked black gown, heavier veiled and more regal than ever. She has one hand on the armrest, clinging to her hard-won triumph. Two men flank her. One is the scoundrel Stanley, the man who betrayed his king in a single fatal heartbeat; the other I do not recognise, but my guess is Jasper Tudor, judging by his weathered face and the knowing looks passing between him and Margaret Beaufort. Jasper is one of the luckiest men I know of, despite his lifetime in exile first with Marguerite d'Anjou and then with his cursed nephew. Somehow, he managed to elude my father's sword, and the stories of his fantastical escapes have mounted to a pretty collection over the years.

Henry Tudor is a tall, wiry man, with brittle auburn hair. His left eye is cast, giving him the eerie appearance of looking both ways, ensuring no detail escapes him. Indeed, I have heard it said he already tends to the finances of his new kingdom as if he trusts no other to manage the work.

My uncle may have been short in stature compared to my giant of a father, and the extravagance of his court may have been forced on his behalf, but at least he looked and behaved as a monarch. Henry Tudor…well, I would have taken him for an accountant or a cleric were it not for the throne he presides on. *Our* throne.

First, he gestures for Young Warwick and John to come forward. John keeps a firm grip on his cousin's shoulder, ensuring he behaves as Meg is left behind for the moment.

'You will both swear an oath of fealty to me as your king and master,' Tudor says. His voice is like wind in January and his accent bears the mark of fourteen years at French-speaking courts. 'The Earl of Lincoln has taken such an oath already. You will do best to renounce your *parenté* to the tyrant Richard, unrightfully late King of England.'

My wretched cousins kneel once more and accede. What choice do they have? Still, Tudor ought to not be so confident of Lincoln's loyalty since he is, thank God, every bit the Yorkist I am.

Once the boys have been dealt with, it is our turn. A year and a half ago, we curtsied on this very same spot before Richard Plantagenet and Anne Neville. If I was reluctant to bow my head and bend my knee then, it was nothing compared to what I feel in this bedevilled moment when I perform the same gesture for Henry Tudor.

Tudor surveys his bride, his cast eye remaining on the rest of us. 'Lady Elizabeth.'

'Your Grace.'

'You are even more *chamant* than I was told. I trust my God-given triumph pleases you.'

'Of course, Sire.' She never falters. It is easy to see how a man might be enamoured with her. 'May I ask when we shall be wed?'

Tudor sits in silence a good while before granting an answer. 'I will decide a suitable date once the matter of my coronation has been seen to. The latter ceremony must take precedence.'

'Oh. I see.'

'You will live comfortably until then. When you give me a son, I promise to reward you.'

'Thank you, Sire.'

I am beginning to understand why my sister might envy a miller's daughter. As much as I yearn for her position as queen-to-be, a husband like this would drive me to the brink of insanity. And to think it could have been me, had anything happened to Elizabeth! I want to laugh and cry both.

Tudor exchanges a handful of words with Mother and then Meg, whom he appears to like a little better than the rest of us since she presents the smallest threat, before sweeping his glance over my younger sisters. When he reaches me, he pauses, because I have risen without his cue and have to push myself down in a curtsey again.

'Lady Cecily, is it?' he says. 'I heard of you also.'

I cannot restrain myself any longer. 'What will happen to the lords you hold captive?'

'Every *traitre* will be dealt with.'

'Pardon, Sire? They were fighting for their lawful king.' I pronounce the word 'king' slowly, delicately, hoping to sway his confidence.

The sinewy man in front of me hardens further to a mask of stone. 'My reign dates to the twenty-first day of August. By the time of Redemore Plain, all who raised their weapons against me were committing treason.'

'But...' He thinks himself so clever, so shrewd! It is *cheating*.

'I'll hear no more of this. Women ought not to poke their noses in politics.'

He cannot be dumber than to note the ambivalence in his own statement. Were it not for women such as his mother and, to certain extent, mine, he would still be kicking his heels in France. Were it not for a woman—Elizabeth—he would not have the vital support of my father's old household knights and would likely not have a throne either.

Mere weeks have passed in our humble existence when Warwick and John are both transferred to the Tower of London for their *safekeeping*, as the story goes. It rings a bell: my angel brothers were to be kept safe in the same cursed place, yet they never saw the light of the day after the summer of 1483. My uncle never intended their deaths, but a misinterpreted word was all it took for the culprits to send them to their graves, because the Tower is reclusive enough, secret enough. If Buckingham and his henchmen could so easily extinguish two innocent lives, my cousins are in perilous danger. Tudor no doubt has men similar to Buckingham in his inner circle, or he might even give the order himself.

Uncle Richard could not afford to kill my brothers even if he had wanted to—indeed, the consequence of the rumours cost him dearly—but Tudor? He would not be murdering his own nephews, causing public outrage, but simply ridding himself of rivals from another bloodline. Well, let him try to root us out. He will never succeed, not when I have a myriad of cousins, not when his own children will be the grandchildren of a Yorkist king. No, he *will* have to accept us as part of his powerbase no matter what his mother might have whispered in his ear about his God-given right to rule alone.

Tudor—or the Pretend-King, as I have begun referring to him as—is crowned in splendour on the thirtieth day of October. Regardless of my personal opinion of him, I had hoped to attend the ceremony, but neither Elizabeth nor I or any of my sisters are invited. This is the third coronation I am denied to attend in less than three years, and we are left listening to the peals of Westminster Abbey from afar. The message in not inviting my oldest sister is an unmistakable slight. Henry VII has no intention of allowing his bride anywhere near true power, let alone make her co-ruler; he has not even made a public announcement reaffirming their betrothal.

'He *has* to marry you,' Mother says several times. 'You are the linchpin of his claim, the sole reason not only Lancastrians support him. You are the heiress to their beloved King Edward.'

Each time, Elizabeth shakes her head. 'He wants me to play the role of any other obedient wife. I can do that, but how am I to fulfil my family's expectations also? How am I to help you if he won't let me?'

'The most submissive of wives can have the greatest influence.'

I find myself chiming in. 'Look at Queen Anne, God rest her soul. She was a model wife and queen in the eyes of the people, yet pulled as many strings as King Richard behind closed doors.'

'Cecily, you mustn't call them that.' She bites her thumbnail. 'And Anne Neville had something it seems I shall never have: her husband's love. Henry loves only his mother.'

She is right. Margaret Beaufort is queen in practice, and I suspect she will fight for that position with teeth and claws even when her son has an actual queen on his arm. The woman fascinates me. I never gave her much notice at Father's court, and since then I have only heard of her through my mother's correspondence, but now I secretly study her. If there are opposites on this earth, she and I must be just that. Beaufort is the most devout person I know, spending hours on her knees in the chapel, calling God as her witness to this and that.

She is Lancastrian to the bone and relentless in smearing Uncle Richard's name, having insisted on the epithet *'tyrant'* since the day of the battle.

I would hate her every bit as much as I hate the Stanleys were it not for the fact that, though she be loyal to the enemy camp, she is at the very least one of the most loyal people I have ever encountered. I cannot stand too look at either brother, but least of all Thomas Stanley, who was the man to be persuaded by his wife and his own self-interest. Even the notorious old Lancastrian Oxford, who led Tudor's army for him, is higher in my favour—but, naturally, my favour counts for naught these days.

In November, Parliament convenes, bringing blessings and curses both. The parliamentary act of *Titulus Regius* is revoked, thus my siblings and I are once more considered legitimate, and I flush with joy over being referred to as Princess Cecily rather than Lady Cecily Plantagenet. I may have my lurking doubts about my own legitimacy, but if I am allowed to style myself as born on the right side of the bed, I most assuredly will. I almost forget my aversions towards the new regime. Then Parliament passes an act of attainder against the late King, denouncing him, and dating Tudor's reign to the day before the battle so that he can label all those who fought for their lawful sovereign as traitors.

By Christmas, the Pretend-King finally confirms that he will indeed marry Elizabeth, and court life settles into routine. Dorset has returned from France and been confirmed in his titles. I tell him about Agnes and their stillborn baby, and am met with a guilty grimace.

Howard's son, the Earl of Surrey, has been attainted from inheriting his father's title Duke of Norfolk, and summarily locked up in the Tower. I am sorry for him and his father, because this is where their precious affinity to my uncle landed them.

Northumberland has also been imprisoned, though there is talk of his impending release and the restoration of his lands and titles. I am no marshal genius, but to me, this is a sign Tudor knows Northumberland's passivity at Redemore Plain was intentional. Just like Stanley, he turned his coat in the moment of truth.

Some of my kinsmen are treated poorly for supporting Uncle Richard while some are handsomely rewarded for aligning with Tudor. In my heart, I belong to the former group, while publicly, I belong to the latter.

I suspect Lincoln shares in this conundrum with me. I glimpsed him at court shortly after we first arrived, but since, rumour has it he has returned to Sandal Castle, avoiding the limelight for once. I must write to him. I know his slimy self well enough. He cannot sit idly with the new order for long, no matter how many pardons Henry Tudor bestows upon him.

Chapter XIV

S OMEONE HAS STOLEN my diamond broach. Some vicious noble recalled who gave it to me and now they have taken it to erase every trace of my old loyalties, or to hit me where it hurts… I rummage through our chambers with increasing desperation. That broach is not just any old trinket. It is a keepsake from days that I am beginning to glorify more and more in my head, a reminder of a time when Tudor's bony backside had never touched the throne.

It is unlike Elizabeth to do such a thing, but I can never be entirely certain. I fling the covers from her bed and crumple her sheets in my search—and, true enough, under her pillow I find a small item. However, a garter can hardly be compared to a broach. I pick up the black ribbon between two fingers and hold it to the light filtering through the thick glass windows. It is too wide for my sister's leg, and the buckle too unfeminine for anything she might wear. I turn it over and, to my horror, a tiny red rose is sown to the fabric on the other side.

Ever since the great battle, Lancastrians have sported a red-rose emblem identical to this one. I cannot tell why they have not simply stuck to Henry VI's golden rose, though it was seldom used, but perhaps they felt red would make a better contrast to our Yorkist white. This must be a cruel jest.

'Cecily? What have you done to my bed?'

I snap around, the garter still in my hand. 'I was looking for something—and I found this.' I dangle my discovery before her eyes. 'Someone placed it there, didn't they, to try to slander you?'

Elizabeth's supple lips part. She can put on elaborate shows of pretence and poise, yet never lie when asked a direct question, and now her fair complexion gives way to a coral blush.

I stare at her. 'Elizabeth? *Tell me.*'

She snatches the garter from me and hides it in between the folds of her gown, refusing to meet my eyes. 'I needn't. I will not have you revel in my shame.'

'I promise I will not, no matter how tempting it is. Please tell me, and if you do, I also promise not to show Mother. If you do not, I might.'

'We are wed in the eyes of God. Henry said it was alright, since the real wedding is within a fortnight.'

'Henry Tudor?' That is a notch better than the Lancastrian noble I expected. Still, dread fills me. 'Did he ravish you? If he took you by force—'

Elizabeth shakes her head, still keeping her glance on the floor. 'No, no. Oh, but I am wicked, aren't I?'

'What motive could you possibly have? If I were you, I'd want to keep him at bay as long as I could.' I smooth the sheets and pull her down to sit on the edge of the mattress with me.

'He is so eager for an heir, a son to seal the merging of Lancaster and York, to secure his crown.'

'I'm...sorry.'

She claps her hands in her lap before I can take them in mine. 'There is no need for your condolences. Henry is not...not so bad. He is calm and still, and very clever. He can be generous when he wants to, but always cautious.'

'I cannot imagine him in bed.' I stifle something between a giggle and a gag.

'Nor should you! Anyhow, perhaps one day I can grow to love him if I try. As long as I do not fail him, he will be a good husband, and then I shan't mind being queen.'

Not mind being queen. If her objections were to Tudor's person, I would understand better, although it appears that she has made her peace with him. During the few months since we arrived at court, the two of them have gradually increased the time they spend together. Now that I think about it, I should have seen the signs. In September it was a weekly, stiff conversation in front of the nobles; now it is daily strolls in the galleries and card games or chess in the evenings.

I coax the garter from her clasped hands. 'Such a hideous red rose. Are *you* going to wear them, too, once you are the Pretend-King's wife?'

'I pick my battles, Cecily, and this is not one of them.'

'I think you pick too few.'

'And you too many.' She sighs. 'He says he has commissioned a new emblem for us, a new Tudor rose. That is what I'll wear, and you too, if you know your own good.'

'Well,' I whisper, defeated for the moment. 'Tell your Henry I'll take a few Tudor roses.'

Elizabeth rises from the bed and brushes imagined dust from her gown, mouth curving in a small smile, the indignant blush long gone. 'I have chosen a motto to use once we are married: "Humble and Reverent." As my lady in waiting, I hope you will abide to it also.'

Humble and Reverent. I try to put the words in my mouth but the taste is sour. 'Your lady in waiting?'

'You waited upon Anne Neville for a short while, though it was less official. You know how to help a queen dress.' Her voice betrays no malice nor mockery, but stings nonetheless.

I stand, wishing desperately that my head reached higher than her shoulder. 'You want me to dress you?'

A tiny frown settles on her forehead. 'Who else would? Mother says you girls will join my household, except Bridget, of course. She'll go to the priory soon.'

I scold myself for not understanding as much without her having to tell me. Of course I am going to be one of my sister's ladies, likely chief lady in waiting, at least until I marry someone other than Ralph Scrope and have a castle of my own. What else did I expect? I can hardly live at court and *not* be part of her household. England's most highborn women will attend to her every whim and need, just as we attended on Queen Anne, and unless I want to cower in Upsall with my half-wit of a half-husband, I have no choice.

I suppose the difference is I that *liked* Queen Anne. I never grew up in her shadow, and she made me feel special.

'You will make a pretty bride,' I finally manage. 'But if I were you, I'd spill a few drops of pig's blood or something of the sort on the sheets after your wedding night, to preserve your reputation.'

The wedding takes place in January, a few days after I found my broach between the folds of a gown I had discarded on the floor. The new Tudor rose is scant comfort: a dominant red rose with a smaller, white one in the middle. I squint at the banners. Let Tudor think us small, for we are still, evidently, the centre.

My younger sisters and I have donned identical apparel with full sleeves of white silk and ermine. For the first time in three years, I truly look like the princess I was brought up to be.

Anne nudges me. 'Is she not beautiful?'

'Very.'

After the ceremony, Mother's face is painted with broad brushstrokes of relief. There is no turning back now. I add 'sister-in-law' to my little list of relationships to kings; 'aunt' will likely come next, once Elizabeth has a son.

Several days of festivities tie onto the wedding, and I have to admit that Tudor knows the components of a successful party despite his miserly tendencies.

Crushing pain pulls me back to reality as my dancing partner steps on my toes.

'Sorry!' he whispers.

I shoot him a glare, but the look in his eyes is earnest. There is something else about those eyes—I cannot put my finger on it. The plain black mask he wears conceals his features, as is the point of a masquerade.

The dance proceeds with its rounds of curtseys and bows and walking in circles. The melody is a little slow-paced for my taste, but perhaps it is a blessing, since my partner would doubtlessly trample my feet black and blue if we danced a jollier, more complicated dance. His palm is smooth against mine, and I thank my good fortune that he does not seem prone to hand sweats. I would rather have a clump-footed man than a clammy-handed one.

Said fortune is short-lived, though, for the dance ends and we are required to change partners.

146

The Pretend-King whispers something to his uncle, Jasper Tudor, and the aging Welshman pushes back his chair with a screech. Not until he curls his fingers around my hand and places a firm thumb on my knuckles do I realise what is happening. No, no, *no!* I cannot dance with him...he is a staunch Lancastrian if ever there was one, he looks like a withering scarecrow, and, I discover, his hands are damper than autumn rain.

I flash Mother an alarmed glance. She shakes her head almost indiscernibly: you may *not* refuse the King's uncle.

I try to keep my eyes averted from Jasper as he leads me in the dance, a *saltarello* this time. Two of my maids tittered a few months ago about how he is hunting for a Woodville girl to make his young wife. Being the King's most loyal and trusted advisor as well as foster-father and relative, he will have his pick of the cream of royalty. Of course, he would be a strategic match himself, considering his great influence, but that does not change the fact that he is the feckless Henry VI's nephew and my complete opposite in opinions. No, I think I will hold on to the possibility of marrying my own kindred or a European lord as soon as my union with Ralph has been dissolved.

'You look disaffected, Your Royal Highness,' Jasper says with a prominent lisp.

I force a smile. 'Not at all, Lord Bedford. Only warm.'

'It seems to me that Woodvilles get warm so frequently. My dear wife is reluctant to light a fire even at this time of year!'

'Your wife?' I meet his eyes at last. How can this possibly have escaped me?

Jasper frowns. 'Your aunt.'

'I have so many.'

'Catherine—the Duke of Buckingham's widow, God rest his soul.'

I make an effort not to gape like a fish. I have been too preoccupied to take notice of every twist and turn on the marriage market, but I should have known my youngest aunt has been traded off again. Poor woman...first the treacherous toad Buckingham and then this Lancaster scarecrow. At least my own dread was uncalled for.

When the tune comes to an end once more, I wipe my palms on my indigo bodice and slip away from the dancefloor, having done my duty for now. Escaping to the nearby gallery, I lean against the wall between the rows of my ancestors' portraits and remove my mask. Closing my eyes, I rest my hands flat against the polished stone. Here, it is cool and crisp, without the bustle of hundreds of guests.

'You've surrendered already? I am sure there is a score of rich men who want a dance with you yonder in the hall.'

My eyes snap open. The young man who stepped on my toes takes a few steps towards me.

I push myself up from my reclining position. 'More than a score, and I have *not* surrendered. What are you doing here?'

'I merely wanted to see how your foot fares.'

'Not ideally, thank you.'

The man leans against the wall beside me with his hands behind his back, nearly knocking down one of the massive gilded frames. 'I thought my steps had improved since last time.'

'What?'

'You do not know me?'

'You're wearing a mask. Pray take it off.'

'Right.' He reaches up and unties the ribbons. 'I knew you at first sight, although you do look older.'

I freeze on the spot. I knew the world was a small place, but not this small. 'What are you doing here? At court, I mean. You did not join Tudor's invasion, did you? Please tell me you did not.'

Thomas scoffs. 'By Saint Edward's toes, I wouldn't risk my life just so one king can replace another. I can hardly tell the difference between this bloke and the last.'

'Of course there's a difference!' I had almost forgotten the incongruous things my old friend can spew out.

'Maybe to you, but not to me, not unless they suddenly give a fig about the Isle of Wight and my own home.'

'You did not answer my question, Thomas.'

'What? Oh, that. Life in the abbey grew dull without you and your sisters, especially the little bouncy one. I never wanted to be a cleric myself, either, so I went first to Lincolnshire and then back home to my father.'

'And then?'

He opens his mouth and closes it again, avoiding my gaze. 'I'll tell you someday. It is of no importance now. Anyhow, he

148

thought I might be welcome at court since my mother served here when she was a very young girl. And I must say this past week has been quite marvellous, even if I have to be an esquire to the Earl of Northumberland. I hope to become a proper household knight soon.'

I hold my breath. 'Then you are close to him.'

'Only physically.'

'But do you have any notion whether…whether it was betrayal or not? At Redemore?'

'Not the faintest.' Thomas shrugs, then backs a few steps, studying the portraits. 'I'm sure you could name all of these people for me, but please don't. Just look at that fabric instead!'

I join him in his survey of the portrait. 'I know. Lovely colour.'

'No, I mean look at the brushstrokes. If I had paint and brushes, I, too, could learn to make it look that real.'

'If you ever do abandon your service to Northumberland for a painter's trade, I shall commission a new portrait from you,' I tease.

'Will you sit still this time?'

'I would not depend on it if I were you.'

Rapidly, I recount to him all I have lived through since we last saw one another little less than two years ago in the gloomy college hall. There are so many details I want to share with him, from my wondrous week at Nottingham Castle to the exact kind of flower I saw on a particularly fine summer day at Sheriff Hutton. I fear I rush through it all, out of breath, but time is sparse. Mother must be searching the great hall for me already.

When I arrive at the laughable sham that is my marriage, Thomas interrupts me. 'It sounds like a complicated plan to me.'

'I suppose so, but I intend to ask my sister the Queen's Grace to petition her husband to annul it. I could manage it myself, but His Holiness would likely reply quicker to Tudor than to me.'

'And then?'

'Then I will do my best to find a far better match.'

'Better? You mean someone who fancies you more?'

I smile. 'That too—kindness never hurt—but you know girls like me never marry for love.'

149

'Your mother did, or so goes the old tale.' He returns my smile, but it lacks the sparkle it so frequently contains, a sparkle I have come to take for granted.

'My mother was lucky enough to love a king.'

'Oh.' He cracks his knuckles in that most irritating manner. 'I always had the impression you were a romantic deep down.'

'I *am*. Romance can be glorious, only not for *me*. I believe Anne can shoulder the role of the dreaming damsel.' I brace myself. 'Thomas, will you be my friend in this place? I do not have very many.'

'It would seem to me you have a small army. Anyone would be a princess' friend.'

'But I'm not asking anyone. You are far more...interesting than the others. With you, I never have to hold my tongue.'

He raises his eyebrows behind the unruly mass of coils. 'That is the lousiest compliment I have ever received.'

'Well, then I'll leave!' I turn on my heel, eyes burning, regretting that I ever asked.

Thomas latches onto my arm and grins. 'I'm not serious, silly! I have been your friend before, so I think I can manage again, although there is one thing.'

'Anything.'

'I'm no more fool than to know you cannot be seen to lavish favour on a man of my standing, but whenever we are alone, I am your equal, no more and no less.'

'My equal? I thought I had not offended you in a long time.'

Thomas is serious when he looks at me. 'No, but I want you to know I am no worse than you, just because of your lineage.'

I ponder this for a brief moment. All my life, I have been taught to view myself as superior in nature to all those below me, because why else would God have graced me with royal blood and anointed my father? Still, I know my person as such is no more charming or more virtuous than most common wenches, less even, and though I cannot doubt my birth right, I wonder if that is perhaps only one layer. Outwardly, on the surface, I am a princess, untouchable; beneath, I am a human like anyone else. I have enough people to play hierarchical games with, and I miss having at least one to be simply Cecily with. Politics can be exhausting if one does not allow oneself a degree of leisure as well. When I look beyond Thomas the chamber servant, I *do* see an equal, for we have always spoken our minds freely, and I have rarely felt the stiffness looming between us which might be expected considering my inferiority as a woman and his inferiority as landed gentry.

'Agreed,' I say. 'You mustn't let me leave you again.'

'Agreed.'

'I do not think I want to go back inside. My feet are aching from dancing.'

'Stay here, then, and I will fetch us some sweetmeats.'

I laugh, shaking my head. 'Tudor sees everything—have you not noticed? You cannot very well steal from the royal table.'

Thomas tucks a coil behind his ear. 'Now you *do* offend me. Just wait and see.'

To my delight, he returns shortly thereafter with a platter of honeyed sweetmeats and two cups of malmsey wine balanced between his fingers. I have always been a little weary of such wine in particular, given my uncle Clarence's fate, but tonight I drink without a second thought. It is quite the treat to have a real friend.

By the time January turns to a February as grey and wet as a woollen dishrag, I deem the time ripe to approach the royal couple with the matter of my annulment. It is a simple task, for it is as much in Tudor's interest as it is in mine to have me back in the clutch of eligible maidens. What does prove a challenge, though, is to have him accept the terms of my new situation. I had hoped to use Elizabeth as a bridge between us, especially now that her husband appears to grow fond of not only her supposed fertility but also of her demure character, but I am sorely disappointed. She says she will not meddle in this sort of affair, and I suspect this is another instance of her picking her battles.

Tudor surveys me with one eye as I curtsey before him in the presence chamber. 'I have a few suitors in mind for you, *Madame*.'

'I will make my own choice of husband, Sire. You have no legal authority over the matter.' I do my best to ignore the magnates fluttering about in the chamber, and rise from my curtsey.

'The King of France is not bound by the law.'

'We are not in France.'

He remains utterly calm, but when he speaks, his voice could turn his breath to ice. 'It is a shame you are so bold. You ought to take after my wife more.'

'I have heard that before, Sire. You misunderstand me. I am in no way refusing your suggestions, merely saying that I intend to make the choice myself.'

'It is you who are mistaken if you believe you may have the same *privilège* as when your uncle the tyrant wore my crown.'

I draw a deep breath, grasping for the thread that is my last resort. These might well be the most dangerous words I have ever spoken, hence I lower my voice. 'How awful it would be if I found myself wed to a man solely of your choice and he fared badly. You have heard of my mother's…gift?'

'I could have you prosecuted for witchcraft for those words alone.'

'That would not be kindly perceived in the eyes of your Yorkist supporters, Sire, nor would it agree with Her Grace.'

At last, the battle behind his eyes is won in my favour. 'Choose sensibly. For all our sake.'

I nod, suppressing a smile, and am about to depart when Tudor raises a hand. 'Everyone out. You stay,' he says to me. When each magnate and even Margaret Beaufort has trotted out of the presence chamber with a chorus of sullen muttering, Tudor rises from his throne and strides towards me. 'Your brothers, the princes. Do you know their fate?'

'I do. And so do you, I should think. That is why you have not made any clear declaration of where the guilt lies: because the truth is that their deaths were very convenient for you.'

'They did not perish by my hand.'

I swallow, staring back at him. 'No, Sire. Nor was it by my uncle's hand, and yet look what the rumours did to him. What is more, I think you knew the boys were dead long before we did, by word of your mother, because for all I know she was private to Buckingham's musings that fateful summer.'

Tudor's initial silence suffices to confirm my half-accusation, before he continues his own inquiring: 'What of the bodies?'

'I do not know, honestly. Buckingham knew, I wager, but he took that secret with him into the grave.'

'I have had the Tower searched, and found nothing. I have to show *le peuple* the bodies, to quench any rumour of them still living.'

'I cannot help you, Sire. Every king has to face pretenders and rivals, especially one like yourself.'

He turns from me, throwing himself down on his throne again, and his knuckles whiten as he grips the armrests. 'I need no reminder of the precariousness of my position. You may go.'

I obey with the sweet feeling of victory, emerging from the chamber and sweeping past the waiting nobles and Tudor's new red-clad bodyguard called yeomen. Fancy what a feigned hint of witchcraft can do.

Chapter XV

'S EVENTEEN—CAN YOU believe it?' I throw another grape at Thomas and he misses for the third time.

'Archaic! Soon, you'll be an old crone haunting these halls, spiteful of every young girl.'

'I'm not afraid of growing old, Thomas. I would have been if my beauty was extraordinary, like my mother's, but I have less to lose.'

He picks up the grape from the table we are sitting on and pops it in his mouth. 'I never heard you so humble.'

'Well, I try. Sometimes.'

We are alone in one of the smaller and more secluded chambers of the palace, a room used to store dusty charts and maps long outdated. I have stolen away from Elizabeth's privy chambers, where her new ladies occupy themselves with needlework, for a moment of ease. Accidentally, the moment has turned into half an hour, and I must have eaten a hundred green grapes from the bowl Thomas supplied.

I cast a glance over my shoulder. 'If you promise not to speak a word of it, I shall tell you a secret.'

'I am rather good at keeping secrets.'

'Marvellous, for so am I. Anyhow, you promise?'

'Right.'

I bend forward and cup my hands around his ear, whispering: 'My sister is with child.'

Thomas pulls back and gives a low whistle. 'Which one of your sisters?'

'Which one do you think? She means to tell Tudor this very eve, which is why she told me not to ruin the surprise. I only found out because—' My cheeks heat as I try to steer away from

154

the subject of Elizabeth's monthly flux. '—because of a womanly matter.'

'I have a feeling the King is not one prone to appreciate a surprise.'

I aim a kick at his foot. 'He is *not* king, and no, I do not think so either, though he is certain to be overjoyed regardless. This must be better than he dreamt of when in Brittany and France.'

'Boy or girl?'

'How would I know?'

'You with your *womanly matters* can tell those things, can't you?'

Had anyone else asked, I would not have hesitated to declare that Elizabeth was carrying a prince in her womb, for any other reply would have been perceived as disloyal. Pregnant queens and those around them always proclaim their hopes to be truth, saying it is a boy before the bulge has even started to show. Mayhap I should do the same and voice my own hopes.

'Girl, then. My sister will have a plethora of girls and love them a great deal, but Tudor will be left without the heir he desires.'

'And then what? You'll spin a web of marriages for all of them to Yorkist lords and reconquer the throne?'

'A lovely idea, truly.'

'You,' Thomas says, reclining on the table and entwining his fingers behind his head, 'are mad. That's what my cousin would say. He's convinced he is the only sane person on this earth.'

'Then *he* must be mad.'

'I told him as much once when we were younger, and he broke my nose.'

So this is the reason for the slight curve in his nasal bone. I have grown so accustomed to seeing it that I have never thought to ask.

'He does not sound agreeable at all,' I conclude as I reach up to correct my headdress.

'He and my father are all the family I have, mind you. We have great fun, too.'

'I suppose madness can be fun if you indulge in it.'

He grins. 'Quite so. Maybe that is why you almost seem to be enjoying your plotting.'

'I do not *enjoy* it, you daft man. I am trying my very best to assist my house of descent, and what's the matter with that?'

'Sorry, then. Nothing's the matter, except I find myself grateful not to have a house of descent, or at least not one whose name is known beyond my pastoral.'

'Kyme, is it not?' His last name feels strange in my mouth, because to me, he has always been just Thomas, at least since he became my friend in sanctuary. Sir Thomas Kyme.

'Yes. Sounds peculiar, does it not?'

'Perhaps a little.'

He reaches for a grape and flings it at my head. Before one can say '*Titulus Regius*', a full-blown war has broken out, fruit scattered all over the otherwise sombre chamber.

Young Warwick and John of Gloucester remain in the Tower. I have not seen them since they were taken from us since they are allowed few visitors, but others have, which prevents rumours from rising. It appears the Pretend-King is careful not to make his predecessor's mistake. By ensuring it is publicly known that they are alive and in good health, he wards off pretenders. However, pretenders are bound to show up regardless of his efforts, claiming the identity of my poor brothers; it is merely a matter of time. What should I do then? True, I wish to see the regime toppled, the political clock turned back, but I do not know if I could support a boy who is nothing but an impersonator. A stranger telling the world he is Edward V, or Richard IV... The boy might be able to pretend, but I would not. No, my hope must rest with those actually of my own blood, my kinsmen. Preferably kinsmen with both maturity and freedom, and the choice is an obvious one.

I sit a good while clutching my goose pen before I take a deep breath and scribble the necessary lines on a sheet of paper. The letter is shorter than customary and my handwriting has not improved, but I dare not use a scribe. The words are dangerous, more dangerous even than my insinuation about witchcraft, and I can only imagine what would happen if the seal was broken by any other than the letter's recipient. Women are rarely put on trial for treason, especially not young princesses, yet women rarely write what I have just written.

I must find a trusted courier, a man of steadfast loyalty, to bring the letter to Lincoln. Time is not on our side. I should have contacted him six months ago, before the new ruler and his confidants had had a chance to settle. I know there are indeed high-ranking nobles with opinions similar to my own, but they are bound to grow quieter with each passing day. Some of them will already have reconciled with Tudor, thinking that they at least have a Yorkist queen, because they have not seen the union up close, and are blissfully unaware of how little influence Elizabeth exercises both publicly and intimately.

She told me she would *act* the ideal wife, but I am beginning to think she has forgotten the act entirely and become one in truth. I want to shake her about and ask her why on earth she is so withdrawn from the political scene, but I dare not, not least because she appears happy. Yes, happy, with her paranoid husband and growing belly.

I have no desire to cause her misery, not for the sake of it, though I believe she would survive the coronet being knocked off her head. This is one reason I pray for the baby to be a girl. If Tudor was removed and Elizabeth was the mother of the Tudor heir, her position would always be fraught with danger, her life infested with scheming nobles trying to use her and her son as pawns. If, on the other hand, she had a hapless girl, she could perchance marry again, this time to a man of the *right* blood and

157

fealty, and not necessarily be bound by this previous union. Lancaster would have no credible claimant to fight for with Henry Tudor gone—that is why he became figurehead to begin with, because he was the last possible alternative alive.

But I am rushing ahead of myself. Lincoln has not even received my letter yet.

Lincoln's reply arrives a fortnight later, by the end of the dreary period of lent, and it is clear as crystal. He writes he is most pleased to hear we have an understanding, yet that is all for now: an understanding, a mutual aversion. We have to bide our time until the tides turn; we cannot act upon said aversion until he has gathered more information and tied more knots with other noblemen. Of course, he has contacts, but there is much dispute in Yorkist circles as to what ought to be done. Those who are willing to risk all in rebellion know not whom to place on the throne in Tudor's stead. While the House of Lancaster faced the issue of too few claimants living, York has too many to choose from. The choice stands, as I suspected, between a grown leader and a child pretender. Perhaps a combination of both would be most efficient. Furthermore, there is the support of the Irish lords—who hark back to their relative independence under Yorkist rule—and my aunt Margaret, Dowager Duchess of Burgundy, who was always fervent to involve herself in English politics.

Mere days after I receive Lincoln's letter, word spreads at court of a rebellion instigated by Francis Lovell, Uncle Richard's dearest friend who once chatted with me at Nottingham Castle, and the Stafford brothers, two other loyal servants. Having fled to sanctuary in Colchester Abbey after the fatal battle last summer, they have now emerged and sparked an uprising. Henry Tudor has travelled north on progress, and I wait tense as a bow string for further news of his eventual encounter with the blessed rebels. Did Lincoln know? Was he privy to the conspiracy without having told me so?

It is not to be. Towards the end of April, Lovell's attempt to seize Tudor in York fails miserably, his forces being scant in comparison to the Lancastrians'. He escapes to Burgundy, thank God Almighty, presumably to seek support from Aunt Margaret.

The following month, I hear the Staffords' part of the insurgency in the Midlands is equally unsuccessful. They are dragged out of a church, and Tudor forces the older brother, Humphrey, to kiss his feet before being taken to be hung, drawn, and quartered at Tyburn. I quake with fury at their treatment. Having spent significant time in sanctuary myself, my brother-in-law's actions feel like a personal offence. Rules must be respected, and he has tempted God's wrath.

Meanwhile, spring is already budding into summer. For months, the sky has been sheathed in dense grey clouds, like a lid trapping the cold fog, but now rays of sun cut through. Thomas says he could smell a change of weather coming, but he says so many ridiculous things.

Elizabeth's pregnancy grows more apparent, until she has to walk with her hands supporting the bulge. Mother rarely lets her out of sight, for they are closer than ever now that my sister experiences what our mother has the greatest knowledge in. The three—or, I should say, four—of us spend many lazy days at the Palace of Placentia, Greenwich, the queen's favourite royal residence. There, we indulge in endless picnics and strolls in the flourishing gardens, accompanied by four servants to carry the canopy protecting our skin from sunburn. Anne, Kate, and Meg, who is warming to us for certs now that she can no longer give her affections to her brother, spend their time supervised by various matronly women and are kept out of Tudor's path. Bridget has been sent to Dartford Priory to to finally begin the religious schooling Father and Mother always intended for her. We bring no other ladies, either, Mother being weary of their chatter.

'Here, Cecily, feel. Can you feel him kicking?' Elizabeth guides my hand to her stomach where the silk stretches tight, clinging to her body. We are sitting on a sheet spread out on the grass near the palace, surrounded by silver platters reflecting blinding sunlight.

I hesitate. Unborn children frighten me a little, though I would never admit it. It is so bizarre to imagine them in there, planted by God's supposed grace, alive but invisible to us. At last, I place my hand on the belly and, indeed, there is a vague poke against my palm.

159

Mother kisses Elizabeth's hands. 'You mustn't tire yourself, apple of mine eye. Your son is strong—methinks he drains much of your energy.'

'I will rest plenty in my confinement. Henry wishes me to go to Winchester.'

Winchester, the place where the round table of King Arthur once stood. No doubt Tudor hopes to make a propaganda statement by linking his dynasty to the revered legends.

'A Prince Arthur born at Camelot. How suitable,' I say with a pout.

Elizabeth gives me a long glance. 'Oh, please let me have my happiness. I thought I wouldn't have it in this marriage, but Henry loves me. He does.'

'Forgive me, then. What will you name her if it's a girl?'

'Perhaps Margaret, if my lady the King's Mother says so.'

'Does she decide everything?'

'Not everything... She merely leaves very little space for others.' She bites her fingernail and turn her face to the sun.

'I have noticed as much. You must resent her.'

Elizabeth shakes her head. 'I cannot ask my husband to choose between me and her. It would be most cruel.'

I know, though, that they are three in the marriage. 'You mean he would pick his mother.'

A black-robed figure towers over us. My breath tangles in my throat and I dare not raise my eyes for fear of how much Margaret Beaufort might have heard of our conversation—too much, that is certain. Her son fades in comparison in regards to keeping every detail of the court and its inhabitants under close watch: she is the judge and the rest of us stand accused, oblivious as to what crime we have committed.

'My lady the King's Mother.' Mother rises, curtseys, and gestures for me to follow her example. As dowager queen and princess, we are far from as lowly as the woman in front of us would like to believe, but Beaufort has competed with us for supremacy for almost a year, and we have been forced to swallow a fragment of our pride. Elizabeth alone may remain seated, for no matter what the private harangue in her marriage is, her formal title of queen is undisputed, and naturally, her pregnancy gives her further reason to rest.

'Your lying in begins within the week, Your Grace,' Margaret says to her daughter-in-law. 'You shall henceforth say another two prayers at nightfall and daybreak until the prince is born. God does not smile upon those who do not repent.'

Elizabeth keeps her gaze and hands firmly on her belly, her most valuable card to play. 'God has smiled upon me already, Madam, just like he once smiled upon you. I hope to receive his blessing again.'

It is impossible to tell whether my sister ever intend to cause damage with her subtle words. I believe she does not, but they often hit a delicate target in me, and it appears Margaret Beaufort is equally unfortunate.

Her lips pucker as if she had bitten into a lemon. 'I dedicated my life to our Lord Jesus Christ. That is why I had only one child, one child destined for divine greatness. I had need of no other.'

Elizabeth does not move a single muscle. 'I did not mean to imply any offence.'

'I have given instructions that your wardrobe shall be left here.'

'I would like to be suitably dressed even if it is a confinement.'

'A plain shroud was good enough for the Virgin Mary.'

I wait for my sister to comply, as she always does in the end regardless of how dismayed she is.

'Then…then it is good enough for me also.'

'Indeed.' Beaufort turns on her heel but does not get far before Mother calls on her attention.

'Madam, I presume you wish to have a hand in arranging the christening? The task might fall to me, but I daresay we can find a compromise.'

A wry smile twists one corner of Beaufort's mouth. 'Ah, the christening. Fret not. My son, His Grace the most august King, has delegated all arrangements to me. Such a special ceremony requires a pious heart.' On that humble note, she leaves us.

I slump down on the picnic sheet again, marvelling. 'She is *unbelievable*.'

Mother follows the departing streak of black with her eyes. 'That woman wants to push me out from court. I do believe there are one too many queens here, though she never was one in truth.'

161

'Won't you tell her so, Lady Mother?' I say.

'And infuriate the King? I'm afraid a confrontation would only lead to my banishment.'

Elizabeth sighs. 'What did I say to make her chide me thus? I try to comply with her wishes, but she is so harsh at times.'

I reach for another filled pastry and gather my veil behind my shoulders to keep it from being dipped in custard. 'Well, have you not heard? I would have thought your husband had told you.'

'What?'

'Your condition is a thorn in her side, even though her Lancastrian dynasty stands to gain from the birth of a prince.' I purposefully drag out my little revelation, enjoying the rare sensation of knowing more than my sister. 'Everyone fawns over you and lavishes comforts on you, and when you give birth you will be surrounded by midwives and ladies tending to your every whim.'

'Try not to slobber with that pastry, Cecily, please. And do get to the point.'

'Of course she's jealous! How could she not be, when she was thirteen and a widow, trapped in *Wales*.'

'Thirteen?'

'And small for her age. The birth nearly killed her and her son—Tudor, that is. I for one think her dedication to Christ is not the sole reason she never had another child.'

Mother grips my arm, though not unkindly. 'That is enough, my sweet. You have been listening to gossip again.'

'Just because it is gossip does not mean it is not true.'

Mother, Beaufort, and I accompany Elizabeth to her confinement in Winchester, as do numerous members of the court. We are to live in Saint Swithun's Priory, an age-old monastery attached to Winchester Cathedral, until the babe is born and the churching afterwards is complete. The diocese of Winchester is enormously wealthy, yet the priory itself with its plain grey walls strikes a note of humbleness in my eyes. It turns out I ought not to have judged our lodgings by the outside alone, though, because every care has been taken to assure that the birthing chamber is of suitable grandeur for a royal child to be born there.

The room is swathed in rich blue cloth decorated with *fleur-de-lis* suspended from the ceiling and the floor is covered in carpets. A luxurious bed dominates the space, its curtains and coverlets made from the same fabric as the wall hangings. Elizabeth's lack of sumptuous gowns and smocks seems trivial in comparison. This is the innermost sacred quarters of the woman's world, which we will guard from all men save Tudor himself, should he fancy a visit to his wife. The last time I entered such a place was almost six years ago, when Bridget was born and I sat and read to Mother, though I was not allowed to be present during the bloody labour, which I was infinitely grateful for.

In spite of all the finery, I can barely stand being trapped in the bedchamber for days on end. September, the lulling interlude between summer and autumn, is not as warm as I feared it might be, yet the atmosphere is stifling. The windows are covered and the candles are lit sparingly so that the room imitates the darkness inside a womb, and it is equally monotonous. In theory, I could emerge from the confinement without breaking protocol since I am not the one to give birth, but Mother is relentless, insisting I remain by my sister's side.

The company is not lacking in merry souls, though, presenting such old acquaintances as the Countess of Surrey, Bessie Tilney, who carried Mother's train at her coronation some twenty years past, and my aunt Catherine, Jasper Tudor's poor wife. Twenty-eight years old, she looks a lesser version of the dragon-eyed beauty my mother was when she wed Father, but her character is the more entertaining. Her thinly tweezed brows come together when she laughs, which is often, and her sense of humour is as wonderfully intricate as an embroidery. She never mentions her first husband, Buckingham, whom Tudor's men have nearly turned into a martyr. Perhaps it is because she would rather say nothing of him than be forced to speak his praise—I recall how he scorned her when I was little.

We pass the time with card games and chess, read to one another, and play music. To my delight, I excel with the lute, before I am obliged to turn to my needlework once more and prick my fingers too sore to play.

Still, Margaret Beaufort circles around us like the hawk she is, ensuring our speech and manners are within her narrow range of approval. She casts stern glances on me several times a day, causing me to dislike her more for making me yawn than for her tireless toil for Lancaster.

Thus, we wait in our ostentatious prison for the blessing of an heir. Of course, it would not be a blessing for everyone.

Chapter XVI

I T IS THE evening of the nineteenth day of September when
Elizabeth's water breaks. The grand bed where she reclines
is soaked, and she struggles to move to a dry spot. Aunt
Catherine and Bessie Tilney support her to the birthing chair in
one of the corners of the room. Once she is seated and her legs
are spread for the midwife's experienced eyes, they remove her
wet smock and hitch up her chemise to her thighs. Catherine
kneels and unplugs the bottle of rose water we have kept by the
birthing chair since the lying in began. With frantic fingers, she
rubs Elizabeth's ankles with the scented water to alleviate the pain
but it appears to have little effect since my sister emits an
uncharacteristic, throaty groan.

I stand paralyzed. I have never before seen her this flustered
nor this uncovered. She can hardly object when Margaret
Beaufort opens the door to the outer rooms of the priory to give
entrance to a stream of lesser ladies. They have been waiting
eagerly since we arrived, loitering around outside the innermost
birthing chamber, and now, they cram around their queen to
witness the birth of an heir so they might testify that the child is
not swapped for a changeling.

Mother turns to me. 'Fetch Our Lady's girdle, my sweet.'

I snap out of my frozen state and collect the holy girdle from
the provisory altar, fastening it around Elizabeth's gigantic belly,
my head spinning.

Her screams tear through the night for several hours while I
flatten myself against the wall, nauseated, desperate to escape. It
sounds as if she is dying. Dear God, do not let her die. As much
as I hate it, and as little influence as she carries, my own and my
family's fortunes depend on her. What is more, she is my sister,

and despite all the times I have wished for her to go away when she has made me feel smaller than a cockroach, I could never genuinely hope for her demise. *Dear, dear God, do not let her die.* Is this what my Agnes suffered? It must have been even worse. I shut my eyes and press my hands to my ears to banish every sound, but to no avail.

Finally—it must be past midnight—the high-pitched cry of a baby cuts Elizabeth's own cries short. Then follows a few seconds of tense silence before a choir of cheerful murmur breaks out among the women present.

A son. We have our Prince Arthur. After eight months of marriage, Elizabeth has succeeded in what many unfortunate queens fail to do for years and years. With all probability, the boy was conceived before the wedding, for he possesses naught of the gravely premature child's slightness, but the public does not know that, and a month too early is not early enough to cross the boundaries of reason.

I cannot curb my curiosity. Before I know it, I have scrambled to the chief midwife's side to assist her. The baby's eyes are large and pale blue-green, the typical Woodville eyes. His skin is warm and tender as I help the midwife to rub him clean from blood and bodily fluids. The chubby arms and legs are comically short in proportion to his body; his head enormous. Despite having seen several of my siblings almost this fresh from the womb, I am always struck anew by how peculiar a newly born looks.

The midwife folds the prepared piece of linen around my nephew and transfers him to my shaky arms before Margaret Beaufort can step forth. I can sense his heartbeats: rapid, like a patter of rain, but strong. As I put him at his mother's bosom, my mouth is dry as withered leaves.

I hate him because he is the embodiment of York's forced union with Lancaster, because he is Tudor's greatest security, yet I love him because he is a beautiful little creature of my blood, innocent of his father's foulness. I hope I can be just towards him and extinguish my hatred.

Four days later, Prince Arthur is christened in Winchester Cathedral. Mother and I take turns holding him during the ceremony and he rests quiet, sleepy in my arms. Now that he is properly swaddled and dressed in his magnificent christening gown, he does not look alien in the least to me. I have carried many of my siblings like this, and although babies have never been my strong suit like they seem to be Elizabeth's, I am familiar enough with the little ones to know how to care for them properly.

I half-expected Beaufort to carry her grandson but she remains seated by her son's side throughout the christening. This must be a moment of triumph for her, second only to Tudor's victory at Redemore. In this child, she has the future of the dynasty whose foundation she has worked so tirelessly for, the continuation of her line. I search her face for a smile and actually find one.

Naturally, Elizabeth is not present for the ceremony. She must remain confined to her bed for another month and undergo churching to remove the sin of conception as well as the pollution associated with the birth itself. I pity her—I do not know how I will bear it when my time comes to be imprisoned thus—but she appears to enjoy this reclusiveness from the public eye. When we return the prince to her after the baptism, she cradles him in her arms, a veil of serenity drawn over her face.

'I could stay here always,' she says.

Mother plants kiss on her temple. 'The wet nurse asks for him.'

'Lady Mother? How can I allow them to take him to Ludlow when even giving him to the nurse pains me?'

'I know it does, apple of mine eye, just as it pained me to surrender my own eldest son. You must remember your duty.'

'Yes.'

Mother sinks down on the bed and puts her arms around her eldest daughter, gazing down on the dozing prince. 'And next time, I daresay it will be a girl. Her you can dote on for as long as you like.'

'Henry wants another son.'

'It matters little. Neither a girl nor another boy will be the heir. After this, you have suffered what is required.'

There is a knock on the door, and I open. The wet nurse—a pudgy woman in her late twenties, with almost no chin and thick rims of eyelashes—marches forward to the bed. She has been carefully selected from a nearby village for her good lineage and virtuous character, as well as for her own multitude of healthy offspring.

'His Royal Highness needs to be fed, Your Grace, else he'll make a fuss, mark my words,' she says in a distinctly southern accent.

Elizabeth nods after a moment of reluctance and puts the prince in the other woman's steady arms. 'You may take him.'

We remain at Winchester until the purifying churching has been carried out. Afterwards, the court travels back to London, while little Arthur is sent to Ludlow to be brought up in accordance with his role as future king, as is customary. I hope this Prince of Wales lives to a more seasoned age than the previous two, my brother and cousin, the unfortunate Edwards. Perhaps he is unusually idle, but nonetheless healthy, though one never knows what God's plan might be, or rather what men's plans are. If a true Yorkist is restored to our rightful throne, Prince Arthur will have to be dealt with one way or another. He may be part York himself, but the other part is Lancaster, and his label is without doubt Tudor. I do my best not to think of the evils that could befall my nephew if my wishes regarding the crown were to be fulfilled.

Lincoln is waiting for us in London. He manages to blend in faultlessly in Tudor's court, yet there is a sly glimmer in his eyes when he meets my glance from across the presence chamber. How I yearn to see the machinations in his mind! Soon, soon I will arrange a meeting so that we might whisper freely.

One of the first days of November, I am sitting in Elizabeth's rooms with Anne, Kate, and a cluster of ladies busy with remaining unobtrusive under my sister's watch. Four spaniels shuffle around our feet, all gifts from Tudor to his wife after the birth of their heir. I adore them, especially the black puppy, Munchie, but I think Elizabeth would rather have had a new set of virginals.

Anne turns a page in The Canterbury Tales with a rustle. 'Beth?'

Elizabeth does not avert her eyes from her needlework. 'Yes?'

'Will you find me a kind husband? One who loves me dearly?'

'Anyone would love you dearly, though you must wait.'

'I'm not *that* young.'

I curse under my breath as I pierce my finger with my needle for the third time this afternoon. 'Eleven is not very old either, Anne. Your knight in shining armour will like you much better in three years or so.'

'Promise?' Her voice is unusually anxious.

'Absolutely.'

Aunt Catherine sticks her head through the door. 'The French ambassador requests an audience, Your Grace. He suggests a walk in the gardens, and he brings two new kinsmen. Frightfully handsome.' She laughs, her eyebrows meeting. 'They brought your favourite apples for gifts, too.'

Elizabeth stands, as do the rest of us. 'I will speak with them presently, and my ladies may come also. Stay and watch the dogs, Cecily, please.' She shuffles Anne ahead of her. 'Let's see if we can find you a French fiancé, as long as the King agrees. Would you like that?'

Kate is the last to exit, jumpy with excitement, and I am left alone with the dogs.

I pluck a honeyed walnut, Munchie's favourite treat, from the bowl on one of the small tables and let him jump after it, huffing and squealing, tail wagging. Once he has gobbled it down, I pick up another treat, and this time I play the silly game with him, jumping my highest.

When I land with the heel of my slipper on one of the floorboards, it emits a slight but unmistakably hollow sound. I falter in my steps and give it a proper stomp. Yes, it is different than the other boards, which all sound solid.

I throw a glance over my shoulder. The guards are posted outside the door, protecting me from intruders although they do not know it. Elizabeth and her throng of ladies have only been gone perhaps ten minutes, and there should be plenty of time before any of them sees fit to abandon the ambassador and his handsome fellows.

Squatting, I knock along the edges of the board in search for where the space underneath begins and ends. The plugs are loose, and having coaxed them out of their holes, I use the tip of my fingernails to lift the board slightly before I can remove it. The gaping black hole is cold as I lower my hand into it, squinting. I have no clue what there usually is under the bottom floor of a palace or how deep the construction is. I am forced to lie flat with my entire arm sunk in the hole before my fingers find something cool and damp.

Gripping the object and pulling it back into the light, I raise myself to a kneeling position. A small silver casket with a lid of painted glass rests in my hands. The lock is feeble and rusty, and I swiftly crack it open, my pulse quickening, my breath stuck in my throat. Might it be hidden jewels, or… No. The object of my stare is a thin stack of folded papers tied together with a frayed blue ribbon. At first, I am disappointed, but as I pick up the paper bundle, a distinct whiff of honeysuckle hits me, and I untie the ribbon in a frenzy. I remember that perfume.

I know that handwriting also: tiny, neat letters, the lines leaning towards the bottom right corner. Queen Anne would not want me reading her letters, but there must be a reason she stored them in such an intriguing hideaway, and better I unveil whatever secrets they might contain than someone with hostile intent.

The first three are love letters. One is dated 20 October 1471; the other two are from the month after that. I blush as I read, for she is more passionate in her written word than I ever heard her. I believe she never sent these letters to Uncle Richard, because at the time she was virtually Clarence's prisoner, and he would not have allowed any correspondence between the two of them.

The latter two are from the late king. If I recall correctly, Anne Neville and Uncle Richard had finally been married in the late spring of 1472. It is easier to read my uncle's words as he is more subtle in his expressions, always careful not to stray from principles of chivalry. 'It would delight my heart, were the Lord to lead you once more into my embrace,' is about as risqué as it gets.

Then follows a series of personal correspondence mainly from the late queen's sister Isabel, which I skim through.

The last letter, however, is something quite different. It is, again, from Uncle Richard, but this time addressed to the toad Buckingham. Perhaps Cousin Anne was tasked with its safekeeping. She would not have wanted to burn it, in the event circumstances turned on their head.

*Ricardius Rex, by grace of God King of England and Lord of Ireland,
calls on his most lowly subject Henry Stafford*

*I have faith you know my displeasure already. You have acted in
foolery like a common knave, and brought immense danger upon the crown.
If you treasure your life, I prithee keep your tongue from wagging. Your
crime against the boys is too beneficial for the rebel Tudor to be known
publicly.*

The short, brutal note has neither date nor farewell, but bears
two seals: Uncle Richard's and Buckingham's, both broken. I sit
with my legs crossed, mesmerized, grappling to comprehend the
full significance of this scrap of paper.

Firstly, there is the greeting. 'Most lowly subject Henry
Stafford.' No title, no duke. The King must have decided to
confiscate Buckingham's peerage and thereby his lands and
appanage, which my Father had once restored to him, as
punishment for his careless actions. Perhaps he intended to
disarm Buckingham by removing him from court, or perhaps it
was an empty threat to frighten his former ally into submission.
All I know is the degradation was never officially proclaimed.
Whatever the reason, the plan backfired profoundly, pushing the
toad over the verge of rebellion.

Secondly, there is the reminder of what Henry Tudor stood
to gain through the murders. With the benefit of hindsight, it was
glaringly unwise to mention it, though I suppose Uncle Richard
simply did not know Buckingham as well as he thought he did.

Thirdly, the toad's seal means he received the letter and sent
it back without reply in defiance, presumably around the same
time he sank himself nose-deep in Margaret Beaufort's and
Mother's schemes.

The letter I now hold in my hand is a confirmation of the
truth in what the late King and Queen told me at Nottingham.
They might have left out details, but what matters is that
Buckingham did order the foul deed. I always believed it, but
these lines erase the last, miniscule trace of doubt.

'What do you think you are doing, girl?'

I turn, the marrow in my bones chilled. Margaret Beaufort resembles the ghost of a nun where the stands in the doorway, striking dread despite her short stature.

'I… That is "Your Royal Highness", to you, Madam,' I manage, forcing the tremble out of my voice.

Beaufort strides towards me. 'I am the King's Mother. I bow my head to no one. Now you will tell me what, in God's heaven, that is.'

'Letters. Just trifles—'

She snatches the paper from my hand with incredible speed. Reading, the lines around her mouth harden, her face whitening further. 'So the wench kept this. What else?'

'Do not call her that, Madam. The rest is of no interest to you, regardless. See for yourself.' I rise and reluctantly give her two of the previous letters, which she reads in quick succession.

'Nonsense, thanks be to God. My son the King's Grace told me you knew about your brothers' true fate.'

'I did, and this confirms it.'

'It shall never see the light of day.'

I try to snatch back the letter but Beaufort holds it out of my reach.

'I could clear my uncle's good name,' I say.

'You could not. This serves as evidence to *you*, because you have already been told the story first-hand. You believed your uncle—but who would believe you? Buckingham never wrote back, or if he did, the letter is not here, thus this is solely the tyrant's words, and they carry no credence with others.'

'I'll show it anyways.'

Beaufort grabs my jaw between her strong fingers. '*You shan't*, girl, is that clear?'

I break free from her and start pacing the room. 'I thought you said no one would believe it. No one would believe you allied yourself with the man who butchered my brothers to pave the way for your own son. If that is so, what is the harm?'

'Your mother was part of the alliance, too, mind you.'

I lose the last of my composure at the insinuation. 'She had no idea, unlike you! She still has not!'

'Can you prove it? So, you see, no one would benefit from this cursed letter reaching the eyes of the nobles.'

'Do you know where the bodies are?'

Beaufort scoffs. 'If I knew, we would long since have dug them up and arranged a lavish state funeral.'

'Because it would make the people view your son favourably?'

'Because it would prove their deaths.'

'So would the letter.'

She purses her lips like a drawstring purse. 'Perhaps you are not as clever as I thought. Now, everything *indicates* the tyrant is to blame; this letter would *indicate* Buckingham, God rest his wretched soul. Only the boys' bodies could *prove* they are dead at all, no matter whom we blame. I won't deny, though, that I knew they were dead, and I promised Buckingham my favour if he would aid us in the rebellion, for the circumstances held far too much opportunity to ignore.'

I want to ask if she also whispered in Buckingham's ear to encourage the murders in the first place, but I am frightened of the answer, hence I stick to the more practical matter of the bodies. 'We both want to find them, surely? I want to see my angel brothers receive the burial due to them.' Tears well in my eyes. 'They…they were the most innocent of children.'

'"Death to the Christian is the funeral of all his sorrows and evils, and the resurrection of all his joys."'

'The Bible rarely helped before.'

A red flare colours the otherwise pale skin stretching over her high cheekbones. 'That is *heresy!*'

We stand measuring one another for what feels like an eternity. She is not the typical English-rose-beauty; on the contrary, she appears ten years older than the forty-five I estimate her to be. There is a hefty dose of knowledge in her dark eyes, the result of a lifetime spent manoeuvring as a woman through a political landscape torn to shreds by men. Despite her fanatical piety and her Lancastrian devotion, she impresses me and has done so since I first saw her standing by her son's throne, if not longer.

Eventually, I surrender and lower my eyes. 'Let me keep the rest, please.'

'Keep the wench's and the tyrant's letters?'

'I do not have many relics from the family I have lost,' I tell her in all honesty. I have nothing from my sister Mary, nothing

173

from Father save the possessions he paid for once upon a time, nothing from my brothers, a mere handkerchief from Agnes. From my uncle and his wife, I have only the diamond broach and the few letters they wrote to me, which Mother has tried to make me burn several times. I have a fondness for memorabilia, and in times of despair, there is nothing so comforting as the past.

Beaufort studies the letters once more, then returns them to me. 'They are yours to keep, but be aware, it is an act of treachery towards His Grace.'

'Does the law truly say that?'

'I am confident we could interpret it in that manner.'

I tie the ribbon around the stack, return them to the casket, and slam the lid shut. 'Well, I think the picture of York and Lancaster standing united under Lancastrian rule is more within your interests, Madam. It might be difficult to uphold if you start spewing out accusations.'

'Imagine if your sister had caught the plague, or a fever. You would have been my daughter-in-law in her stead.' The rare trepidation in her voice is plain as day.

'I know. I suppose you are grateful for her now, in contrast to what might have been.'

'There is nothing more unattractive than to think oneself inferior, girl.'

I cross my arms, clutching the casket in one hand. 'I do not—I simply think you would have had a fair amount of issues with me.'

'I will keep you close, make no mistake. A treacherous heretic like you has to be turned to the path of light,' she hisses and closes the distance between us, enveloping me in a cloud of fumes: lavender and marjoram, too strong to be pleasant.

'And you intend to undertake that task?'

'Henceforth, you may accompany me on my morning walks, mass, and, naturally, morning prayers. You will rejoice to find your unwieldy character turned compliant.'

I remain nailed to the spot a long while after she leaves me. Having pushed the floorboard back in its place, I scurry back to my own bedchamber with indignation burning hot in my chest. If there is one single way in which I *do not* want to spend my early mornings, it is being subjected to Margaret Beaufort's schooling, regardless of how much she impresses me.

Chapter XVII

LINCOLN AGREES TO meet with me in a sparsely furnished, small solar near the great hall. He greets me with a slight bow, as custom demands now that my legitimacy as a princess has been restored, and I grant him a tense smile.

'You want news?' he says in a hushed voice. One never knows who might be on the other side of a door.

I brace myself. 'If you have made any progress in solving the issue of Henry Tudor, then yes, I want news.'

'Got the perfect candidate.'

'A candidate for the throne? Prithee tell, Cousin.'

'The Earl of Warwick.'

I gape at him. 'What? But he's...' So simple-minded, so young, so imprisoned. 'Why not yourself?'

'Think. He descends through the male line. I stand a better chance to rule through him than on my own.'

'Does the male line trump the fact that his father was a traitor both to York *and* Lancaster?'

Lincoln gives an impatient shrug. 'Irish lords think so. Not everyone's as bitter about Clarence as you.'

'Yet you seem to have forgotten one pivotal thing: Warwick is as safely locked up as he has been for the past year.' I clutch my elbows, jutting my chin forward.

He takes a step closer, his breath humid against my face. 'Do you think me witless? We will conjure a new Warwick. I have a man in Oxford who has found a boy of the right age and with the right looks about him.'

'An...an imposter?'

'That's generally what they call it.'

'And what of the original? If you help this…this pretender seize power, what happens to our cousin?'

Lincoln rubs his thumb against my wrist, a twinkle in his eye. 'Then he will be king, obviously, with me as his regent and chief councillor. Once the original is set free, we can do away with the pretender easily enough. A boy without means like him.'

I stare at him. Is he completely out of his mind? Did his horse throw him and trample him on his head? He thinks we can fool the public with an imposter boy until we get our hands on Warwick himself, then murder the innocent boy to keep him from telling, and presumably rid ourselves of Prince Arthur as well. It is madness, it can never work. However, what makes me weary is not the sheer likelihood of failure, but the fact I have been pushing from my thoughts for a while now: it is impossible to destroy Tudor without more or less destroying my sister and nephew also. Before the prince was born, or if the child had been a girl, it might have been possible to detangle the knots our family has tied with theirs, but when the alliance has been sealed through an *heir*… There is nothing I want more than to see Elizabeth humbled and the clock turned back; there is nothing I want more than to see Tudor as dead as Uncle Richard and all those loyal Yorkist men—but this would be the cost. Elizabeth would be more than humbled. Her son, whom she loves more than anything else in this world, would likely be smothered or dropped by *accident*. I fancy myself a better person than to willingly let children lose their lives over what they cannot influence.

Lincoln must not know my reluctance. Unless he trusts me, I will have no power either to aid or to prevent his plans.

'You may keep me informed, Cousin. I will do what I can to assist you in this most…glorious quest,' I say.

Lincoln scratches his trimmed beard. 'Good. Yes, you know your own good, don't you?'

Before I can reply, he has grabbed my chin and pressed his lips against mine for a vile moment. I freeze in his grip. This is not how I imagined my first kiss. It tastes of wine, not just any wine but the distinctive, expensive Italian sort which I recall to have been his favourite when visiting Sheriff Hutton.

'Never received your congratulations on my wedding,' he says after releasing me.

177

'Your wedding?'

'To Margaret FitzAlan.'

I remain frozen. Perhaps I ought to be glad he has married, because I like him less with every passing second. 'You do have my congratulations. As I said, keep me informed.'

A smile crosses his lips, though his voice is tinted with irony. 'Your wish is my command. Hope we can resume these pleasantries soon.' On that note, he leaves me. In the doorway, he has to stoop low and fall on one knee for the pretend-king, who appears to have left his yeomen behind for a little tour of the palace. Knowing Tudor, I have no doubt he seeks to inspect every corner of every room for the hundredth time, searching for a way to cut down costs of maintenance. I try not to heed rumours, but I am inclined to believe the one reporting that a servant found him elbow-deep in the royal coffers, biting the pennies to assure himself of their validity.

Tudor keeps one eye on Lincoln and the other on me. 'What is the meaning of this?'

Lincoln smiles again, having risen. 'Meaning of what, Your Grace? I wished to bid a proper farewell to my dear cousin.'

'You are leaving court again?'

'Indeed.' Perfectly polite.

'*C'est dommage.* I trust you will keep us informed of your whereabouts.'

'Sire.' With a bow he is gone.

Tudor turns to watch him go, and I seize the opportunity to wipe my mouth on my sleeve, fearing Lincoln's lips might have left a trace like slugs do, and at the same time relishing in the fact that the Pretend-King did not notice my lack of curtsey.

'And you? Do you grieve to see the back of the Earl?' he asks.

I force a shrug. 'It makes no difference to me.'

'I will not have any sinister scheming in my court.'

'No, Sire. Though I cannot imagine why you would tell *me* that.'

We stare at one another in silence a moment before Tudor breaks the spell by reaching up to adjust the black velvet hat on his thinning hair. 'You should spend more time tending to my queen and less time wandering around unchaperoned.'

'With all due respect, Sire, you are as unchaperoned as I, and if there is an assassin lurking, he would be daft to attack me rather than you.'

'I was not thinking so much of assassins as of your reputation, *Madame*.'

'Naturally.' I fail to hide my sarcasm. 'If you permit it, I will leave you to your *inspections*.'

'I do permit it.'

With my slippers clicking against the stone as I descend the staircase and my headdress peculiarly heavy on my head, I feel more split than ever. My fundamental, personal allegiance to my sister and nephew battles with my allegiance to York, and I cannot even tell where my rationality is. Damn Mother for arranging Elizabeth's marriage and damn Elizabeth for delivering a son! Perhaps most of all, damn Lincoln for marrying—that is the last grain of sand that tips the scales for me. If he plans to be regent and rule England through the simple-minded Young Warwick, and if he had promised to make *me* his wife, queen in all but name, I could have endured his character and perhaps even my own scruples regarding Elizabeth's fate. But no, the fool has dispensed with my support. As much as it stings in my eyes, it appears I have become the new regime's spy without them knowing it.

I recount the meeting to Thomas later that evening, having snuck away from Elizabeth's company once more to our room of old charts and maps. To my chagrin, he is livid.

'You let him kiss you?'

'There was not a great deal I could do about it, Thomas. Besides which, I have to stay in his good graces if I am to find out anything more about this insurgency.'

Thomas cracks his knuckles. 'But he's not going to wed you.'

'I know that. Which is why I will not assist him in his plotting—only on the surface. And *please* stop that habit.'

'What if he wants more from you? What if he wants to make you his mistress?'

I do not know whether to laugh or cry at the thought. 'Do not be ridiculous! I am not fool enough to agree to such a thing.'

'Right. I just don't think that man is considerate enough to care whether you agree or not.'

'Why do *you* care?'

He opens and closes his mouth twice before at last muttering, 'Because I don't think well of it!'

'Will I have to beg for your approval when I do marry, too? I asked you to be my friend, not my guardian.' I straighten my back and square my shoulders like I have seen Mother do when caught in a quarrel. Of course, Mother would rarely have to fear losing an argument, unlike me.

Thomas clamps his jaw. 'You have made that perfectly clear. Though you are being unfair—maybe it's my horribly low birth that does it.'

'Now *you* are unfair. I have never treated you as an inferior, at least not since I grew to know you.' My words are genuine: I have tried my very best to be his equal, and have been successful despite my initial misgivings.

Thomas rounds the table standing between us and halts a few feet away from me. 'Do you know what I'm tired of? Your meddling…just like your mother. Why can you not simply watch the events unfold from afar, be they to your liking or not, and remain safe?'

I frown. 'Because…because they affect my life too much.'

'Though that is not all, is it? You have lived in splendour under *every* king since you were born except for that little interlude in the abbey. This is about you trying to control the order of the world.'

'Well, I want to see York restored to the throne, that is all. I cannot leave something like that to chance! You know I hate uncertainty…'

'*Life* is uncertain! And that crown is nothing but a stupid piece of gold anyhow. It was never worth dying for.' He kicks the table leg; the blow appears to be worse on his foot than on the wood.

'You dare to suggest my uncles, and my grandfather, and everyone else, died in vain? You are saying my father risked all since for a *stupid piece of gold?* I draw a trembling breath, balling my fists. I cannot recall the last time I was his enraged, this scandalised. He has crossed the line. 'No. No, you are not allowed to say that. You have not known the pain in my kindred's eyes when they spoke of heads on pikes at Wakefield Bridge, nor have you known the hardships my mother has suffered, the fear that has dimmed her spirit forever. Have you any idea how many thousands of people's blood that has watered England's meadows?'

'That is precisely my point! And my words are not yours to command as you please.'

'Like you try to command me?'

He scoffs. 'Sorry. You know I am right, though. You would be so much happier if you left court all together and settled down in the countryside with someone who could love you.'

'Am I so difficult to love?' I barely dare to hear what he has to say.

'That is not what I meant.'

'What *did* you mean?'

He grapples for words. 'Only...only that your dear cousin Lincoln does not love you.'

'I was never under the illusion. Have we not already established that he is married and I'm not inclined to be anyone's mistress to cast off when I'm no longer pleasing?' I march past him towards the door, and turn to look at him as I reach the threshold, my vision foggy with tears. 'You are an insolent, thick-headed rascal, Thomas Kyme.'

He stares back at me through a shield of dishevelled black hair. 'And you an arrogant, senseless brat.'

I sprint from the room, tripping on the embroidered hem of my gown during the flight, bruising my knees. A few wide-eyed servants watch me, but fortunately, the courtiers who matter are nowhere to be seen.

I shall never speak to him again, *never*. How did I think he could be my companion when he opposes the very fundamentals of my being?

November passes in a clammy haze of grey. Thomas and I avoid each other with equal determination, which turns out to be easier than it was to find opportunity to meet. I chase him out of my thoughts as well, with varying success, but every nasty word exchanged between us sticks to my memory like a splinter in my finger, always hurting just a little. It feels different from all the

181

times I have quarrelled with Mother or my sisters. Kate is the only one who argue back as boldly as I do, and furthermore, with them I usually forget the squabble within a day or two.

I spend more hours with Margaret Beaufort than any living soul should have to suffer. She keeps me close, constantly prattling in my ear about her God and her son and the shortcomings of the York girls. She does approve of Bridget, but as far as I know, they have never exchanged a single direct word, and Beaufort takes a kind view on anyone living in a priory, destined to take holy vows.

I make an effort and finally discover two things we share: our fondness of dogs and our fear of childbirth. Beaufort's fear springs from experience, my own from expectation, and it is an unfortunate combination since the stories she tells me only increases my fright. She says a few tight-lipped words about how her midwife tried to force out a child heavy as a tenth of her own weight—and unlike my own kinswomen, she was thin as a stick except for the belly itself.

The dogs are a far happier topic for us. I will try to find the right moment to ask Elizabeth to give me Munchie for my New Year's Day present, for the dear little creature already trots at my heels, sniffing at Margaret's own two spaniels as we walk down the galleries.

'Your sister should appreciate her husband's gifts more. It is a good thing she has not yet been crowned,' Beaufort says during one of these walks.

I force myself to slow my steps as I have an unseemly habit of walking too fast. 'Her Grace is sometimes unaware of the things others do for her.' I occasionally find myself chiming in with Beaufort's snide comments about Elizabeth, although they are often a little strong even in my taste. She, who never truly aspired to it, is queen, while we, who both have wanted it more than anything, are not. The situation has become a third link between myself and the King's Mother, although I try to remind myself it is Tudor and Beaufort who are and always must be my main adversaries.

'How is your husband Lord Stanley?' I say.

'Lord Bedford,' she corrects me. 'His new title was well-earnt.'

I cannot stop myself; the resentment bubbling up inside me is scorching, fired on by my lingering anger towards Thomas. 'Yes, treason can do such marvellous things for one's carrier, or so I hear.'

'Watch your tongue, girl. Do not think yourself immune because of your sister's position. I—I mean my blessed son— saved your lot from the gutter!' Her voice rises to a familiar pitch.

'You would be nothing without us!'

We keep walking and this time I make no show of restraining my steps, but rather surge ahead of her in a way she never allows anyone equal to or beneath her station to do.

She catches my arm and locks her fingers there, hauling me in like a naughty toddler. 'Let us not make a scene before the nobles. Speak with me about something suitable.'

So that is what we do, revisiting the topic of spaniels as if there was no rift between us, like so many times before. At first, I grit my teeth, but I soon give in to the conversation. This is what is so devious about Beaufort: she is the most agonizing, irritating, strange woman I know, and yet I always succumb to her command.

Advent and the Twelve Days of Christmas come and go. Tudor puts on a surprisingly lavish display considering his miserly nature. The garlands of holly are entwined with tiny gold bells, the food is aromatic with expensive spices, and the velvet wall-hangings depicting the Tudor rose have been made for this occasion alone. I see now that he knows how and when to spend, except the times he does so are too few and far between for my liking.

I join Elizabeth and Anne—and the Pretend-King, naturally—on one of their visits to Ludlow to fawn over Prince Arthur. He has grown since I last saw him, and gained quite a bit of weight, as babies ought to. Still, he is the calmest child I have ever seen, apart from Bridget, on the verge of feeble. I have been taught boys are supposed to scream and show signs of strength early, but when I mention this to Elizabeth, she brushes off my concerns, saying the prince is merely being kind to us all. His pudgy wet nurse exchanges a glance with the two rockers but says nothing. Afterwards, the court moves on to Greenwich to spend a few months at the Palace of Placentia.

I manage to curb my disappointment when I do not receive Munchie on New Year's Day as I had hoped. My gifts are sumptuous enough, true, yet I wished for nothing more. Perhaps my sister forgot I asked—I shall have to try again.

I have found that the only way to escape Margaret Beaufort's clutch during the morning hours is to venture outside while she says her private prayers before dragging me with her to mass, early in the morning. One of those mornings, I extend my previously brief outing to a proper walk. The garden is coated in frost, the tiny crystals reflecting glints of white sunlight. The silver birches stand naked, bereft of their magnificent greenery, their thin branches poking the churned grey sky. Gone are the roses so vibrant in summertime, gone is the russet glow of autumn. A blackbird picks at the hardened ground with its beak but the search for food is futile.

I pull my fur-lined sleeves down over my hands and wrap my arms around my torso to stem the shivers running through my limbs. If one were to see through my layers of clothes, the goose bumps I feel would make me look like a plucked bird ready for cooking.

I raise a hand to shield my eyes from the blinding light. A figure is leaning over the edge of the fountain further down the gravel path, throwing something in the water. As I close the distance between us, there is no mistaking the plain doublet and hose, not to speak of the broken nose and sharply contoured jaw. Two ducks are swimming in the ice-cool water of the fountain— I am close enough now to see their orange feet paddling below the gleaming surface—and Thomas feeds them from the loaf of wheat bread he cradles in one hand. His priorities do puzzle me, for while he wastes his best bread on ducks, he still refuses to buy himself a finer set of clothes.

What puzzles me more, though, is the way I feel when seeing him. Mayhap the weather has cooled my anger as well, or the passing of time has done its work, because my sole sentiment is nervousness, jittery nervousness. Is he still sullen? He has not yet noticed me, though it should be easy enough since the garden is void of people other than us—or is he purposefully ignoring me?

Before I can think any further, Thomas leans too far out and loses his footing, dropping the loaf of bread with a *splash*. I lunge forward and grab his sleeve just in time to prevent him from tumbling face-first into the fountain and presumably upsetting the ducks. He is heavier than me and nearly drags me with him in the fall, but after a critical heartbeat we both stand on firm ground again.

Thomas shakes his head. 'By Saint Edward! You frightened me.'

'I *saved* you.'

'What, from the fountain's evil grasp?'

I pout. 'If you want to bathe in water that filthy and cold, I shan't stand in your way.'

'I'm sorry.'

'No matter.'

'I mean I'm sorry for what I said, about you and...everything.' He reaches for my hand and I accede more swiftly than I perhaps should.

'Likewise,' I say. The relief is immediate, the weight of dispute lifted from my shoulders, and I cannot help but notice how his face is at once free from shadows.

Thomas squeezes my hand. 'Friends?'

'Yes. Friends.'

A glance flashes between us and I at once sense how close we are standing, too close. His lips brush against mine, a warm summer breeze in the midst of winter, even softer than his hands. Neither of us move. This is not how I imagined my second kiss, but I want to stay forever.

Thomas pulls away and emits a quivering sigh. 'It's an imprudent idea, is it not?'

I force my head to a mechanical nod. 'It is the very quintessence of imprudence.'

We break apart, slowly, like detangling a knot, our eyes turning simultaneously to the ducks and our blurred reflections in the fountain.

I shift my weight now that the summer breeze has left me. 'Did you...did you bring any more bread?'

He clears his throat. 'I am afraid not.'

We stand in silence a long while before I muster the courage to take his hand again and lace our fingers together. A dalliance would risk my reputation and prospects of a good marriage, and put him in grave danger, to mention only the most obvious impediments, yet as foolhardy as it sounds, I hope we can indeed still be friends.

Chapter XVIII

B Y THE END of February, Mother empties a figurative bucket of cold water over all our heads, or at least my head. She has decided to retire from court life to live out the years she has left in Bermondsey Abbey, an old monastery in the southeast of London.

I simply cannot fathom it: my own mother, the Dowager Queen and once upon a time the most praised beauty in England, living in squalor! Of course, not everyone would define it as such, and dowagers do have a habit of retiring to abbeys, but still… She has fought so hard for her place in the sun these past two decades, especially after Father died, and now she hands every ray of sunlight to Margaret Beaufort. Indeed, the King's Mother will surely rejoice in the new arrangements, for she will be the undisputed first lady of the court and country except for Elizabeth, whom she steps on easily enough.

'Is this Beaufort's scheme, Lady Mother?' I ask her as we stand watching the servants pack her coffers. Many of her rich garments and beauty concoctions belong to a time gone by, before she was a widow. I doubt she will ever use them again once she settles in the drab abbey, and these days I can barely spot any of the vainglorious flair she used to represent to me when I was a little girl.

Mother puts an arm around my shoulders. 'No, you must not blame her. It is His Grace's wish.'

'But he only wishes what his mother tells him.'

'That is not entirely true, my sweet.'

'I still think she whispered in his ear. Though it does not matter. They are villains, both of them, for sending you away from us. Kate is not yet eight years old!'

187

'She is a brave girl, and too giddy to miss me for more than a fortnight. I dare say she will manage.'

I take a step back to avoid colliding with one of the maids hurrying forth with a stack of folded cloth. 'I was more concerned about how *we* will manage *her*. She never truly listens to me, not even to Elizabeth.'

'She will learn to listen.'

'If I were you, I would refuse to leave.'

Mother strokes the back of my hand, a hint of her characteristic smile playing on her vermillion lips. 'One cannot refuse a king, as you know very well. And you mustn't worry, for I have been promised a pension befitting a woman of my status.'

'How much, Lady Mother?'

'A yearly sum of four hundred pounds.'

I frown at the number, which is not exactly beggar's scraps but neither is it what I hoped for. 'Less than the yearly income of a minor Earl, is it not?'

'Methinks you forget I am not the Queen any longer, and have not been for a while now. It is time I accept it.'

She baffles me like never before. This show of docility is so utterly unlike her, so outlandish, when I have long been accustomed to her ambition. I can only presume it has been brought on by the turning of the years and the realisation that she has little left to fight for now, having achieved her goal of seeing Elizabeth on the throne.

'You *should* be queen. You or Anne Neville, not meek—' I stop myself before her name crosses my lips, however, it is too late.

'Take care not to speak ill of your sister. This is not her fault.'

'Tudor loves her, or so she says. If it is true, he ought to listen to her if she asked for you to remain.'

Mother sighs. 'She has asked, and he has told her no. His love for her is…it is the kind of love which will only last when he is the lord and master.'

'Then he does not love in earnest. I think that is what Anne would say, and she knows these things best even at her age.' I wish my little sister were with us now to chime in with me.

'Everyone loves differently, yet that is of little importance in this instance. I am leaving and you shall learn to live with it, just like I have, bless you.'

I accept her hasty blessing with an expanding cavity in my chest. I have not always agreed with her, and I have felt more animosity towards her than befits a dutiful daughter, but her presence has provided me with security. Regardless of whom she loves best in the moment of truth, she has protected each of her children with teeth and claws. Without that protection, I am left to my own, admittedly dubious, devices. Moreover, I do not know how my sisters and I will be able to keep the peace between us for long once she is gone, because we will have lost the unifying force that has so often cut our petty arguments short. And Margaret Beaufort… Does she not prance around enough as it is? Tudor, also. It appears to me they have rid themselves of yet another reminder of an older, rightful regime, another imagined threat. Perhaps they have forgotten it was Mother, unfortunately, who made Tudor's ascend to the throne possible by granting him Elizabeth's hand and with it a chunk of Yorkist support.

That particular thought obscures my surge of affection the slightest, but I nevertheless have to make an effort to remain composed and dry-eyed as I watch her carriage roll away the following day. I must visit often, as often as the Pretend-King and his mother will allow.

Mere days after Mother's departure, Tudor hosts a joust. He will not compete himself—it is a risk he refuses to take, especially while his only heir is barely six months old—but many nobles mount their horses most eagerly.

We ladies take our place on the spectators' bleachers among the men who are too old or too young to participate, wrapping our thick cloaks tighter around our shoulders to ward off the biting cold. The Pretend-King sits on his dais in the midst of us, presiding over the competition like a hawk.

Meanwhile, the contestants mass in the roped-off tiltyard, preparing for their turn, prancing in their colourful coats of arms. A handful sport ribbons or handkerchiefs tied to their lances: tokens from wives or sweethearts.

189

The horses' speed and force send cold rats' feet of fear skittering down my spine. The highest standing magnates use destriers, the most prized kind of warhorse, while the regular nobles and knights have to contend with coursers and even all-purpose rounceys. I used to think of every creature simply as a horse of varying fineness, but Thomas has refreshed my knowledge of the proper terms. The animals' muscles rise and fall under their glossy hair as they scrape their hooves in the tiltyard, stirring up clouds of dust, their nostrils flaring and their eyes like pearls of black glass. One single kick from those hooves could smash my skull to mush. The wooden tilt-barrier is to keep them from crashing into each other, however, it looks feeble from where I am sitting.

I always find the joust itself thrilling, though, for it is a remnant of a time when troubadours and knights competed for the fair maiden, and it is an excellent way to exhibit what is left of chivalry in our age. I suspect the men who fight love it more for the violence it allows them to participate in without judicial consequences, but no matter. It *is* violent, yet also an art of perfecting technique. My family have mastered the joust since before I was born; Father and a number of my uncles, both Woodvilles and Yorkists, were reckless enough to enjoy it. I have heard many stories during my childhood about a particular joust where my uncle Earl Rivers excelled. It was part of a tournament to cement an alliance between England and Burgundy, furthering marriage negotiations between Aunt Margaret and the Burgundian duke. Rivers made the nasty mistake of killing the Burgundian representative's horse, whether it was an accident or not, but the marriage did come to pass in the end.

Anne, who is sitting on my left, takes my hand. Her eyes are glittering in the crisp sunlight. 'It is so very similar to the romances, isn't it, Cecily?'

'Are you looking for your own knight again?'

'You make me sound so silly.' She lowers her eyes.

I squeeze her hand, a smile playing on my lips. 'I did not mean to. But I happen to know something you do not.'

'What?' She frowns. 'You just mock me.'

'No! Well, perhaps a little. I suppose you know Bessie Tilney? The tall woman who is always forgetting her rosary in the most peculiar places, the lady who was with us at Winchester?'

'The Countess of Surrey?'

'Yes, her. I have heard it said that she intends to petition Tudor—His Grace, I mean—for your hand in marriage on behalf of her eldest son.' I revel in my little sister's wide-eyed gaze. How I love to be the deliverer of gossip and secrets, as long as they are not harmful.

'But our betrothal was broken...?'

'It faded into nothingness, that was all, when Uncle Richard was no longer alive to protect our interests.'

'Then I hope His Grace concedes. I like the Earl of Surrey's son, yes, I like him very much.' A peach blush tints her cheeks.

I laugh. 'You've never met him. But you are fortunate, for both the earl and his father the Duke of Norfolk were loyal to York till the end.'

Margaret Beaufort, sitting on my right in a pompous black gown, interrupts us. 'Do not fill your sister's head with nonsense, girl. You listen to too much gossip. The Howards are still in disgrace, and my son the King's Grace shall not bestow this match on them.'

I roll my eyes at Anne and she hides a giggle behind her hand. Beaufort cannot possibly control *everything* in our lives.

Thomas Stanley jousts against his younger brother William, flustered like the hellish brood they are; Northumberland defeats a myriad of lesser knights; Dorset topples three opponents from their horses. Several of the contestants are on the verge of old age, yet their physical prowess is undeniable.

A man called Viscount Welles, Margaret Beaufort's younger half-brother, competes against Jasper Tudor and is marvellously victorious. I know very little of the man other than that he is an unyielding Lancastrian who rose in rebellion along with Buckingham and then fled to join his nephew's provisory court in exile. Now, he is without doubt a royal favourite and handsomely rewarded.

Beaufort nods toward the viscount just as he dismounts. 'His father was killed at Towton, and our brother and nephew both beheaded in the year of our Lord 1470.' Her voice is bitter as almonds.

I crane my neck for a better view. When the viscount removes his helmet, I spot a weathered man, perhaps approaching forty, with wisps of light reddish hair fluttering around a square, dimpled chin.

Beaufort continues. 'You ought to know this already, for said brother and nephew rebelled against your father.'

A wave of cold washes through me. 'Then their deaths were justified. They defied their rightful king.'

'They defied a usurper.'

'I refuse to listen to your slander, Madam.'

We exchange a glare. What I cannot bring myself to say is that I do feel sorry for his father, Lancastrian or not. The twenty-six-year-old ghost that is the Battle of Towton is deeply carved in our collective memory. The wound has not yet healed even in those who were not born at the time, and once it does heal, there will be the tissue of an imperfect scar. Twenty thousand dead, or so I have heard it said. The bloodiest battle ever fought on English soil. My own father was scarcely older than I am now, king though not yet formally crowned. He hacked his way through the Lancastrian ranks, fierce as he was in his youth, winning a decisive victory for York. After that fateful day there could be no doubt as to who the new monarch was—but the incomprehensible slaughter still overshadows the triumph to this day.

'He is in need of a wife,' Beaufort says, interrupting my lament.

A few seconds pass before I catch the insinuation in her words. 'No. I shan't wed a man who is among the foremost of my enemies.'

'We will see, girl.'

'You need my consent, and I will not give it.'

'I *said* we will see.'

Eventually, Welles wins the joust, and Tudor grants him another piece of land for prize. It cannot be a significant grant compared to what the viscount already holds, but it is a significant gesture, since Tudor so rarely loosens his grip on crown property, preferring to keep it under his own watchful control rather than deal it out like his predecessors did.

I sneak away to find Thomas, who is brushing Northumberland's sweat-soaked destrier, humming to himself, his strokes with the brush long and firm.

'What are you doing?' I ask.

'What does it look like? I volunteered to care for the lord's horse.' He strokes the white stripe on the animal's mule.

'*Volunteered?* But you are an esquire. The tasks of a groom are far below you.'

Thomas shrugs. 'You know I love the creatures. Just look how beautiful this one is.'

'They are terrifying.'

'I beg to differ.'

A painful silence settles, a silence filled with smiles withdrawn before the other has a chance to respond, a silence which has become habit. It has been like this ever since that day by the fountain and it tortures me, because it is not as easy as I hoped to be friends and nothing more, nothing less. At least, that is what I try to convince myself we must be, though my heart yearns for that 'more'.

After a while passed in this manner, I leave him with his precious horse and join the other ladies.

Court is ablaze with whispers, saturated with hearsay. Henry Tudor's first real challenge in the shape of a Yorkist claimant has materialised: a young boy who states he is Edward, Earl of Warwick, eldest living nephew to Edward IV and Richard III descending from a male line. We all know him to be a pretender, since the real Warwick is clapped in the Tower, but the rest of England cannot be quite so certain.

The boy would not be cause for concern if he was alone, but as the courtiers soon gather, a band of influential nobles back his claim. Foremost among them is the Earl of Lincoln.

I have been writing to my cousin occasionally since he left court again in autumn last year, and received short messages back every so often. Francis Lovell is with him. They intend to have the imposter—whose actual name is Lambert Simnel—crowned Edward VI with the support of the Irish lords and Aunt Margaret of Burgundy, then march to face Tudor in battle. The more I hear, the gladder I am to not be on their side other than in his thoughts, because this is indeed madness. Lincoln asks me to send details on how many men his opponent might be able to muster and whether there is any support for "Edward VI" in London. I believe he overestimates my closeness to Tudor.

I deliver the details he requests, but they are all false, a product of my imagination. Let him try and arrange a usurpation based on made-up information. I thought to reveal my position to my sister and her husband long since, so that I might expose Lincoln's strategy in turn, however, I am caught in the thrill of having a perilous secret, of being the sole privy to a grand plot. This combined with my lingering reluctance to approach Tudor with friendly words causes me to delay much too long. At the point when rumour of the rebellion spreads at court, I have still failed to utter a word of my involvement, and this proves to be a fatal mistake.

I am sat in my bedchamber writing one of my messages to Lincoln, the letter he sent me spread out before me for reference, when Elizabeth gives me a start. I was too absorbed in trying to correct a spelling mistake to hear her enter, and before I know it, her slender fingers rest on my shoulder.

I shuffle to hide my papers, placing one of the books lying on the desk over the note from Lincoln—too late.

'What is this, Cecily?' She pulls out the letter from underneath the book.

I attempt to snatch it from her but she is too tall. 'Nothing. Give it to me!'

'What have you done this time?' My sister's glance wanders over the paper, slowly, while I watch in agony. 'Oh, what have you *done?*'

'I was going to tell you, I swear I was! I had no intention to conspire with him, not truly.'

'Yet conspired with him you have.'

I shake my head, panic sizzling in my stomach. 'No. Only…only at first. I wanted a king of our blood on the throne.'

'Was a queen not enough?'

'Queens have so little influence—or rather you do. But then he told me of the imposter and his choice of Warwick and…and I never wanted to support him from that moment! I never wanted you and the little prince to suffer so we could have *that* kind of king. A simple-minded boy-king, the son of a traitor, brought to power in this way—'

'Would you have let us suffer if his plan had been another? If your own gain had been greater?' Elizabeth's voice is low, causing my own to sound frantic. It is the dreaded voice of a parent telling a child they are not angry, merely disappointed.

I clutch the fabric of my gown, clenching my fists. 'I cannot say.'

'How weak your love for me is, how fickle your loyalty.'

'I chose you in the end, did I not? Were it not for my love for you and your son, I'd picked Warwick and Lincoln, even if it was unlikely to succeed, even if I stood little to gain.'

'But you didn't choose me. This letter proves it.' She holds it up high in the air once more, as if to proclaim my supposed betrayal to the whole world.

'It proves the opposite. I was going to show Tudor and thus give him all the information he needs to win. You have to believe me,' I plead, disgusted at the note of desperation.

Elizabeth raises her chin. Strokes of sunlight filter through the stained windows and illuminates the soft contours of her face. 'I do not *have* to do anything. I am your queen and you would do well to remember it.' She picks her battles, and she has picked this one, against me rather than all the struggles against her husband and mother-in-law.

'Well, all the details I have told our cousin are false tracks.' I hand her the letter I was halfway through writing and point at one of the paragraphs. 'See? Why would I write him this if I wished him to succeed?'

Elizabeth is silent a moment before announcing her decision. 'I have to take you to His Grace so that he can pass judgement on all this.'

What follows are three days of raw fear. The Pretend-King is as suspicious as ever, and his general opinion of my character does little to alleviate said suspicion. It would cause unrest at court if someone as close to the royal bosom as me was seen to be alienated before he is certain of my crimes, hence he interrogates me in person with only Elizabeth as a quiet witness. He reads through every letter I have received from Lincoln these past months, his expression set in stone, before moving on to the one I was writing myself. He asks a thousand questions regarding my intentions and whether I know anything more than what the letters spell out, and by the end of the third day, I could weep from exhaustion. He does not raise his voice a single time, which serves to frighten rather than reassure me.

Elizabeth sits by his side, eyeing me, face pinched. A tiny spark of hope ignites in me, because I think I spot a flicker of pity in her face. I used to loathe her pity—I still do—but if it can soften her again and make her come to my rescue...

Margaret Beaufort is summoned on the third day. After listening to a lengthy recounting of Elizabeth's discovery, she grabs my face like she did the time I found Queen Anne's silver casket, and turns my head from side to side as if searching for a sign of truth or lie. I hate her even more than Stanley in that moment, though my hatred quickly shifts to relief when she releases me and speaks.

'Let the girl swear on the Holy Scripture. You know, do you not, what happens if you take a false oath or break a true one?'

I nod several times. 'I do, Madam.'

Beaufort turns to her son. 'Then she will either tell the truth or be punished in hell for all eternity. Let it rest at that.'

'Are you certain, Lady Mother?'

'Please, Your Grace,' Elizabeth says. 'I believe my sister has committed a blunder, that is all.'

Beaufort orders a servant boy to fetch her personal Bible, which the Pope himself once gave her, and I take the required oath. The shadow of a doubt creeps upon me. Would I really have burnt in hell if I had lied? It does not matter, because my three temporary foes believe it, and they at last believe me as well.

With the crisis averted, Tudor can turn his attention to his greater dilemma.

Chapter XIX

I BEGIN TO dread being alone with Thomas, dread it because I know not what I might do or say, dread it because I adore those moments. I dare not kiss him. I always wished I was more courageous, like Queen Anne, both in matters of the heart and in the face of danger. However, my wish has not been granted, and although I can say or do any rash thing when I do not think first, I am now thinking too much to even move my little finger. I feel infinitely small where I sit on the table in our room of charts, my feet not reaching the floor.

'I should go,' I say.

Thomas keeps his gaze on his drawing. 'Must you?'

'I think I must. My sisters will be expecting me.' I slip off the table and out of the room, stumbling over my own feet. The moment the door closes behind me, I breathe a sigh of alleviation. How much longer can this go on? Forever, I hope, but I do not think it is possible to maintain a brimming infatuation while keeping it from ever erupting into a full-blown liaison. I want nothing more than to let it, yet the risk is too great.

An urge to lift the weight off my chest washes over me. There is no one I could tell, though, no one except... I am not certain what council I can expect from a man of the cloth other than a scolding and an instruction on how I may repent for my shortcomings in chastity, but priests are bound to silence, and I doubt the cleric will care about my little follies anyways—and it *was* too long since I last took confession.

That afternoon, I relieve my feelings in the shadows of the confessional, as well as the story of my brief second kiss. The priest tells me to give myself ten lashes with a frayed leather whip and ask God's forgiveness for my wickedness. I do not mind asking forgiveness, but the lashes sound unnecessary to me. After all, it is not my conscience which troubles me.

I am walking down the empty gallery two days later when the King's Mother appears like a demon from a side entrance and latches onto me.

'I have been informed of your potentially disastrous affair,' she hisses.

I stare at her. 'You've made a *clergyman* your spy? Is there any corner of this palace where your sticky fingers are *not* poking? It is hardly an affair.'

Beaufort still holds my arms in a grip of steel. 'Tell me this instance, have you committed further carnal sins with that man, or are you still a maid as was the Holy Virgin?'

My cheeks burn and I struggle to break free. 'I am still a maid, if you must know.'

'Good—if you lie, it will show. You may still fill a purpose.'

'I assume you have picked one for me?'

'You have to marry before the years damage you as they have damaged me.' She touches her cheek where a web of wrinkles has sprung forth.

'My mother and I will decide whom I wed. My father entrusted her with the task before he died.'

'You foolish girl. You will have Viscount Welles.'

I laugh joylessly. 'I will *not*.'

Ever since the joust, I feared she might press this matter, but she has not brought it to the surface until now. The idea may not seem outlandish to an ignorant onlooker; we both hold positions close to the throne. However, it takes a single glimpse on any hereditary chart to spot the obvious: Welles is the son of a baron while I am the daughter of a king, once destined to be Queen of Scotland. I might have been robbed of that particular destiny, and Father lying cold in his grave might have lessened my leverage, but a marriage to a duke would still be entirely reasonable.

There is also the subtler, though perhaps even stronger, impediment. When I agreed to the temporary union with Ralph Scrope, Uncle Richard said I could pick a Lancastrian noble if Tudor took the throne, should it please me to do so. I almost considered it for some time, but there is a limit to how much I can take. A great magnate with vague Lancastrian connections, I could have stretched myself to accept. But Welles' wealth and status are not sweet enough to overpower the tart taste of his allegiances. I simply cannot wed a man who is so *evidently* my enemy.

Beaufort continues with a dangerous gleam in her eye. 'If you persist in this impertinence, I shall announce what I have learnt, and more, to the world. You will be known as a fallen woman, not fit to be the wife of any gentleman, and your *friend* will assuredly lose any position he holds at court.'

'You cannot do that,' I whisper.

'I can do more. I can charge you both with fornication—you remember what happened to Jane Shore?'

I do remember. I remember her penance and fall from grace all too well. Of course, Beaufort could not prove what has not happened, but I do not doubt the lawcourt would take her word on pain of thwarting Tudor.

'Welles is not an advantageous match.' It is the only thing I can think to say.

'He is of my blood, of the King's blessed blood, and in high favour.'

'But not even an earl! And even if he were a prince, he is everything I am not. His family have fought mine for decades.'

Beaufort finally loosens her grip of my arms. 'He is Lancastrian to the bone, it is true. Let us pray he can sway your own foul affinity.'

'Our heirs…' I have to pause for a deep breath at the thought. 'Our heirs will have as much York in them as Lancaster, if not more, because I intend to raise them as such. Is that what you want for your nephews and nieces?'

'Unfortunately, there is no way to keep the Yorkist line from blending with my own, as your sister's marriage has already proven. Indeed, we have always shared blood through both ancestors and marriages.' She is right, but it does not ease my pains.

I clench my fists, fighting back tears. 'You're cruel. A cruel old crone, too fanatic for anyone to love, too embittered to realise you belong in a time gone by.'

'My son the King loves me, Jasper does—and God. I am *as good as your queen!*' Her voice could shatter glass just as she shatters dreams.

Tudor summons me to his privy chambers. 'Lincoln and his Flemish mercenaries have landed in Ireland. Lovell is with them. Apparently, his last failed rebellion was not enough to discourage him.'

I pace before him. 'How many soldiers, Sire?'

'Two thousand, I am told.'

'That is less than half what you had at the time of your own usurpation. It ought not be as great an obstacle as I expected.'

'Be careful with the words you use. You are, furthermore, incorrect in your assumption.' There is a knife-sharp edge to his voice.

'How so, Sire?'

'*Le prétendant* may have had two thousand troops at the hour they landed, but you can be certain the Irish are flocking to his cause as we speak. Lord Kildare might raise another five or six thousand, and then there are the English.'

I shake my head. 'With all due respect, if the Yorkist lords of England believed this rebellion to be worth the risk, I would know. No, you have caught us all under your yoke by begetting Prince Arthur. We see all the future we have in him now: half York.'

Tudor drops down in the wrought oak chair and studies the rings crowded on his bony fingers. 'Do you mean *no* respect when you say due respect, *Madame*? The prince is all Tudor. Now, you may leave. I have business to attend to.'

As it turns out, the business involves arranging a public display of the rebellion's invalidity. To prove Lambert Simnel is nothing but an impostor, Young Warwick is brought out from his cell and paraded through the streets of London like a trophy, though he is far from shiny. For more than a year and a half now, he has been isolated in a damp little room, barred from warmth and company. I never liked him, still pity stirs in my chest as soon as I lay eyes on him. His boisterous spirit is gone without a trace, his shoulders are scrawny and slumped, his complexion pasty and pale from lack of sunlight.

200

Warwick's sister Meg, who has blended into the court as if purposefully avoiding attention, can only stare as we stand watching the procession from a window. Anne wraps her arms around her friend and her shoulder is soon sodden with Meg's tears. Our brothers may have died in the flesh—hers has died in the soul.

A fortnight later, we receive the news of Lambert Simnel's coronation as Edward VI in Dublin. Lord Kildare, the leader of the Irish lords, is steadfast in his support, as appears the Irish public, and naturally neither Lincoln nor Lovell wavers.

Tudor amasses his men, or rather his magnates do, managing to scrape together an impressive force of twelve thousand. Twelve thousand Tudor rose badges, a deadly rose garden, where the white is mere dots in a sea of red.

I am made to sit and hold Elizabeth's hand as they ride out. Her otherwise enviable fingers give the impression of having been shortened, since she has once more bitten her nails to the skin at this point. Her grand bedchamber no longer feels so grand at all when she dismisses all the lavishly dressed attendants except for me. I cannot for my life understand why she would want *me* in this hour, but I have little choice, and it is my sisterly duty.

'Oh, it is only his second battle, *ever*.' Elizabeth sinks down on the bed, gesturing for me to do the same.

Thought I know it to be true, the fact startles me. 'Yes. Isn't it remarkable? He won the crown in his first, then. I never thought we would have a ruler with neither experience of the sword, nor of governing.'

'My mother-in-law says it is a sign of divine intervention.'

'She likes to play God.'

Elizabeth sighs. 'I believe she is right in this. It is one of the reasons I found it easy to accept him as my lord and master: God wished for this to happen.'

'God, or Stanley? Stanley and Northumberland, Buckingham and our own mother. You do realise, do you not, that unless it was divine intervention, it was treason that brought King Richard down? Anyhow, if God is truly almighty, everything which happens is His wish.' I look at her for affirmation.

'Naturally.'

'Well, then it was his wish also that our uncle should be king, and that Tudor should fail in his first attempt. And how can God have wished for our poor brothers to die? It seems frightfully intricate to me.'

'He works in mysterious ways.'

I tilt my head to gaze up at the gilded canopy, where flowers are embroidered in silver thread. 'If God wills it, your husband will return unscathed. If not, I shall remind you of his mysterious ways.'

Elizabeth leans back to study the canopy with me, her face fallow as marble but her eyes animated. 'Have I told you that Henry still suffers from nightmares about Redemore? About the cavalry charge, the man racing like a demon towards him… Pray do not forget that my husband is as human as you and I, Cecily. As human as our uncle was.'

'It is difficult at times. Forgive me, but it is.' I frown, though there is a spark of queer delight in my chest. 'You called him our uncle. I haven't heard you say that since before Father died.'

'You know I am one with Mother in my opinion of him, but…but I did really love him once, as you still do. Before.'

Once again, the deceitful 'what if' takes possession of me. 'If he had only withdrawn his soldiers, sent for a new horse, ridden north to Yorkshire, where every man would have rallied to his standard—'

'He was ever the gambler, unlike Henry, too careless.'

I grant her a joyless laugh. 'He cared a great deal, dear sister, but not for his own life, not during those last moments. Not when it counted the most.'

During the following month, we receive scraps of news from messengers. Lincoln and his army—eight thousand strong, we hear—spend three days skirmishing with the Lancastrian cavalry, which is under the command of my uncle Ned, Lord Scales. The Yorkists having been delayed in their march, Tudor is able to join Lord Scales in Nottingham, and on the sixteenth day of June, the battle stands outside the village of East Stoke.

York is crushed.

Elizabeth concerned herself in vain. Tudor leaves the fighting itself to his vanguard, led by the seasoned Earl of

Oxford, much like he did at Redemore Plain. It is a sensible choice, but it does not exactly fume with glory or bravery. What happened to the days when kings defended their realm with their own sword? I suspect that era died with Father and Uncle Richard, if not before.

Lambert Simnel, the Yorkist figurehead and pawn, is pardoned and placed in the royal kitchens. There, he is sentenced to labour as a spit-turner for an unspecified amount of time, a humbling enough task to wipe out any glamorous illusions he might still have. I have to admit it is a stroke of genius on Tudor's part, since he can add a sheen of clemency to his reputation while degrading the child as far as is possible without harming him and thereby angering the public. Furthermore, unlike the real Warwick, Simnel will be seen constantly, preventing rumours of his escape.

The Irish lords are pardoned as well, for Tudor cannot risk their opposition again.

Dorset is released from the Tower after having been confined there during the uprising. I do not know if there is a grain of credence in Tudor's paranoia regarding my half-brother, if he truly was involved in any way, but Dorset has not been entirely trusted by the Pretend-King ever since he tried to abandon exile back in 1485. Whatever was spoken on that day of interception in Compiègne, Tudor's suspicion remains, and not without cause, considering Dorset's skittish character.

Francis Lovell's fate is a mystery. When I ask, some say he was killed, others that he was merely wounded and could escape back to Burgundy. Naturally, I pray for the latter.

Lincoln is not as fortunate as to have his death doubted. I never hear how it happened, other than that he was slain on the battlefield, and I doubt he received a proper funeral. Mourning my cousin is beyond me after all that passed between us, yet it stings to know another Yorkist claimant lies mowed down. We do have his younger brothers, as well as the real Warwick and John of Gloucester still languishing in the Tower, but my hope dwindles with each passing day. Could any of them succeed, and do I want them to? I cannot tell.

If I had been born a boy, I would make my own claim; I could trump both Tudor's and Elizabeth's, do away with him and treat my sister with kindness. But no—if I had been born a boy, I would be long dead. Mother once told me men fight on the field and women on the marriage market. I have rarely been glad to be a girl, but in this moment, I am. We face our share of danger, true, but at least it is rarely as fatal as if we had been of the opposite sex.

I have pondered my own words to Elizabeth that day when Tudor left for Stoke Field. I have not said it out loud before, but I have thought of it often: treason. Tudor should never, *never,* have been able to defeat his opponent at Redemore. His troops were inferior in number and he himself was inferior both in experience, skill, and bravery. Oxford, who held chief command over the soldiers, was and is a seasoned warrior in truth, but not even he could have brought victory for Tudor without the rippling chain of treachery both before and during the battle. As I go about my daily pastimes, I explore the subject in my head.

There are the more subtle treasons, such as my own betrayal of Lincoln which might have lessened his chances of success, and the Countess of Warwick's betrayal of her daughter when she left a fourteen-year-old Anne Neville to more or less fend for herself at Tewkesbury.

There are the coat-turnings out of pure necessity, such as when the Woodvilles abandoned their former Lancastrian allegiance when Mother caught Father's eye, or when the Howards started to gravitate towards becoming Tudor's new lapdogs. It is difficult at times to draw the line between betrayal and mere loyalty to one's own house or even common sense.

Treason was what nearly killed Father several times during his reign, and it certainly did kill Clarence, though he inevitably chose that for himself. What Uncle Richard said about his fate lives with me still. *He crossed every boundary during a decade, yet the punishment did not come until…until it did.* Could there indeed be something more to it? To me, the reasons I already knew of—one failed rebellion, one restoration of Lancaster to the throne, another suspected rebellion, having a sorcerer predict the King's death, opposing the King's justice on more than one occasion—always seemed plentiful enough for any gruesome death, and that was notwithstanding his abhorrent treatment of Queen Anne and his never-ending arrogance. But Father forgave a great deal of those *unpleasantries*, the way Father alone could forgive, though he never forgot any man's lapses. Clarence's death sentence made no mention of the woman against whom he was charged with having committed judicial murder. I know this because Mother basked in finally having her vengeance for the brother and father Clarence took from her, and she thought it was her persuasive tongue—not to mention her persuasive smile and carnal appeal—that brought it about, recounting every detail to me.

I doubt it was thus. For nigh on nine years, she wished for her brother-in-law's death before the wish came true, and as far as I can recall, Father was no more infatuated with her then than what was considered status quo. No, there must have been something more, like Uncle Richard said.

A shadow of a memory resurfaces one night as I lay staring into the dark. Was not Bishop Stillington, the man who confessed to having officiated a plight-troth between Father and the late Lady Eleanor Butler, kept under arrest around the same time as the execution in 1478, allegedly for association with Clarence,? If he spilled his secret to Clarence, Father would have seen no other choice but to put Clarence to death, for he would not have risked his fickle brother turning on him once more, this time in the knowledge that he was the rightful heir to the throne seeing as we children were all baseborn. Or am I getting a headache over an imagined connection, musing over something that never happened?

The sheets at once feel coarser against my skin, frustration prickling me. I would ask Stillington myself, but having no favour with Tudor, he involved himself in the recent insurgency and has sought refuge at the University of Oxford.

I know of one truth alone: that this could be a mere fanciful speculation of a sleepless night, soon forgotten when dawn breaks. I shall have to leave the matter to the mists of the unknown.

Chapter XX

I PAY MOTHER a visit, but she has come down with a cough and a fever, and I leave her to the care of the nuns at Bermondsey Abbey to avoid contagion. I had hoped to ask for her advice regarding my marriage, or perhaps merely for her to confirm that I must indeed wed Welles. Crestfallen, I decide to turn to the only other person I can think of who might have anything truly sensible to say, and who would never spill a secret: Bridget.

I have had precious little correspondence with my youngest sister, but she is not yet seven, and was never one for mindless prattle. The half-day journey to Dartford Priory is a relatively trivial enterprise, though, and guilt stings me for not making it sooner. When I step out of the carriage onto the farmland, my slipper sinks deep into the grassy mud. I cast my eyes at the rural building in front of me.

'Is this where my sister lives?' I ask the coachman.

He nods, picking a speck of dust off the Tudor rose badge stitched to his sleeve. 'It is indeed, Your Royal Highness. I will wait for you here.'

The priory resembles a small, run-down country manor, the home of a modest gentry family. A lone cow is scratching its flank against a nearby oak and a cat as black as charcoal lies stretched out in a pool of sunlight by the main entrance. The only indication of human life is the plumes of smoke curling from the chimneys, contrasting against the bruised purple sky.

I hitch up my skirts to my ankles to protect the hem from mud, just like Mother would have reminded me, and approach the door. A long while passes after I have knocked before a nun opens and grants me entrance. Her face is wrinkled like a raisin, her eyes small and buried between folds of skin, her apparel the black habit of Saint Augustine…or is it Saint Dominic? I cannot tell the difference.

After the necessary introductions, she gestures for me to follow her. 'Come hither, Madam. Your sister is tending to the candles.'

We pass through a gloomy corridor and a series of dusty little rooms, encountering streaks of black, silhouettes shuffling along the walls, made identical at first glance. Then we emerge into a dining hall dominated by a single table.

The raisin-faced nun nods at a small, dark figure bent over the altar by the end of the room. 'I will leave you in privacy.'

I walk down the side of the table, my gown brushing against the bench with a soft rustle. 'Sister? Bridget?'

The figure turns, an unlit candle in her hand. 'Cecily? I did not expect you.' Her voice is deep and melodious, so unlike the child she is. I had almost forgotten it, having heard it so rarely, just as I had forgotten how beauteous her face is: heart-shaped with clearly defined jaw and cheekbones, her hooded eyes the only brown ones in the family except for Mother's. She looks as if sculpted by a master of the arts—only her hideous garments dull the impression.

I kneel and take her in my arms. 'Forgive me for leaving you so destitute.'

Bridget withdraws. 'There is nothing to forgive. I cherish the peace here, and the knowledge I am surrounded with daily.'

I am tempted to laugh, baffled by the stream of perfectly composed words coming from her rose-petal lips, but manage to resist the temptation. If the nuns have somehow brought speech to her tongue, I will not be the one to frighten it away.

We sit down together on the bench, Bridget's feet dangling above the floor.

'Would you like to hear the latest gossip?' I ask.

My sister gives a barely noticeable shake of her head. 'Elizabeth writes to me sometimes. I believe I know of the events that matter.'

'Well, of course you know of the battle at Stoke Field. I still cannot quite understand why they did not claim Simnel to be either of our brothers. Tudor could hardly have paraded *them* through London to prove it false.' A tremble sneaks into my voice.

'You still mourn. I can tell.'

'Don't you?'

She shakes her head. 'Alas, I do not remember. I was but two years of age the last time I saw them.'

'I forget that sometimes. You sound so…old.'

Bridget frowns. 'I do?'

'No, wise, rather. A bit too wise for your years, really, and I doubt the nuns encourage frivolous games and the like.' I press forth a grin, tracing patterns in the wooden table with one finger.

'I have no desire for frivolous games.'

'Then…what do you do to pass the time?'

'I study the Scripture. I sew, and sometimes I collect herbs.' She smiles—I cannot recall ever seeing her smile this wide before.

'Herbs?' This time I fail to suppress a genuine giggle, though Bridget remains composed.

'Yes. They are very useful.' She cocks her head. 'Something is troubling you. I can tell that too.'

I hesitate a moment. Perchance her young shoulders are too frail to share my burden. It appears, though, that she is anything but frail, and has few other burdens to bear. Therefore, I allow my secret and my conundrum both to drop from my lips in what feels like blunt, clumsy words. Once I finish, flushed, Bridget takes my hand in her small, cold one.

'You should wed the viscount. It's the sensible choice. You can grow to love him if you are willing to let go of your aversions,' she says. 'If you think you can do that.'

There is the familiar burn in my nose, warning me of my impending tears. 'I do not think I can do that, no, but I suppose I will wed him. I have no other choice.'

'You always have a choice.'

'If so, I cannot see it.'

I stay the night at the priory, for the hour is too late to travel safely. I thought Mother was unfortunate in Bermondsey Abbey, but her residence is a palace compared to this place. The nuns are kind, doing their very best to find me the thickest mattress and the smoothest blankets, however, I do not sleep a wink where I lie in my little guest chamber. My skin prickles with sweat in the summer heat; my nose stings with the unfamiliar scent of herbs I do not know the name or qualities of; I twist and turn. Should I ask Bridget if she wishes to return to court with me? If I were her, I would want nothing more intensely in this world. Yet I am not my little sister, in fact we are more different than a cat and a dog. She has already blended into the black mass of solemn-faced nuns, become one of them. It should not surprise me, since her spirit is too idle for her to be tossed around in courtly intrigue. I can only imagine what her future husband would have thought, had she been intended for marriage. He might have been outraged at her cleverness, or thought her a witch, considering her herb-gathering and the rumours surrounding our maternal side of the family.

It is strange to think she does not remember the glory days when Father was king and all was well. I suppose she remembers Uncle Richard's reign, but those glory days were brief and more mine than hers. Perhaps it is a blessing to be so young as to not remember much of our angel brothers, since she can hardly have had any nightmares or ghosts to exorcise.

I turn over on my side again and try to plump up the pillow for the fourth time. I am not certain what I expected or indeed wanted either Mother or Bridget to tell me—that I should remain unmarried while Margaret Beaufort drags my good name in the dirt and Thomas' with it? That I could possibly find a duke or indeed any lord to marry after such slander, after charges of fornication? It is Welles or a fishmonger from a Southwark alehouse. My youngest sister said I always have a choice, but if that is what she meant, she has a very loose grasp of the term.

In the morning, after attending mass with the nuns and sharing their grey, sticky oatmeal to break the fast, I kiss Bridget farewell and hurriedly depart. My poor coachman has been incubated in the stables since no man can be allowed inside the priory except when it is absolutely necessary. He must be as eager as I to return to London, because we roll inside the city walls in two-thirds the time it took to travel to the priory.

I find Margaret Beaufort on her knees in Saint Stephen's chapel. These days, she kneels before the Almighty alone.

I clear my throat, but to no avail. I know she can hear me, yet I have to wait half an hour, if not more, sitting in one of the stalls before she at last struggles to her feet, visibly stiff-jointed, and turns to face me.

I grant a tiny curtsey along with my sweetest smile. 'It shall be as you wish, my lady the King's Mother.'

'Yes. Naturally.' She wraps her rosary around her hand.

'I only ask you let me enjoy my…friendship a little longer. My friend is very dear to me—I'd rather not lose him until I must.'

'Did your wet nurse drop you on the head?'

I meet her stare. 'You will not tell, because if you do, I am useless to you.'

'No, I will not tell, but if you are discovered, you will be equally useless as if I had.'

'I know that. Thank you, Madam.' My voice is strained with contempt.

I turn to leave, but Beaufort speaks again before I have the chance to escape. 'You will be *pleased* to know the Earl of Warwick's sister will be your niece through marriage. She is to wed my own sister's son Sir Richard Pole.'

I clench my jaw. *Of course* she is. The spider has trapped yet another fly in her web, allowing her own family to rise higher still. Meg Plantagenet, daughter and granddaughter of traitors, but nonetheless a Yorkist herself, and nonetheless my cousin. Perhaps she does not mind, having lost such a great portion of her willpower after seeing her brother fade away…she is hardly in a position to object, anyhow.

I depart without another word.

Tudor embarks on a hunt a fortnight later, unwieldy and time-consuming though it might be to shepherd a hundred men and a few women from Westminster to Waltham Forest. It is more apparent than ever that he did not spend his adolescence as a prince or even as an Englishman. He ought to know by now that the best hunt can be found in the Sherwood Forest at Nottingham.

I accompany the fluttering party of nobles and gentry on Margaret Beaufort's command, since she considers it an apt opportunity for me to exchange a few words with Lord Welles. I avoid him like the plague, and he does not seek me out.

As it happens, I end up falling behind, as I am prone to do on hunts, hoping to avoid the sight of prey being slaughtered. Thomas, who has joined the escapade solely for the chance to ride one of Northumberland's best horses—a chestnut stallion with glossy black mane and a feisty temper—tarries with me.

'No one will notice if we sit here awhile,' he says. 'The weather is too lovely not to, right?'

I squint at the figures in the distance that are the other horses. They are some two hundred feet ahead of us; it is a risk, but one I cannot resist taking. 'Only a little while, then.'

We trail off the main path and dismount by a thick-trunked oak whose branches stretch far and wide to create a canopy of green. I try not to blush as Thomas lifts me off my horse and my skirts get caught on a notch in the saddle, exposing my stocking-clad calves a little too long.

We tie the animals to another tree before making ourselves comfortable under the oak.

Thomas' arms rest around me like the most natural thing in the world, his hands on his knee, creating a circle for me to sit in. His doublet against my back and his cheek brushing against my hair somehow feels more intimate than I imagine my wedding night will be.

My wedding night. My wedding. I thought I was doing us both a service, leaving Thomas ignorant of what the future holds for me, but I am not so certain anymore. What has been budding between us since the beginning of the year must be cut down before it blooms, or it will be all the more painful. I know little of life and less of love, yet I know this.

I fumble for the right words to tell him. I do not get the chance.

'Marry me.' Thomas' voice is sheathed in forced calm.

I duck under his arms and turn to stare at him. This time, he has gone *truly* insane. 'What?'

'You heard. Marry me.'

'If you're attempting a jest, you should pick another theme.' I stand, furiously brushing the grass stains from my gown, avoiding his eyes.

211

He scrambles to his feet as well. 'Is it so unthinkable?'

'*Yes.*'

'We could live of my father's land, or find a home of our own in the countryside. We could have as many dogs as you like, and my horses, and maybe a little one. You could be the prettiest girl in the village and—'

I cannot help but to laugh out of pure disbelief. '"The *prettiest girl in the village*"? Are you out of your mind? If I wed you, I lose everything.'

'You wouldn't lose me.' The solemn note strikes a chord in me.

'I know. And I do not want to lose you, not one bit. But there is something you must know. I have agreed to give my hand in marriage to Viscount Welles.'

Thomas runs a hand through his hair, lustrous as lacquer in the summer sun. 'I see. Then he is of high enough standing to satisfy you?'

'Well, no. It is as high as Margaret Beaufort will allow, though, for she intends to raise her own lot. She *knows*, Thomas. She has eyes and ears everywhere in this court, and if I do not adhere to her wishes, she will see us both ruined.'

'And how, pray tell, does she intend to bring that about?'

'You would be dismissed from your position, and I steeped in disgrace, both of us put to the hand of justice for trumped up charges of fornication,' I whisper.

'Don't you understand, silly? You could still marry me! I may be no canon lawyer, but she could not have us punished for…*that*, if we were already husband and wife. It would be as easy as to claim we had been plight-trothed before it happened. I would gladly leave court if you would leave with me.'

I bury my face in my hands. Why, why did he have to ask? The thought had not crossed my mind for a second, and now my will is torn, brutally divided. I cannot allow emotion to take the upper hand rather than my ambitions, not this time, and I have to say it out loud.

'Then it is either no one and disgrace, you and impoverishment, or Welles and—if nothing else—a decent living?'

'You make it sound so… Where is your heart in all this?'

'You know it is with you—but it is not as simple as that. All my life, I have prepared to become the wife of a great lord. Welles and his allegiance are abhorrent to me, and he is no duke or prince, but at least he is *something*. My heart can have no say in the matter.'

Thomas takes a step towards me. His face is blank but his eyes burn on me. Then, he puts forth the second worst question he has ever asked me: 'Do you love me?'

I draw a shaky breath. 'Do you love *me?*'

I count the heartbeats of silence. Thirteen, fourteen, fifteen. If only I could read his mind and watch the battle there—is it as merciless as my own battle? He will not say he loves me, I know he will not, for just like me he is too proud.

Twenty. I turn on my heel and scuttle through the cluster of trees surrounding us, for once eager for my horse.

'I will ask once more and never again. Cecily, will you marry me?' Thomas calls out after me.

I halt for a moment without turning to look at him, before resuming my flight.

My wedding takes place five months later, on the twelfth day of December. The preparations have been thorough: I have had my measurements taken for a dress of peach-coloured silk generously lined with ermine, I have been scrubbed in rose water, I have received Mother's blessing. She is not overjoyed—she knows I am in agony, though not the whole reason why—but has vowed to make an appearance at the wedding feast.

Cousin Meg has faced her own trial already and been packed off to Ludlow, where her new husband, Richard Pole, serves in Prince Arthur's household. I do not envy her having to live in Wales; I will be taken from court as well, but at least Welles resides in Lincolnshire, and I have missed the Midlands since leaving Sheriff Hutton.

I ride on a barge adorned with white and—to my dismay—red roses to Westminster Abbey, where my betrothed is waiting for me at the western entrance. Westminster Abbey, that pinnacle of grandeur, of dread as well as triumph. The days of sanctuary are like something from a past life, yet I am always weary when attending ceremonies there. The nave may be glorious with its gothic vaults, but my thoughts often drift to the time I cowered in the college hall in fear that the soldiers would disobey orders and break inside. The time Mother refused me to go with Dickie, and I never saw him again, the bouncing cloud of gold around his head as he left us... The time we listened to the coronation held on the other side of the walls, all the times I yearned to escape into the open and fill my lungs with freedom. There is only one set of memories I can no longer allow myself to revisit: the crease of concentration on Thomas' forehead as he tried to sketch my portrait in the Chapel of the Pyx.

Welles' crimson hose and cap embroidered with gold distinguishes him from the rest, as if his considerable height was not enough. 'Princess Cecily,' he greets me.

I keep my gaze pinned to the doorway. 'Lord Welles.'

It is the second time we speak; the first was when we formally agreed to the betrothal. His voice reminds me of opening an old wooden coffer in need of oiling, and it betrays no emotion. Neither do his posture or his manners, and from what I have observed, he never abandons courtesy.

I let him take my hand, his thumb resting lightly against my fingers as we proceed inside the abbey. Dear God, do not let him be a palm-sweater.

I study the flat of his back and his neck as I walk slightly behind, for I do not wish to see the brackets around his eyes or the lines searing his face. He is older than Uncle Richard would have been today, as old as several of my other uncles, and like his nephew Tudor, the years have taken their toll. What I told Thomas is true, I do not fear old age, but that does not mean I find it appealing, especially in one who is to share my bed.

The ceremony feels eternal, and not in the way an enchanting evening can feel eternal, no, but rather like an agonizing lecture. We have five witnesses apart from Archbishop Morton: Beaufort, Northumberland, two of Welles' brothers, and Elizabeth, who has finally been crowned. Tudor himself is preoccupied with matters of state, as is so often the case, which I am grateful for. Why make a wedding any worse than it has to be?

My vows come mechanically. Welles has more wit than to stumble on the words like Ralph Scrope did, but that is the last thing on my mind.

The wedding feast is truly a feast, and even Tudor attends, conversing with my husband about hawking while I sit clutching Mother's hand under the table. For the first time, I am afraid, afraid to leave London and my sisters. Even Elizabeth would be a comforting presence to bring with me, although she appears oblivious of my unhappiness. I have wed a Lancastrian nobleman just like she did, and she is content, hence she sees no reason for me to complain.

Anne—dear, sweet-faced Anne—is not with us. She has taken to her bed with a headache, which might have been an empty excuse coming from anyone else but which I know is genuine. The physicians say it is nothing to be concerned with; like poor Mary, Anne's health has always been a bit frail, but not in the extreme. She sends her regrets instead of her congratulations, and for that I love her all the more.

A chamber has been prepared for us, the newlyweds. Welles' estates are too far away to travel there at once, thus this is where we are to spend our first night as husband and wife. The room is swathed in candlelight and ember sparks in the fireplace, spewing specks of red over the smouldering cinder. Despite this, I am shivering where I stand by the bedpost of beautifully carved pine, dressed only in my chemise and stockings. I have a sneaking feeling the light is illuminating the contours of my body through the thin fabric of my garments, making it an impossible task to retain my modesty.

Welles clears his throat. 'Let us proceed, Lady Welles.'

'Yes.'

'If, perhaps—' He hesitates, then gestures towards the bed. 'Would you mind terribly if you sat down? In fact, be so gracious as to lie, please.'

I throw myself on the thick coverlets, lying stiff as a stick, my arms crossed over my chest. 'So. Is this how you usually do it? With your mistresses, I mean?'

Welles scratches his dimpled chin and sits down by my feet. 'Oh dear. I hope we need not discuss indelicate matters, my lady.'

'Well, we are not in public view, *Husband*. You can be as indelicate as you like. Are you happy your sister hauled me in for you? Am I a pretty enough present?'

'I have no doubt we will both benefit from this arrangement.'

I scoff. 'Really? How, in God's name, am I to benefit?'

'Surely, you are eager to beget children, as is every woman. The joys of domesticity will calm your nature.'

'Is that what you assume of all women? I have two decades to reproduce! I wager you have heard of the Woodville fertility.'

Welles takes my foot in his hand. 'May I remove your stockings?'

I pull off both my silk stockings, wrap them to a hard ball and fling it across the room. 'I suggest we leave this to another night.'

'Pardon me, Lady Welles, but the marriage must be consummated. My beloved sister is bound to interrogate me in the morning, and I am afraid I lack the disposition to lie.'

'Just get it over with,' I whisper.

Chapter XXI

ATTERSHALL CASTLE IS the grandest wedding gift of
them all. Margaret Beaufort has been generous, or rather,
she has wrapped her sinewy hands tighter around my
neck. 'A place to enjoy a calm life. You may remain as long as
your conduct pleases my son the King. Else, we may have to send
you somewhere humbler, to humble your spirits also, for your
own good.' That is what she told me after handing the keys to the
castle to her brother Welles. She is still in control of our new
home, and so my fate is at her mercy for the time being. I cannot
deny, though, that the thought of Tattershall makes my mouth
water, for I have a clear memory of Father once praising it as the
finest among castles. Whether this was an exaggeration or not
remains to be seen. Welles has numerous other estates and
manors we might choose to live in, but many of the houses were
lost in a split of inheritance.

We travel three days after our wedding, me in a carriage and
my husband on horseback, exchanging nary a word during the
lengthy journey to Lincolnshire. A tail of loyal servants and carts
containing our most valued belongings and furniture follows. The
roads have been partly wrecked by winter storms, and it is a full
fortnight before we pass the city of Boston and arrive at our
destination of Tattershall Castle.

The carriage rolls across the bridge of the outer moat and I
stick my head out the window. The water is glassy teal, fat geese
gliding in flocks on the surface. I have never liked geese. When
they open their beaks, all one sees are rows of tiny teeth.

Having crossed the moat and been seen through the
gatehouse at the end of the bridge, we arrive in what I assume is
the outer ward. To our right are the stables, where I spot two grey

217

horses chewing frost-bitten grass and a groom pausing in his tasks to watch us. I withdraw my head into the carriage. Our little entourage turns left and continues between the outer and inner moats until we reach another bridge and gatehouse. Once we have passed over these also, arriving in the inner ward, I can only gape at what I see.

The castle itself is situated half in the ward, half rising from the moat. It is neither broad nor far-reaching, but perhaps six or seven stories high, towering skywards. The cool sun illuminates the fashionable red brick, bringing Sheriff Hutton to mind, and I am glad it possesses this spark of colour, because I am tired of palaces built of limestone and granite. From what I can see, there is one tower in each of the corners, though they may well be turrets. Trying to lean out far enough to turn my head, I count to five more towers wedged in the wall surrounding the inner ward. At the top are battlements, strengthening the impression I already have of Tattershall Castle as a fortress fit to withstand most trials, unlike anything I have lived in save Nottingham Castle.

I do not know if I should be delighted or intimidated. A little bit of both, perhaps. I was promised a castle out of the ordinary, and this I have been given. However, I do get the sense my husband could lock me up in one of these massive towers and close the gatehouses, and I would be a damsel in distress as good as in any of Anne's books. Of course, he could lock me up in a regular pleasure palace as well, so I suppose my concerns are not particular.

The coachman offers me his hand but I climb out of the carriage without taking it. Winter immediately plunges its claws in me, sending shivers through my every limb, and I wrap my sable furs tighter around me. My breath creates whiffs of mist, the grass crunching with frost as I take a few steps towards the castle.

'It is called the great tower,' Welles says, dismounting beside me and handing the reins to one of the servants. 'The castle itself, I mean, my lady.'

'I see. It does not look like a single tower. Which floor is mine?'

Welles dabs his runny nose with a handkerchief. 'The basement is for storage and the ground floor for communal business—tenants coming to pay rent and the like. Then, let me see…' He counts on his fingers. 'Ah, yes, we have the great hall, the audience chamber, and the private chamber. Then, there are the battlements and roof gallery.'

I raise my eyebrows. 'Is it that small inside? Truly?'

'I am confident you will find it to your liking, my lady. I have been told it looks like a fortress from without, but palatial from within.'

I do not know what to say to this. I think the outside is splendid but the inside sounds modest, while my husband appears to think the outside the rough end and the inside the real prize. We shall have to see which one of us is in the right.

The steward, an old man with two strands of hair on his head and alarmingly red earlobes, opens the door in one of the turrets and lets us inside before dispatching a group of servants to collect our belongings from the baggage carts. We step directly onto a spiral staircase, presumably running all the way up to the battlements.

'This staircase will take us to the great hall,' the steward squeaks like a rat being stepped on. 'We have another entrance leading to the communal chamber. There is a third door, to the basement, but God forbid you use it.'

I frown. 'Why?'

'The chief cook stores her spices down there. Spices! Nasty things, they are.'

I decide against lecturing him on how wrong he is, turning my attention to the room we emerge into on the first floor. My initial impression of a small interior is swiftly disproven: the rooms may be few, but since each floor consists of a single chamber, said chamber is sizable, offering space that thick walls might have occupied otherwise. The inner walls are of the same red brick as the outer, though hung with rich tapestries—Flemish, if I am not mistaken, like the ones Father used to spend lavish sums on. The ceiling is chalked white and supported by rows of beams, creating a striped pattern. Vaulted windows allow for rays of winter sun to flood through the painted glass and cover the floor in rich reds and greens and blues, the room being lit up also by the iron chandelier.

I round the hefty, polished table and the cushioned chairs dominating the great hall and arrive at the enormous fireplace ensconced in the wall. Cinder is all that is left from the fire itself, providing next to no warmth. Badges and crests line the mantelpiece, several of them identical replicas.

I point at one of the crests. 'This belongs to Baron Cromwell, the man who had all this built, does it not?'

The steward bobs his head, hands clasped behind his back. 'Indeed, my lady.'

'What happened to the castle after his demise?'

'It passed to his niece, Joan, and her husband, Humphrey Bourchier. I was a young lad back then. Chamber servant, I was.'

I freeze, and not just because of the fireplace being unlit. 'I know that name! Humphrey Bourchier was my late father's cousin.'

Welles avoids my eyes, his expression blank. 'Yes, my lady.'

'I heard…I heard he was a treacherous man. His fate served him right.'

Dense silence settles between us. Humphrey Bourchier benefited greatly from Father's rule before swapping loyalties during Clarence's and Warwick's attempt to re-establish the Lancastrian line on the throne little less than two decades ago. He was slain at the Battle of Barnet, where Father's and Uncle Richard's victory paved the way for the return of York.

'Not for me to say. Ever since, the place has belonged to the crown, until my lady the King's Mother was gifted it, that is,' the steward says at last.

I swallow, tracing the smooth stone with my finger. 'There is room here for another crest. We'll put a white rose there—in fact, we could have the rest removed, and commission a whole line of white. It will brighten the room.'

'Pardon me, but I cannot allow such a thing,' Welles says.

'What would you have, then?'

'A Tudor rose or nothing, Lady Welles.'

'In that case, Cromwell's old badge will do nicely. At least you cannot keep me from the garden, dear husband. I think I will have the gardener plant roses in summertime, and white ones do have the sweetest fragrance.' I glare at him, my words an intended provocation more than anything, but he refuses to meet my challenge. Instead, he turns from the fireplace and stand looking out from the window.

'You would do well to remember my sister's words regarding conduct.'

I push back my more violent impulses and march towards the staircase. Although neither of us speaks the fact, he does have the authority to keep me from the garden, to keep me from whichever room of his choice. Mayhap he hopes it will not have to come to that, and neither do I, but it is the bitter truth.

The three of us—I first, then the steward, and last Welles— climb the staircase to each floor. After the great hall comes, as Welles predicted, the audience chamber, where only the most highly esteemed guests are entertained. The second floor is the sole subdivided one, a brick corridor leading from the audience chamber to a smaller room with three chairs around a chess table and a cushioned window seat. I can see myself there, playing the lute, with Anne and Meg playing chess and Kate wiggling on the third chair. In all likelihood, they will not come, not the three of them at once, if at all. The distance is too great, Tudor will hardly let my sisters out of sight for long, and though Meg is now married to Welles' nephew, she only lets her guard down to me entirely in Anne's company. If this was Sheriff Hutton… If this was Sheriff Hutton, I would have turned the clock back to our merry household the summer three and a half years ago.

On the third floor is the private chamber, a massive bedchamber serving as solar in equal measure. My stomach turns at the sight of the intricately carved wooden cradle standing in one corner, prepared with blankets and pillows.

'Prithee, where shall we host visitors staying the night, or children past the age of swaddling?' Welles asks the steward.

'The other three turrets house additional lodgings, my lord. Much smaller, mark my word, but fine and dandy for those of lesser rank or lesser size.'

I wish I could shut out their conversation and erase the cradle from my vision. Welles does not have to be frightened of childbirth, for it is not his life that is at stake. My cousin Katheryn, Duchess of Huntingdon, died in childbed a mere couple of months ago, and she was around my age.

As long as the baby lives, Welles would be in a leisurely position with me in a grave: father to a prince or princess, free to wed a woman who suits him better, his status elevated by his last marriage. If we both live, I shall love my children endlessly, though I fear I might not prove the most patient of mothers, yet nothing can change the fact that they will be of my enemies' blood. I vow never to hold it against the dear creatures, but I feel sorry for them already.

At last, having climbed the last step of the spiral staircase, we emerge on the roof. A vaulted colonnade stretches around the rectangular, open space, creating a covered walkway. From there, we proceed up a smaller stairway to the battlements.

I place both hands firmly on the coarse brick, gazing out over the flat Lincolnshire landscape. The height in itself sends a note of delight all the way to my fingertips, because I have rarely been allowed to stand on the battlements of the castles where I spent my childhood, were there even any, and the view over Lincolnshire is equally spectacular.

Icy winds tear at my hair, trying to pull it from the gold-thread caul.

I turn to Welles. 'You can go inside if you like. I think I will stay awhile…it is refreshing up here.'

For once, he does not object.

That same evening, I lie curled up in our bed with the deep blue covers in a knot by my feet, not because I have suddenly developed a tolerance for the cold of winter but because disorder is a thorn in Welles' side. This night, he has spared me my mechanical wifely duties and even agreed to dismiss the squire who usually sleeps with us in the room, but it is scant comfort.

My pillow is warm and wet with tears. My eyes hurt from staring into the bright flames licking the logs in the fireplace and my fingers ache from clutching the blanket. I should never have left court, never agreed to wed the stiff man lying awake beside me. I should have been braver and fought Margaret Beaufort harder. Now, it is too late.

'Please, my lady, must you weep? I cannot work if I cannot sleep,' Welles says.

I prop myself on my elbow and wipe my eyes with the back of my hand so that I can glare at him. 'My apologies if it is inconvenient for you. I really am keeping as quiet as I can.'

'Yet you have no reason to grieve.'

'*I don't want this.* What is it you fail to grasp?'

He sighs. 'Pray have consideration for the rest of us, my lady, and cease this foolery. I may be no great prince, and we may have certain differences, but there is no reason we cannot live perfectly content.'

'You do not understand.' I pile my pillows against the wall behind the bed and recline against them, arms crossed.

'Oh dear. Marriage is an arrangement to profit both parties, as all matters in life. I believe we have had this discussion already, and I am not fond of discussion.'

'I can tell.'

Welles pats my shoulder before I can shuffle out of his reach. 'Cherish this castle, if nothing else, my lady.'

'It's magnificent, but I miss Westminster.'

'In my humble experience, missing is cured with the passing of time.'

'Indeed?' My voice drips of irony. 'I would have thought the passing of time would only make it worse.'

We say nothing more that night, or the next, or the one after that. I think my husband obtains his much-needed sleep.

The days turn into weeks, then months. In budding spring and blooming summer, Tattershall Castle transforms from imposing to genuinely glorious, especially once the sun warms the rooms. The garden does become a place of roses: pale pink, a middle ground.

Much in the same manner, my husband and I find our own middle ground. I am reluctant towards the concept, but it has its uses. I must be the obedient wife Beaufort wishes me to be, and in time, she and Tudor will have to relent in their view towards me. They like me little better than I like them, but I have come to realise, if not made my peace with, that I will get nowhere unless I start smoothing the rough edges between us. One day, my children will be King Arthur's cousins, albeit through the female line of descent, and I remember my family's history well enough to know what kings' cousins can achieve. I will not have them put at a disadvantage because of my own scruples.

Welles is not unreasonable. He is many things, but not that. I lose count of the times I lash out at him or indulge in tears, yet he never once responds with violence. He neither hates nor loves me, not yet, but continues to treat me with distanced courtesy, the quarrels I attempt running off him like water off the geese in the moats. In the beginning, it frustrates me to the verge of madness, but, eventually, I am too exhausted by his lack of temper to try to provoke a reaction. Him being almost a score of years my senior has never shown itself clearer than in these moments.

To my amazement, I manage to put aside our political and familial differences, secluded as we are from courtly intrigue. My husband will always be as staunch a Lancastrian as I am a Yorkist, as mellow as I am impassioned, but there are very few to remind us here, and at the moment I can achieve nothing by dwelling. I discover he shares my love for music, and in this we find a sliver of compatibility.

Tattershall is not infinite, thus we are made to spend more time in each other's company than I have done with anyone except my immediate family and Thomas. Thomas... As much as I try, he is impossible to forget. His eyes, his hands, his horrible knuckle-cracking and the baffled look on his face when I pulled him back from tripping into the fountain. Even the time he launched a grape at my nose lingers in my memory.

Welles does not know, or if he does, he meticulously avoids the topic, as do I. I think he has a mistress, a woman in nearby Boston, because he travels there often and always returns with a guilt-stained gift for me, avoiding my questioning glance. It wounds my pride a little, but I expected nothing else, and I have enough pride to survive it. As he said, our marriage was and is a business arrangement—let him have his dalliance.

Missing is the most difficult part: Mother, each of my sisters, including Elizabeth. I write to them, but it is not the same as seeing their familiar faces. Finally, in late autumn, Welles brings me with him for a few weeks' visit to court. I delight in the experience—he promises we can go soon again—and absorb all the news and gossip like a sponge.

Both the Duke of Brittany and the King of Scotland have died during the year, leaving eleven-year-old Anne of Brittany and fifteen-year-old James of Scotland to inherit their domains. If only I had possessed what they now possess at such a young age! It could have been thus, had I married James as Father intended during my childhood.

Thomas is nowhere to be found at court, but I dare not ask anyone of his whereabouts. Perhaps he is simply avoiding me, and I could not blame him.

All these things fade to the background, though, when I learn my own piece of news: I am with child.

Lord Welles—or John, as he now allows me to call him in private—is bursting with joy in his own subtle way, as is Beaufort. I cannot share their sentiment, yet there is one benefit of my condition, namely that my husband will demand nothing but to sleep next to me for several months, both because the goal has already been achieved and for fear of harming the baby in the last stages of pregnancy. It presents less of a challenge to be his friend than it does to be his wife. We return to Tattershall in time for the Christmas and New Year celebrations on Tudor's instruction, to avoid traveling when I am too far gone. To my surprise, I rejoice to see my own castle again, because although I do not own it, I know every corner of every room except the kitchens and basement like the back of my hand. It gives a sense of security.

John, Beaufort, Tudor, and the rest of them all pray for a son, naturally. I do not know what I hope for. My whole life, I have been taught that boys are the road to success, and they can achieve so much more in their own right. At the same time, my own experience has planted a seed of doubt in me, for while my brothers were thought to be the greatest success of my parents' marriage, they are gone, while Elizabeth wears a crown. Cousin Meg is the wife of Prince Arthur's trusted servant while Young Warwick wastes away in his prison cell. Aunt Catherine is Duchess of Darby while her brother Rivers had his head cut off, and Aunt Margaret is Dowager Duchess of Burgundy while three of her four brothers met violent and premature ends. Girls may have to take the road to good fortune through marriage, but they are infinitely safer, and what is the use of success if one is not safe enough to maintain it? Yes. Yes, I do believe I want a baby girl.

Chapter XXII

LADY MOTHER!' Annie's auburn locks are powdered with a dust of snow, her cheeks rosy from the cold, feet kicking up clouds of white as she tumbles towards me.

I take her in my arms and scoop her up from the ground. Six years of age now, she is too heavy to be carried on the hip like a toddler, and I have to put her down again.

'What happened to your sister?' I ask, offering a gloved hand for her to cling onto as we walk along the outer moat.

'She wanted to build a snowman to show Father. I said, I said I didn't want to.'

'Why not?'

'It wasn't very pretty the last time we tried.'

'You mustn't give up then, darling. Come, shall we try together?'

Eliza—or Elizabeth, as John still insists on calling her despite my grumblings—is easy to spot in her new frock, like a dot of red in a landscape of ivory. She is rapidly growing, too, more than a head taller now than her little sister. The snowman is already half-finished; her hands work in a frenzy, as always, as if every project was a battle against the clock.

I stroke her hair with my free hand. They ought both to be wearing something against the weather and to guard their modesty, but they are still young enough to get away with going bareheaded, especially since we have no visitors at the moment.

'Look! Do you think Father will like it, Lady Mother?'

I smile. 'I will have him beaten about the head if he does not.'

Both my girls, but my oldest especially, thirst too much for John Welles' approval. I have tried to tell him thus many times, but he struggles to show his love in ways other than a friendly nod and a pat on the shoulder.

Annie bends down for a handful of snow and pats it onto the snowman's belly.

Eliza pushes away her hand. 'I can do it myself!'

'Be nice!' I say, though I do not expect her to listen. I understand perfectly well that she wants to manage on her own.

Half an hour later, we stand dishevelled before a snowman more handsome than any of us might have hoped. Annie has tied her own scarf around his neck and stuck two sprawling sticks in the body for arms.

I wrap one arm around each of my daughters: so small and warm, and mine alone. 'We should go inside for supper.'

'Not without Father!' Eliza pouts. 'He will be back soon, I know it. I can almost hear his horse yonder.'

'We can wait a little longer, if you are truly not too hungry.'

The three of us take another stroll along the moat to pass the time. The winter is hard this year, forcing the geese to waddle on the strand rather than swim, the water having frozen. If the ice was thicker, we could skate on it, like we did a few years ago. Even my husband joined Eliza and me in the merry-go-round, falling over more often than gliding. Annie was too small back then to participate—she was always small for her age, but I do not consider it a disadvantage. It means I can perhaps keep her with me a little longer before she is considered ripe for marriage, and her birth was a trivial matter compared to the first time I endured such a thing.

In all honesty, the dull confinements were worse than both my childbeds. I was mistaken to dread them so, because while many others have bled to death, my maternal heritage did not fail me in my task. However, I have not conceived for many years now, and Welles is beginning to despair, fearing God may be withholding his blessings from us. He never speaks a word about the fact that we do not and perhaps never will have a son and heir, but I can read it in his face late in the evenings. I think he has come to love me in his own way. Yes, he loves me, and he will not cast off a wife of my status, hence I feel secure despite not fulfilling my purpose. Our daughters will be wealthy heiresses, as were Isabel and Anne Neville, and wealthy heiresses are the most sought-after commodity on the marriage market. Indeed, they not having a brother puts them at an advantage in this.

At first, I was distraught over my so-called failure. Elizabeth has given Tudor two sons and three daughters so far; her little Prince Harry is around Annie's age and a fierce boy. Yet the more I held each of my baby girls, watching their tiny fingers curl around mine and their precious peachy lips form gurgling sounds, the more my sense of failure subsided. To me, they are the essence of perfection, and I would not trade them for any of Elizabeth's boys. Furthermore, they will be safe from harm, as I have long known, for who would endanger two little princesses?

Their Lancastrian blood also protects them, as much as I hate to admit it. Nonetheless, they are Yorkist to the bone—except the colour of Annie's hair, that is. Welles does not realise it, but Eliza has Uncle Richard's pebble-grey eyes, and both she and her little sister devour the bedtime stories I tell them about glories gone by. They know the details of the conflict now called the Cousins' War, although I make certain to cast it in a fairy tale shimmer and omit the goriest parts. When they are alone with me, they call Tudor by his name rather than his regal title, while in the presence of others, they show the respect needed if they are to remain in favour as they grow older. I daresay they might be cleverer than I give them credit for.

Once did I suffer a miscarriage such as I have heard other women tell of, but it was too early to tell the sex of the babe, and I found myself unable to lament my loss for very long. Either I am heartless, or these incidents affect some to greater extent than others. I pray it is the latter.

The muffled sound of hooves in snow interrupts my musings, and soon Welles reins in his horse at the sight of us and dismounts.

Eliza lets go of my hand and surges forward. 'Father, we built another snowman! Will you come and look?'

Welles looks at me. 'Er, ye-es. Yes, I believe I will.'

After a few minutes of pointing and explaining, we all return indoors, I with a pleasant feeling in my chest.

That evening as the girls are about to sleep, Annie, who fancies a good adventure as much as Dickie did, asks me to tell them again about the battle at Mortimer's Cross, which paved the way for my father's assumption of the throne.

'And your grandfather looked to the sky, and there were three suns burning bright,' I say, sitting on the edge of the bed the girls share in one of the turrets. 'That is how he decided on his emblem, the Sunne in Splendour. One sun for each brother.'

Annie knits her brows. 'But…if one was King Edward's, and another was King Richard's, there should have been a King George, too. Otherwise it's just two suns.'

'Well—' I hesitate. I cannot very well tell them that the third sun, Clarence, was put out in a barrel of wine.

Welles' voice from the doorway saves me. 'You ought to leave these things to the nurse, my lady.'

'I enjoy it.' I place a kiss on each of my daughters' noses and rise from the bed. Having closed the door between their room and ours, I cross my arms. 'I was not telling them anything they shouldn't hear.'

My husband sighs. 'Alas, I doubt it, my lady.'

'My sister will be visiting. I had a letter from her this morning.'

'She is most welcome.'

I nod. 'Good. And how was court? I wish I could have gone with you, for I miss it dearly.'

'You had my permission.'

I cast a glance at the door to our daughters' bedroom. 'You know I cannot bear to leave them for such a long time. Two months is so…much!'

I come to think of my own mother, put away like an outdated piece of jewellery in Bermondsey Abbey. I never had the chance to introduce her to Annie before she passed into God's hands one heat-ridden day the summer five years ago. Her burial was fit for a church mouse rather than a dowager queen, and she had only her blessing to give us in her will. Such was the result of Beaufort's and Tudor's workings—or at least I think that was it. Three years later, I marked the passing of my paternal grandmother, Cecily Neville, who I believe was only too happy to have outlived Elizabeth Woodville.

My husband and I sit down by the fireplace. The old crests engraved in the stone are as familiar to me now as those of my own kindred. I pat my knee and my spotty spaniel, called Munchie after my old favourite, jumps to my lap. His fur is smoother than velvet under my hand, his tail wagging slowly.

'Come, tell me all the news,' I say.

'Oh dear. I am afraid it shan't please you.'

'Now I *have* to know.'

'His Grace treats Perkin Warbeck with the most generous clemency. He has, at last, confessed to the falsehood of his claim and will be allowed to reside at court.'

'*What?* Not in the Tower? Tudor—His Grace, I mean— would keep Warwick and John of Gloucester under lock and key while letting the scoundrel Warbeck prance around freely?'

'You forget your cousins are a threat because of their supposed claims, while Warbeck is harmless, having confessed he has no such claim.'

'But…but he deserves it, and they do not! After everything he has done…'

Perkin Warbeck, the young man who for many years now has styled himself as my long-lost younger brother, the young man who seeks to dethrone Tudor, the young man who has caused me so much pain. At first, I wanted to believe it. Every report about his looks—the blond hair, the handsome face, the Yorkist features—sounded like Dickie grown up. He was the right age, knew the right things. Aunt Margaret of Burgundy even acknowledged him as her nephew and declared she believed every word of his story: how he had been spirited away from the Tower, made to swear to not reveal his true identity for a certain amount of time, and lived on the continent under Yorkist protection.

Of course, there was always the gnawing, increasing doubt sprung from what Uncle Richard and Queen Anne told me as well as from the letter to Buckingham that I found under the floorboard in what seems like another life. My brothers are both dead. I never believed Warbeck's imposter wholeheartedly, yet it was an immense temptation, because he lit a spark of hope in me. Nothing hurts as badly as hope being squashed, and mine certainly was through his actions, for I knew they were unlike anything my little brother would have done. He, who was always humbler than I, would not have pursued the crown at the cost of others' lives; he, who was always valiant, would not have deserted his own army.

Welles takes my hand and it strikes me how much he has aged. 'Calm yourself, my lady. There is nothing you can do to change what the King has decreed.'

'That is the very cause of my distress.'

'I see.'

There is naught more to be said.

Anne arrives a week later. It was long since I last saw her, and how I have missed those fairy-like limbs and those floating steps. She brings gifts: silk for a new gown for Eliza and a delicately crafted doll for Annie. I suspect my sister likes her namesake best, since my oldest daughter is perhaps what some would consider rowdy. Welles and I had a bicker over what to call our youngest, but since he had decided on Elizabeth for our first, I finally prevailed with the name Anne, for the late Queen and for my favourite sister alike.

Darkness falls early, as it is wont to do in this season, enveloping the landscape in a gloomy embrace. From outside, Tattershall looks like a haunted castle, its red brick turned black; inside, hundreds of candles emblazon the vast spaces. Anne still does not like the dark, hence we sit in the most well-lit room of all, the one adjoining to the audience chamber, tucked up in the cushioned window seat. On a round table slightly below sits a bowl of dark red winter apples from the garden.

'Did you hear about the Pope's daughter?' I ask. Ever since her father became the Head of Christendom, I have indulged in the scandal that is Lucrezia Borgia.

Anne's eyes widen. 'I know. They say her husband was made to sign a confession of impotence.'

'Not that bit, everyone knows that. I mean did you hear about the baby? Word is she had a baseborn son of her own while the annulment was being negotiated.' I bite into an apple, the juice both tangy and sweet on my tongue.

'She did? I wonder who her lover was.'

'Some say t'was her brother. Regardless, I hope he realised his luck, catching Christendom's so-called greatest treasure.'

Anne pulls her knees up to her chin and rests her arms on them. 'I think the Catholic Monarchs would consider their own daughter to be that.'

'Catalina?'

'Prince Arthur calls her Catherine—that other name is so...Spanish.'

I shrug. 'She *is* Spanish. I hope Tudor is finally satisfied with her Spanish gold, too, though I doubt it. The more he can stuff away in his coffers...'

'They can afford it, surely, with all the riches from the New Land.' My sister's gaze is distant, perhaps set on the continent we have heard so many fabulous tales about. 'Aren't you excited to meet her? She sounds so wonderfully clever.'

'If she is, she'll know her luck. Just imagine coming here, escaping her parents' horrid slaughtering of the Jews and Moors! I wager our weather is better, too. Our summers are more temperate, and the sunshine is not scorching, like it can be in Spain.'

'You will come to the wedding, will you not?'

'Of course I will. Elizabeth must give me some role to play in the ceremony if I am to be Catalina's aunt.'

Anne smiles. When she reaches for an apple, the lining of her voluminous sleeve slips back, revealing a broad stroke of bruises encircling her wrist. The skin shifts in bold shades of yellow and purple, the kind of bruises I can only recall seeing on men returning from combat.

Anne pulls down her sleeve as quickly as possible but she must know I have seen what she is hiding. A moment passes with the sole sound coming from either of us being the chewing of apples.

I put mine down on the table and take my sister's arm in a gentle but steady grip, pulling up the sleeve once more. She winces at first yet does not try to stop me. I study her arm in the candlelight, searching for more bruises, but find none.

'Who did this?' I ask, forcing myself to remain calm.

Anne shakes her head, blushing. 'It is of no importance.'

'*Yes*, it is.' I catch her other arm, and to my horror, the battering is mirrored there. 'Tell me this very moment, Anne.'

'I was terribly insensitive, stupid even. I spent all evening listening to one of the minstrels, which I should not have, it was just he sung such pretty songs and had written such pretty poetry. They were not intended for me, but Tom could not know that.'

I gape at her. 'Howard is to blame?'

'*I* am to blame. It's just he loves me so, so much, and I should not have hurt him thus by lavishing attention on another man.'

I also thought my sister's husband, the Earl of Surrey's son Thomas Howard, loved her 'so, so much'. I thought she had been blessed, him being both adroit and charismatic, only two years her senior, not to speak of the son and grandson of trusted Yorkists, despite their buttering up Tudor recently. When they were wed a few years ago, he had eyes for none but her. He was not the knight in shining armour she had always dreamed of, but it mattered not, because he compensated for his lack of chivalry with a hefty dose of adoration. Now, the thought of him makes fury burn hot in my stomach.

I cup Anne's hands in mine. 'Can he truly love you if he beat you?'

She withdraws her hands. 'He did not beat me. He merely held me firmly and said I mustn't act as if I were not his wife. And then he kissed me, and I think he forgave me.'

'But—'

'Forget it, Cecily!' she snaps. 'Just because your own husband is not as passionate.'

'No, no he certainly is not.' I have never seen her this defensive—I will get nowhere by pressing the matter further. 'Well, won't you tell me about something else? How is Kate?'

Anne smiles, our spat apparently forgotten. 'She is glowing, God's truth. Little Hal and Teddy are chafing against her nerves, though.'

I can imagine it: eighteen-year-old Kate, still every bit the sprightly young girl, trying to talk to her friends over the noise of wailing babies, pouting at the helpless wet-nurse and rockers. Still, two healthy sons in two years of marriage is a feat most women would drool over, and in due time, her husband William Courtenay will inherit the earldom of Devon.

The rest of the evening passes in idle chatter about everything from Kate's new daring headdress to European politics. I take care not to mention Thomas Howard again, for I do not want to lose my sister's confidence and affection. However, I shall have to keep as close an eye as I can on their marriage. If he does not behave in the future, then…then there is very little I can do about it, but I have an obligation to poke my nose in it at the very least.

In the morning, I write to Elizabeth, hoping she might be able to persuade Tudor to reconsider his leniency towards Perkin Warbeck. Though she does not show it as far as I know, she has been as wounded by the impostor's existence as I have. Her hope, too, must have been lit and extinguished; she, too, must have spent endless nights lying awake wondering whether she has failed to support her long-lost brother or whether it was all a cruel trick.

I seal the letter and give it to one of the servants with instructions to ride to Greenwich, where the court currently resides. The pained look in his eyes almost makes me change my mind, but no, he will have to live with the cold, lengthy ride. Perhaps, just this once, my eldest sister will adhere to mine and her own wishes rather than Tudor's.

Anne, Welles, and the girls are waiting for me in the great hall. The table is decked with bread and cheese, milk and spiced wine, and porridge. I take a seat, ravenous as always after a night on an empty belly, reaching for my spoon. This being my own household, there is no need to follow to the norm of having a feather-light meal or nothing at all in the mornings.

Welles coughs into the crook of his elbow for a good while. When he has finished, he appears mortified. 'Pardon me, ladies. I believe I have contracted a chill. It was not my intent to make such a fuss.'

I swallow a laugh. 'Do not concern yourself with us, Husband. We have survived worse.'

'Perhaps I ought to take to my bed.'

'Do so. I'll have a tray sent to you—some tea and honey, and the rest of your bread.'

He pushes his chair back, gives my hand a squeeze, and retires upstairs.

Anne frowns, slowly stirring butter into her cloggy porridge. 'Your husband does not seem healthy, not at all.'

234

I dab a smear from Annie's cheek, secretly glad Welles cannot tell me that this, too, is the nurse's task. 'He is prone to sore throats and runny noses, and always has been. He says he enjoys winter, but I doubt it.'

'Will you go to him?'

'He can sleep awhile first. I promised the girls we might show you the puppies in the stable—did I not?'

Eliza nods fervently. 'Yes, yes, please let's.'

Having finished our meal, the four of us embark on our little expedition: across the inner ward, through the guardhouse and over the bridge, to the stable on the other side of the outer ward. One of Welles' greyhounds gave birth to nine squealing little bundles of fur and wet noses a week ago. Apart from my own babies, they are the sweetest thing I ever saw, and the others share my opinion, squatting in the rushes.

Once we return to the castle, I order the tray for Welles and follow the Irish kitchen maid to the main bedchamber. She puts the tray down on the side table, curtsies, and scurries back to her safe domain in the kitchen.

I sit by the foot of the bed. 'Are you awake?'

Welles grunts something before erupting into a fit of sneezing, and I shuffle farther back as discreetly as I can.

'Oh dear... Do forgive me,' he says.

'No matter. Take your remedies and we shall have you on your feet tomorrow.'

However, Welles' ailments are slow in passing, in fact, they increase rather than pass. Five days come and go, and he is still tucked up under four blankets with a fever and hoarse voice. The children, Anne, and I do what we can to brighten his spirits, but to no avail.

On the sixth day, my sister departs early, for fear of contagion. I am reluctant to let her return to Thomas Howard, but what can I do? Her eyes sparkle when she mentions him; perhaps she is leaving due to longing, not merely risk of infection.

'Promise to write to me, and spare me no details of how you fare,' I tell her while the carriage is being prepared.

She kisses my cheeks. 'Of course I will. Prithee do not worry about me, but think of Lord Welles instead.'

Chapter XXIII

TOWARDS THE END of January, I summon a physician from Boston to Tattershall for the second time. He brings leeches, hoping to balance the humours in Welles' body. I stand flat against the wall while the crook-nosed Bostonian applies the greenish-black, slimy animals to my husband's exposed, pasty arms and stomach. It is a good thing he is sleeping heavily—and better still I gave him an extra glass of our strongest wine—for he shares my disgust of the ungodly beasts. I have to press my hand to my mouth to stop myself from vomiting as I watch the leeches draw blood. I would have picked ordinary bleeding myself, but the physician knows best.

'Have this, Lady Welles. Be certain Lord Welles takes it every morn and eve till he be healthy again,' he says once his work is finished, pressing a small wooden tub in my palm.

'What is it?'

'Seeds of celery mixed with honey, anise, wine, and pepper. It is a useful remedy for those suffering from coughs.'

I nod. 'I shall give it to him. Grammercy.'

I pay the physician his costly fee, and he departs, leaving me standing by the bedside. I have to sleep in one of the turrets from this point forward, perhaps in the little room below that of my daughters', to avoid catching the disease. Unlike some of my sisters, my health has always been strong, and when others have crumbled under sickness' yoke, I have remained standing, but I would rather not tempt fate.

Eliza and Annie are intrigued, though fear lurks in their eyes like a shadowy cat sneaking on its prey. They have seen their father ill in bed before, and have suffered similar ailments themselves, but this is different. For almost three weeks now,

Welles has shown no signs of improvement, rather the opposite, and I know the chills sometimes shaking his body scare our daughters, hence I keep both my girls away from Welles as much as possible. To my despair, though, it is too late, because Eliza is soon overtaken by similar symptoms as her father. Is it my fault? Should I have been more restrictive regarding her whereabouts earlier? In such a small child, fever and lung diseases are all the more dangerous, this I do know. Children are always vulnerable—that is the first thing one learns as a mother.

I spend my days switching from my husband's bedside to my daughter's and back again. I spend my nights twisting and turning in my own provisory bed. I move Annie down two floors and set up a temporary new bedchamber for her as well in a desperate attempt to protect her from the evil spreading in our household. Is it God's wrath over my lack of proper piety, at last spilling over? Or is it a curse laid upon us, or perhaps merely nature's cruelty? It is impossible for me to tell.

Eliza appears smaller than ever as she lies ridden with painful coughs and burning with fever. Gone is the fiery, thriving girl I used to know. She squeezes my hand relentlessly, her little fingers red from the effort.

One day, she tells me: 'Lady Mother? I'm afraid.'

'Afraid of what?'

'Of dying. I do not want to die. I want to do so many *other* things.'

Her words bring tears to my eyes, for I am every bit as frightened as she is. 'You shan't die, my love. We just have to wait for the worst to pass, and then you will feel better.'

'Promise?'

'Promise.'

A knock on the door. The Irish maid, Joan, sticks her head into the room. 'Pardon, m'lady. You might want to see to Lord Welles. He's not doing so nicely.'

I sigh, push the chair back and rise, then blow Eliza a careful kiss. 'I will be back before you know I was even gone.'

As I enter the main bedchamber, I am nearly blinded. Dust dances in the streaks of white sunlight, the dark velvet curtains surrounding my husband creating a stark contrast to the otherwise bright room.

237

Joan was certainly not exaggerating. My husband's breaths come quick and shallow; he presses a hand to his chest as if to stem pain. He has lost weight, too, over the past month, and the bones jut out under the chemise from his already skinny shoulders. The sight brings images to my mind of Queen Anne shortly before she died.

'Come,' he wheezes.

I comply, halting halfway through the room. While I do not have the heart to deny my daughter my immediate presence, I lack the courage to take as great a risk for my husband.

Welles continues, his voice unrecognizable. 'I have made a will...I bequeath all my castles and manors to you, dear wife.'

I fail to form any proper words of gratitude. I could never have guessed he held me in such high esteem, nor that his love was so ardent. Perhaps a person's true colours only show on their deathbed—for that is what this must be—if they have lived a too restrained life.

'Do not leave me, John,' I say, hiding my clenched fists between the folds of my gown. 'Please. The girls need their father.'

'You are the most capable woman I could have married. They shan't lack anything in the way of protection or riches.'

'Your sister will have us removed from Tattershall. What if she and Tudor pick another husband for me, and our daughters are made someone else's wards? What then? Their new guardians would marry them to their own sons and take their inheritance before I could so much as wink.' Widows are rarely granted the custody of their own children, and this frightens me beyond anything.

'There is a letter...in my desk. Give it to the King. He will know then that my last wish is for you to be free to choose both your own and the girls' husbands. Tattershall...it is true. You may have to move elsewhere, but the other castles are not of poor standard. I have committed my last wishes regarding the burial and so forth to paper also.'

A cold trickle on my cheek. I reach up only to discover my eyes are leaking. After everything this man has cost me—my freedom, my ambitions, a large chunk of my pride—he now gives me back my own agency. I may be approaching twenty-nine and am not as fertile as my husband and Margaret Beaufort might have wished, yet I have maintained my appearance, and as a wealthy widow I will be more independent than ever before. I will be in a position to wed whomever I like, or at least have a far more free choice than last time. And still…I mourn Welles already. I never grew to love him as a husband, but he was—no, he *is*—a friend and has been kind when it has been within his power. Without him, Eliza and Annie would not have entered my world.

I swallow my tears and tread the last steps towards the bed. Kneeling, I clasp my hands in a feeble prayer.

'Forgive me, Cecily.'

I turn my eyes to him, hesitating a moment. 'There is nothing to forgive. I mean it.'

'Then you will pray for my eternal soul?'

'I will, though I do not think my prayers will do you more good than your own record of actions.'

He moves his head in what could be interpreted as a nod.

I do not have to deliver Welles' letter, nor break the seal on his official will. It is a miracle. The morning after what I thought would be our last words to each other, the disease loosens its grip on him ever so slightly. I can only gape along with Joan as we watch him eat a bowl of turnip soup without coughing it up. Perhaps the leeches were just slow in working, or perhaps it is divine intervention. Whatever the case, nothing is the same. He has exposed the sentiment closest to his heart in the clutch of death, and I have known the anguish losing my husband would bring. The air between us is thick as the castle walls. If this bout was to test our marriage, we have passed, and still, a sense of embarrassment tarries. I understand the blessing granted me, truly, but I wish I had not pleaded for him not to leave me. Despite the length of our union, despite all the emotional bursts I have put on display, I have never before felt this vulnerable under his gaze. He must be wondering whether I love him. I do not know yet if I do, but I have a sneaking suspicion. Surely, there are many ways to love a person. He is neither a lover nor a father figure to me, and not like the friends I have previously had, but

239

he does play the third most central role in my life and that does entitle him to a kind of platonic affection.

Although he improves a little day by day, Welles is still too weak to rise from the bed for another fortnight. His breath may have begun to calm, but his strength remains diminished, and I wonder if it will ever return entirely. Like a bird with broken wings, he is a tad broken himself. Someday I *will* lose him, for his powers to resist death will not always be what they were on this first stroll along the edge of the dark abyss.

A few days after Welles eats that first bowl of soup, I spend the night in the chair I have drawn up to Eliza's bed. The governess, two servants, and I have tried to feed her broth and bread, but what she does manage comes up again moments later. With each passing hour, she fades a little further and I grow a little more fearful. The sound of her merciless cough and exhausted lungs is starting to creep into my nightmares, just like when Queen Anne perished.

The physician from Boston visited once more yesterday, extracting another heavy fee. I would pay him every single penny I have if he could cure my girl, but the bleeding does not seem to help and she refuses to swallow the herbal remedies. The physician says this sickness is very common—I know it well enough myself; I have seen chills worsen like this before—and we can only wait. I loathe waiting. It is the worst kind of torture of the mind.

When I wake, Eliza is looking at me. The windows are still curtained and the darkness casts heavy shadows on her taunt little face.

'Lady Mother?' she whispers. 'I'm afraid.'

'I know, my love. There is no need.'

'Tell me a story.'

'Which one would you like to hear?' Her hand stirs but she says nothing, hence I pick one myself. 'There once was an evil queen called Marguerite d'Anjou. She had come from a faraway land across the sea to wed a king called Henry when she was very young. Now, Henry was not really a king, for his grandfather had taken the throne foully from a tyrant. Sometimes we need to remove a tyrant, but this was not done in the right way, because

240

the crown should have passed to the usurper's cousins, who were first in line. What was more, Henry was too feeble and too indecisive to rule, rather like a small child, caring only for saints. So, Marguerite married him, and the years went by. After a time, the kingdom was very tired of the King's silly non-rule and people had started to fight. So, do you know what happened?

'Your great-grandfather, the Duke of York, said he could rule and then the kingdom would be a happy place again. But the evil Queen said no, she would rule. Some people thought this was a very nasty thing because she was a woman, but the truth was it was bad because she was from another kingdom across the sea, and so she had no right. Evil Marguerite had a wicked son, whom she had had through a wicked love affair with a man who was not Henry.

'Marguerite and your great-grandfather fought very hard and very long, and her army was known to pillage and loot the country. At last, your great-grandfather died and your grandfather fought on in his stead and won—' My words fall flat.

Eliza does not move. Alarm bubbles in me as I bend forward, hoping to feel her short breath against my cheek—and nothing.

'No, no, no...' I murmur as I put two fingers to the place below her jaw where I have seen physicians check the pulsating of the blood. Again, nothing.

No. No, no, *no*. A strange hollowness fills me, then pangs of panic. I want to cry out but no sound emerges.

Is this what my own mother felt when Mary died? What about all the others...baby George and baby Margaret who passed away in infancy, my brothers in the Tower, Grey on the scaffold? How could Mother survive losing six of her twelve children prematurely when I can barely breathe having lost one? Perhaps she was made of sterner stuff than I am. Perhaps she found comfort in Christ, or something else pushed her to go on.

I close my eyes. Eliza's hand is still warm in mine, yet limp. I see her against the black of my eyelids: swaddled for the first time, the midwife placing her in my arms, her grey eyes gazing into mine as if she already knew my every secret. I recognised those eyes instantly, and how I cherished the fragment of my uncle that I found in them.

241

I see her smiling for the first time. I laughed then, as did Welles. I see her taking her first wobbly steps in the nursery, like a fawn on ice. I see her face sticky with strawberry juice in summertime, her fury when anyone tried to manage anything for her. Was it all for nothing?

Mayhap I have failed. I tried to not let my slight favouritism for her sister show one wit, because I know how painful such a thing can be. Annie took an extra ounce of my love because of her sweetness and her dependence on me, but Eliza will always be my oldest, my first, the one most like myself.

No, not will be. *Was.*

Judging by the burnt-down candles, several hours pass before I struggle to my feet and let go of my daughter's hand. The warmth is gone now. My knees are sore and flattened, my cheeks clammy with tears. I bend down and pull the covers up to Eliza's shoulders, smoothing the wrinkles and arranging her arms neatly by her sides. There. Prettily tucked up in bed, prepared for the night.

A flock of wide-eyed servants await me outside the door. They should not be here, in the main bedchamber, without having been summoned, certainly not the wench I assume is one of the scullery maids, but I cannot be bothered to chide them for it. No doubt they have amassed out of curiosity to know what I have been doing for such a long time, or out of empathy. It is possible that they, too, are grieving, if they understand what has happened. I care not one bit. They can all go to Hell-everlasting as long as they leave me be.

'Lady Welles?' the steward asks. He is ancient at this point, his earlobes even more scarlet than when I first met him ten years ago. 'Is there anything you'd have me do for you?'

'No. Nothing.' I push past him.

With numb tongue and feet moving mechanically, I walk downstairs and open the door to Annie's provisory room in the north turret. At first, the sight of her lying still on the pallet makes my heart jump to my throat, but no, she is merely sleeping, her torso rising and falling with every deep breath. Thank God. Apart from Welles and my four living siblings, she is all I have left to care for. Everything else has lost its importance.

I sink onto the pallet next to Annie, stroking her silky hair. As I lie down and encompass her with my arms, burying my face in the soft curve between her neck and shoulder, cold claws of fear and grief tear me to shreds.

I will never let her go, *never*.

We travel to London, to court. Welles says it will do us good to escape the stale atmosphere of sickness and death now present in Tattershall's every corner. He says speaking to my sisters will lift the bars of iron I feel weighing on my shoulders and chest. I insist on bringing Annie—I have no intention of breaking my vow—and he cannot refuse me, not in this.

My daughter has not yet turned seven, but she is a clever little lady, and she knows her sister's fate. When we lowered Eliza into the ground in her alabaster coffin, Annie held my hand hard, as if she could squeeze out my sorrows and thereby dry my tears. If a face can rot from constant dampness, mine ought to be on the brink of ruin. I do, however, regain a sprinkle of mirth eventually, if only for Annie's sake. I suppose this is what kept Mother on her feet after her losses: the need to live for the children one does have left, and the joy they still give.

Elizabeth and Tudor receive us in the presence chamber at the Palace of Westminster. Since my wedding, I have mainly visited for ceremonies and celebrations, and it is strange to think it will be my home for a few months if not more. Annie has never seen the palace, nor has she smelled the stink of London's streets. She manages to dip down in a pretty curtsey before her regal aunt and half-cousin, one of the very few real curtseys she had performed in her life.

'She is charming, Cecily,' Elizabeth says, poised on her throne.

'I know.' I kiss Annie's hand. 'Perchance Prince Harry can provide some company.'

'My Harry may be the same age, but I believe you will find him too strong-willed for a girl to play with. Princess Mary is more suitable…is she not, Your Grace?'

Tudor nods. 'I shall see to it your daughter is properly lodged in the royal nursery.'

Welles bows his head. 'Sire, you are most bountiful.'

Just as we are leaving, treading through the crush of nobles swarming in the chamber, Elizabeth speaks again. 'Sister? We heard rumour of your loss. I am sorry God saw it fit.'

I swallow and nod, then pull Annie with me and depart. Elizabeth must know something of what I am feeling, having lost a daughter of her own a few years ago, but she has *four* children left, and without doubt another one under way soon. Two—Arthur and Margaret—are with their own households, being raised to their most probable futures as King of England and Queen of Scotland respectively, while the other two—Harry and Mary—are here at Westminster at the moment. None show signs of sickness. My sister cannot understand what it is to have a single gem which one has to guard with one's life for fear of God deciding it fit to snatch it.

I accompany Elizabeth to the royal nursery the following day to visit Annie as well as greet my nieces and nephew. Princess Mary is two years old and a stunning little thing. I was present at her christening but have not seen her since, and she is rapidly growing into a dark-haired beauty.

'His Grace hopes to wed her to the heir to the Duke of Burgundy, if he has a son,' Elizabeth says as we stand watching Annie show Mary her finest doll, the one Anne gave her.

I search my mind for a chart of European relations. Philip, Duke of Burgundy, is the son of my aunt Margaret's stepdaughter, and his wife Juana is the older sister of Catalina de Aragón, Prince Arthur's intended bride.

I frown. 'Despite this eventual heir's mother? Juana is insane, or so they say.'

'People say so many things, Cecily.'

'Well, what of Prince Harry?' I turn my eyes to the big-boned, red-headed boy kicking a leather ball against the wall. In a few months, he will be taken from the care of women and brought up by male tutors.

Elizabeth shakes her head. 'I know not. He shall have to put his attention to governing his dukedom first, I believe.'

Henry Tudor, Duke of York. Our grandfather held that title, as did our brother. It is the dukedom dearest to me and the one closest associated with my house of descent—and now Tudor doles it out at will. The prince is deserving, though. He is infinitely unlike both Tudor and Elizabeth; his temper is that of his grandfather, Edward IV, hot and fickle, and even at this young age he is eager to show off his athletic disposition, yearning for the day he can join the joust and the hunt. How different England's future would be if Harry had been the heir and Arthur the spare! The country would not be as mildly ruled, but court would be far more entertaining.

Welles was right: London does help to distract me. One of these days I might go to Dartford Priory and speak to Bridget, whom I have missed sorely since I was last here. Her words of wisdom have only grown since she was a little girl, and the Lord knows she is a hundred times more sensible now than I was at seventeen.

The days of my youth feel like a dream. The crinkles around Thomas' eyes when he laughed and the silly games that we used to play are indeed naught but that, a dream, for he is nowhere to be found at court. When his master Northumberland died, the household men were either sent home or took up service elsewhere; this is all I know.

If I could have anything, anyone, back in my arms in this instance apart from Eliza and Dickie, it would be my old friend.

Chapter XXIV

ONE CLOUDY SUMMER day, Kate bursts into my bedchamber and takes me by the arms. 'Cecily! Cecily! Did you hear about the impostor?' Her hair is in disarray, her eyes lit with excitement.

I shake loose. 'Warbeck?'

'Him!' She raises herself up and down on her toes, a habit I had hoped she would grow out of with time.

'Would you mind *not* bouncing while you're talking?' I ignore the sour face she makes.

'Pardon me, then. Anyhow, he climbed out his window and sought sanctuary at the Charterhouse of Sheen. Can you believe it?'

I grapple for words. 'No, not quite. Is he a complete blithering idiot? Does he not know how fortunate he was to be spared the first time?'

'He's in the Tower now—no windows this time.'

'I'm glad. He deserves that and more.'

'You are not always very nice.'

I give my sister a glare. 'Should I have to be pleasant to a coward who has used our brother's memory for his own gain?'

She shrugs. 'I never believed he was genuine. I knew all along he pretended.'

'I am sure you did.'

She sticks out her tongue at me, a flash of pink like a cat's, and is gone. It is a wonder Tudor has not chucked her and her husband, William Courtenay, out of the palace already, considering how her bubbly manners contrast to the Pretend-King's preferences. It must be Elizabeth who has spoken a few kind words in his ear.

246

Anne melts into court more easily, since her behaviour is decorous and her views are more moderate than my own. As far as I know, her qualms regarding the regime changes of the past decade are minimal, and she has always kept her attentions to personal matters rather than politics. As long as she has her growing collection of literature from Caxton's printing press and her husband, Howard, she is content, although I think she wishes for another child. Perhaps she hopes that would stabilise her marriage. Her only son is approaching his second birthday, a sickly boy, and I understand her concerns well enough. Anne is rarely at Westminster, though, as she retired to Howard's estates after their wedding.

I have observed my sister and her husband ever since Howard returned to court, taking a brief pause from his Scottish campaign. He treats her with the greatest courtesy in public, presenting her with gifts as costly as he can afford. However, each time Anne appears with a new set of sparkling emeralds around her slim throat, I swear there is the hint of a new shadow in her face. If I could see through the velvets and brocades of her gowns, I am certain I would also see the bruises those jewels serve as apology for. I may be suspicious, but I would rather be that than naive and enamoured like Anne herself. Twice or thrice I have approached the issue and been brushed off. With my sister refusing to cooperate, there is very little I can do, and even if she appealed to Elizabeth to have Tudor reproach Howard, no monarch has legal authority over the private affairs between a husband and wife. In all likelihood, Howard would merely be enraged at her supposed betrayal, and punish her for it as he pleased.

During the autumn and winter, I ensconce myself more and more in the companionship of my sisters, even Elizabeth, when she is not on Tudor's arm, because they provide the sole close family bonds I have left from my childhood. Uncles and aunts and cousins still swarm England's counties along with a sprinkle of Father's other bastard offspring, but I have grown estranged from them during my lengthy absence. Of course, there is Dorset, but he is no more likeable than he was when I was a child. Elizabeth keeps him at arm's length according to Tudor's instruction, since his lack of backbone showed clearly during his time in exile.

Although I would never dream of going a single day without spending a few hours with Annie in the nursery, Welles grows more and more remote in my life. During the first months after Eliza left us—the thought smashes me to pieces all over again—our relationship warmed, a bond being forged in our grief. Now, my husband is away on his nephew Tudor's errands increasingly often, and the distance makes it difficult to keep the warmth from cooling, at least on my behalf.

Speaking of distance, it is high time I visited Bridget. The New Year's celebrations keep me from traveling, but on the last day of January, I kiss Annie goodbye and set out on the journey to Dartford Priory.

The priory is far from as horribly impoverished as I remembered it being the first time I came here. Perhaps it never was—I cannot tell. I have visited four times in total, and each time it grows in my esteem. As long as Bridget is content, it does not matter whether she lives as a pauper.

To my astonishment, I recognise the ancient woman who opens the door and shuffles me inside. I would have presumed her dead from old age, yet here she is, five years after I saw her on my last visit.

My sister, a full-fledged nun now, receives me in the humble bedchamber she shares with two other members of the order, a room bright with daylight. On a small table stands a ceramic vase with a clutch of herbs and flowers, exuding a vague fragrance, and above the wall hangs a wooden crucifix where the gold paint has begun to flake off.

I sink down on the squeaking bed opposite the one where Bridget is sitting. 'Who is it you share this room with?'

She smiles—she is the only one I know who has really inherited Mother's smile. 'Sister Martha and Sister Alice.'

'And they are good to you?'

'Sister Martha is of a very respectable age and very prudent, too. Sister Alice is…' Her cheeks flush pink. 'Graced by God in every manner. One would think it was her divine task to make one mirthful.'

The description brings my Thomas to mind, except he is not mine, and I should not think about him. I have rarely, if ever, seen my little sister blush; I assumed she did not have the capacity for it, being too serious, too old in her spirit. Now, though, she looks just like any fanciful young girl, and chiselled to perfection. How strange—surely, I must have missed something.

'This Alice sounds lovely,' I say. 'Is she pretty, also?'

Bridget knits her brows. 'Not particularly, although I'm oblivious as to why it is relevant. Beauty flees so quickly.'

'I suppose so.' I am glad my sister has found a new friend. My own greatest friendship ended badly to say the least, but Bridget will not be at risk, since Alice is, after all, a woman.

'Will you stay awhile?'

I nod. 'If the nuns have no objection. You can show me all those…herbs you speak of so frequently, and I can tell you everything new from London.'

'Is the activity so fervent yonder?' Her gaze is cryptic as a coded message written in invisible ink despite the plain question.

'You know me. I can talk for days if you let me.'

'I shall ask the prioress to have a bed made for you.'

I am a widow. Welles' health was never the same after his bout of consumption, and his body could not resist the disease this time.

I wish I could recount the moment he passed. As it is, the day a year ago when he almost died carries greater significance with me simply because I was there. Thinking of my husband's last words and breaths, I tend to imagine it was just like that almost-death; I fill in the gaps with the memories I have which might fit.

My ten-day trip to the priory was thoughtless. I should have returned sooner, I should have realised, I should have been more attentive to Welles' state… Would he have wanted me to be with him when he died? I think he would. He was not alone, thank God, since Margaret Beaufort sat by his side, although whether it is best to die alone or in her presence is debatable.

At the burial in Westminster Abbey, where such a great number of my ancestors and relatives already rest, I try hard to weep, yet no tears heed my command. I hope I have not become like Mother once was: too drained by past sorrows to muster anything but a tight-lipped paleness.

Death continues to hunt and slay when another young man claiming to be Warwick emerges and is brought to London. His fate is quicker and more brutal than that of Lambert Simnel or the real Warwick, because Tudor orders his execution at once. The incident might have upset me in the past, but I am too preoccupied with the changes in my own life to spend much thought on it.

I shall miss my overly polite Lancastrian, this I am certain of, but what tugs the most mercilessly at my heartstrings is Annie's silence. Throughout February and March, she barely speaks, and when she does, her voice is bereft of merriment. I cannot blame her, because I know the ache of losing both father and siblings within a short time. Whenever I try to make her laugh, it fails miserably. One day, a possible solution strikes me.

'Would you like to go home, Annie?'

She hesitates, then nods. 'I miss home. Here is…too much.'

I find Margaret Beaufort alone in her lavish chambers, seated by her solid oak desk with a pen in her hand. When the page announces my entrance, she instead picks up her pope-given Bible and keeps her eyes on the beautifully illustrated text as if to mark its precedence over me.

I take a few steps into the room and grant her a small curtsey to oil the wheels. The air is thick with incense being slowly absorbed by the crimson tapestries draping the walls.

'My daughter and I wish to return home, to Tattershall Castle, Madam,' I say.

Beaufort closes her Bible with a smack and turns to look at me. 'Tattershall was a conditional gift for the duration of your marriage. It is not your home.'

'Then what is?'

'Here, at court, until you wed again.'

I scoff. 'You cannot force me this time. My…friend is long gone from here, and no one would give any credit to accusations of twelve-year-old adultery without witnesses or proof, not even if you laid out the charges yourself. You lost your chance to ruin me.'

'I *chose* not to ruin you, girl.' Her voice reaches a pitch, then settles down. 'I have no need to force you this time. You know as well as I do that the clock is ticking for you. No one will wish to take you for his wife once you are beyond childbearing years.'

'Mayhap you forget I have other attractions: my name and title.'

'Who is it you have set your hopes on?'

'I do not know yet. My husband has been dead less than two months.' It is Eliza's death rather than Welles' that has kept me from devoting my thoughts to the marriage market, but hopefully the mention of her brother will strike a chord with Beaufort.

'You need not inform me.'

I draw a deep breath 'Let me return to Tattershall, Madam. *Please*. Are you incapable of guilt, of pity? God must be wretched over the way you treated me. Your actions were not those of a merciful adherent to Christ's preaching.' If nothing else, this ought to do the trick.

She licks her lips, frowning. 'You would speak to me of the Lord?'

'Yes. Your eternal soul would benefit if you showed me a grain of indulgence. What is more, it was your brother's dying wish. I assume you read his letter.'

A moment of tense silence passes. If I could see through her skull, I would no doubt behold the cogs in an intricate machinery trying to work out whether I am right regarding her eternal soul.

'Go to your castle and take your daughter with you. And pray write to me when you have pondered whom you might seek to wed—we will discuss it in a civilised manner.'

'Thank you, Madam.'

I follow these instructions more than willingly. When I tell Annie, she smiles for the first time since Welles' death. Court is infinitely exciting for a child her age, yet exhausting, and she is worn from having so many eyes on her. After taking farewell of Anne and Kate, as well as Princess Mary and Prince Harry and a cluster of courtiers I would rather forget at the moment, we embark on the journey north.

'Look, Lady Mother! A baby sheep!' Annie exclaims more than once, sticking her head out the carriage window.

Each time, I follow her pointing finger and nod. 'I think you mean a lamb, darling.'

'Yes. A lamb.'

Not until we arrive at Tattershall do I realise how much I have missed the red bricks and turrets, the double moats and the rose garden waiting to bloom yet another summer. London did me good, but I find it impossible to truly think of Westminster or Greenwich or Eltham as my permanent home these days. It is strange to confess it, but domestic life has transformed me, just as Beaufort and Welles said it would. But no...I can still cause mayhem if I want to; I can still dance the *saltarello* with twenty magnates on a masquerade ball, and I can still engage in secret schemes. I refuse to grow too sane and too plain—this is merely for the time being. Once Annie is of marriageable age, I will dive head-first into court intrigues again, all to lay out an advantageous future for her.

We can be happy here, she and I, alone as we are. The idyll of a complete family has faded long since, but as long as we have each other, I can keep every ghost at bay.

Sunshine gathers in golden pools on my skin and warms the nape of my neck. July is a fine time of year, the grey skies clearing at last. I have discarded my heavier gowns and bought a set of light silks and linen for both Annie and myself, exchanged the cumbersome gable headdress for a caul with only the thinnest of veils billowing around my head as I walk through the garden. Pale pink blossoms create a soft atmosphere, and next year, there shall be stark white roses as well, whether Margaret Beaufort likes it or not.

Annie tugs at my hand. 'Lady Mother? Can I go and look at the fishes?'

'Tell them I said hello. And Annie? Don't go too close to the horrid geese.'

She nods, then speeds away towards the moat where she so often stands gazing at the bright orange fishes flickering beneath the surface. I should commission someone to dig her a pond of her own where she might keep the slippery creatures as pets.

I continue my stroll, tilting my head back to bask in the pleasant light. Widowhood is more demanding than I could have imagined. I have to spend hours every day managing my late husband's estates in addition to my previous tasks of overseeing the household finances and my daughter's education. Despite this, I enjoy my new life more than what is proper considering my losses. I ought to marry again, for it is true my clock is ticking, and I *do* long for the opportunity to climb another step on the hierarchical ladder, add another fancy title to my name. Still, if I do, I will have to give up this temporary haven sooner rather than later.

I have written to Thomas but not dispatched any messenger with the letter. How could I, when I have no clue regarding his whereabouts? For all I know, he is either a household esquire to a peer living far away from court, or perhaps more likely, long since settled on his father's lands near Friskney or on the Isle of Wight with a wife and children of his own. I can be naught but a bleak memory to him at this point.

A scream slashes through my thoughts. When I dart across the grass and round a corner of the wall surrounding the inner moat, I catch sight of Annie's bonnet floating in the water like a chip of bone against the olive-green surface. Farther from the strand, her head sticks up, hair floating around her face, hands splashing in the attempt to keep herself from sinking. She must have wanted to have a closer look at the fish and not understood the risk.

My feet beat against the grass, sharp little stones hurting through the thin soles of my slippers as I hitch my skirts to my knees. My heart thuds against my lungs, bruising my chest from the inside. I gasp after air, throat burning dry, vision blurring.

'Lady Mother! Mother!' Her screams turn to clucking noises as water fills her mouth. They cut through the distance between us, that cursed distance, urging me to accelerate, but it is impossible. I have never run faster my whole life.

'Mother is coming, Annie!' I press forth over my own panting as I start to wade into the moat. The water is cold despite the warmth in the air. I know no more of swimming than she does; I have only seen men do it in lakes when I was younger and accompanied Father's household on summer progress. The moat is deeper than I thought, perhaps twice as deep as I am tall, and my feet kick without finding anywhere to stand. I paddle and tramp, draining my energy rapidly, yet I get nowhere. Filthy water fills my mouth and nose, pushing down into my lungs, making me cough and gasp for air.

'Mother!' Annie is drifting away from me, though she is flailing to get closer. A spasm of pain twists her face in a grimace and she stops splashing. I have heard of this horrid phenomenon before: people being swallowed by lakes and rivers when their muscles stiffen from effort.

I flap my arms and trample the water furiously—it is futile. 'Help! Help me! Help *her!* For the love of God!'

Annie's head bobs up and down until I can only see her bonnet on the surface. My throat hurts from shouting and I swallow even more water. At last there is commotion at the bridge leading from the garden via the postern to the inner ward. Through the haze of water in my eyes, I discern a small group of guards headed by the old steward and two grooms scurrying across the lawn, some holding down caps on their heads or clutching swords out of reflex. By the time the first four reach the moat and dive in, my legs are aching from kicking water.

Annie's cap floats towards me—but no Annie.

The men manage to pull me ashore and leave me, sitting with my arms wrapped around my knees, dripping, to search for my daughter. I am paralyzed, until the moment the steward kneels before me with bowed head and lowers her into my lap. The world blurs around me. I sense the soaked men standing a few feet away, exchanging glances in silence. The clear blue sky and green grass dotted with pink are at once offensive to me. How can the roses be allowed to live?

Her little body is limp and cold. I rub her arms and cheeks furiously in an attempt to bring back the warmth. It refuses to return. Her lips, the colour of lavender, remain slightly parted and her eyes stare glassy into mine as if through a mist. Auburn hair slicked to her scalp, pearls of water encircling her head like a coronet. Fingers that once clutched a single one of mine when she was a babe.

I cup my daughter's face in my hands and turn it left and right in the hard sunlight. It cannot be. It simply cannot; I forbid it. She is all I need in this world, all I want. I cannot lose another child, not my youngest. My *only*.

Chapter XXV

I BURY HER in Saint Botolph's Church, Boston, next to Eliza. The coffin is fresh from the carpenter, still smelling of paint. I wanted it white, not for the sake of my family name but because it made her look just a little less pale herself. I place her favourite doll beside her, the one her aunt gave her, and clasp one of my sapphire necklaces around her neck. I intended to let her have it on her wedding day.

I understand now, perhaps for the first time, what crushed Queen Anne. The disease in her lungs may have driven her towards her death, and the vicious rumours about Elizabeth may have quickened the process, but if her only son and hope had not already died, she could have resisted the rest. I am older now than she was then, but I may yet meet a similar fate.

There are so many people waiting for me in the afterlife: Father, Mother, my sister Mary, Rivers and Grey, my brothers, Agnes, Uncle Richard, Queen Anne, Welles, Eliza...Annie. There are more than the people I love who are still living. If I were to join the dead lot, I could perhaps be reunited with them. The only issue is that they will not all be in the same place, since some were bound for Heaven while others are likely struggling to escape the chains of Purgatory. That is where I would go, too, I am confident of it. I have not always been as humble and obedient to God and my elders as I ought to. I have sinned more times than I have taken confession—yet I cannot think myself foul enough to be plunged down to Hell. There is naught to be done than to hope for death to seek me out, though, because if I hurried it along Hell would at once be the only possible destination, and then I would be no less lonely than I am now.

I cannot stand to look at Tattershall. It is no longer my shining haven. Annie's presence managed to gloss over Eliza's absence for a time, but now that she is also gone, the castle and the garden are covered in death's heavy cloak, infested with crawling milk-white worms.

Inside there is the smell of disease reeking from Eliza's old bedchamber where she drew her last shallow breaths, and when I venture outside for relief, there is the treacherous water glaring back at me. How can I ever cleanse this place? It is impossible. With only the servants around me, there is no one whom I can talk to in order to fill the void of silence. If I had a friend here, I might stay, but all my living acquaintances are either scattered across the country at their various estates or, more commonly, pinned down at court. Court... The hub of companionship, as well as the dirtier side that is intrigue and schemes, may not always be the kindest of places, or one where I am afforded the freedom and independence I enjoy tucked away here in the Midlands, but one can never be lonely there. The dances, the banquets, the jousts—all these things used to spark joy in me as I was surrounded by chattering ladies and lords in bright apparel, and if I try, I might be able to draw some small pleasure or at least distraction from that life once more. It will take time, no doubt, and come gradually, but I will never return to the world of light hearts if I do not attempt it.

After having taken a dear farewell of the old steward and watched the carts with my coffers of belongings roll ahead, I step into my own carriage and sink back in the velvet seat. Resting my cheek against the smooth window pane, I cast one last glance at the place I considered home for such a long time. Home, however, is where the people one loves are, and there is nothing for me here anymore. The sound of hooves against the road is oddly comforting as I travel south, the days passing in a haze. I grow stiff as a stick, and it is an immense relief when we pass through Aldersgate and continue through the flurry of activity that is London.

The Palace of Westminster towers before me, its spires poking holes in the sky, the stone tinted dull gold in the splashes of late August sunshine. I have beheld it like this more times than I can count, yet its beauty never diminishes. The inside of the palace is filtered with the same golden light, owing to the high windows. I wish it were not thus, for I am not ready to step into this shimmering world when I have spent the last month in utter darkness. However, I have come this far, and Elizabeth will be expecting me.

My sister receives me in private this time. She is alone, for once, standing making peculiar wiggling movements, her back toward me. When she turns to face me, it is as if someone tightened the screws on an iron cage around my chest. The baby in her arms, whom she is apparently trying to rock to sleep without great success, is a cherubic little thing with downy hair and cheeks round as apples. I had almost forgotten my nephew Edmund, Elizabeth's third son. He should be around six months old now, though a little small for his age.

Elizabeth smiles. 'Welcome, Cecily. It will be wonderful to have all my sisters under one roof again. Anne is come from Howard's estates for a few months. You do not mind your old lodgings, do you?'

'No,' I press forth. 'No, I do not mind. How…how is the baby?'

'Oh, rather difficult—he simply refuses to sleep. I ought to return him to the nursery.'

'You have been blessed.'

'God is kind.'

I nod while Elizabeth sweeps past me on her way to the nursery, leaving me with the sour bile of envy burning my throat. Two accomplished girls and three seemingly healthy boys, the oldest of which is already fourteen and an inch away from sealing a triumphant marriage match. Yes, God has indeed been kind towards my sister. If I were her, I would not let anyone else care for baby Edmund in my place; I would not let him out of my sight. She is merely doing what is considered natural and proper for mothers of our status—she is even *more* involved in her children than ideal—but I cannot wrap my head around it. And not once did she mention my Annie.

Life goes on. Each evening there is a dinner or a dance or an entertainment for foreign ambassadors, and it does me good to be kept busy and under the public gaze, because it prevents me

257

from dwelling more in my bedchamber than is socially acceptable. Tudor has certainly learnt what ruling a kingdom requires in terms of display, and although he still holds onto every penny he can, he knows when he has to spend. This is in no way the sparkling court of my father or uncle, but it is a hundred times more than what Tattershall had to offer. Underneath, though, my youngest daughter is a constant, prickling presence in my mind.

Just as Elizabeth said, it is wonderful to have her, Anne, Kate, and myself under one roof. Of course, she forgot Bridget, but my youngest sister is close enough for me to call on any time. By remaining near this knot of women, I grasp a sliver of life as it used to be two decades ago when we were giggling little girls making merry in these same halls, despite or perhaps because of Elizabeth's innocently masked supremacy and Kate's annoying bursts of energy.

One chilly afternoon, Tudor summons me to his privy chambers. Begrudgingly, I leave Munchie by the fireplace in my bedchamber and march through the halls and galleries, trampling the hem of my dark blue gown more than once—the seamstresses must have confused the measurements.

Tudor is waiting for me in his favourite armchair. 'I have information for you, *Madame*, that I would rather not deliver in public.'

I arch my eyebrows. 'Why not, Sire?'

'Your reactions are not always fit to be seen by the court.' He takes a deep breath. 'Warwick and Warbeck are to be put to the justice of the law.'

I gape at him. 'What? Why now, after all this time?'

'They thought they could escape. It shows they have not yet given up their foolish claims and accepted their fate.'

'One is a repeatedly failed pretender, the other a simple-minded youth who cannot tell a goose from a capon after fourteen years of imprisonment. They present no danger to you, Sire.' My line of defence is only half-true, since nothing can guarantee that the men would not at least be used as figureheads for a rebellion, but it is without doubt the path most likely to succeed.

258

Tudor studies his rings. 'I thought it would please you to see Warbeck dead.'

'I will not mourn him. Warwick is my cousin, though, of my blood.'

'His blood is his death sentence. The same applies to John of Gloucester.' He says it with such casualness that I almost miss the new fatal blow he has dealt.

My words grow thick and clunky on my tongue. I remember John clearly: his intense glances and sweet smiles. I remember how ghostly pale, on the verge of transparent, he turned when we received the news of his father's defeat. Shall I lose not one but two cousins? I decide to grasp a straw. 'He was never legitimised.'

'Bastards have risen to power before.'

'If you seek to wipe out the Yorkist line, you'll have to wipe out your own children. Who shall be next—Prince Arthur?'

The Pretend-King grips the hilt of his very real, very sharp, gold-studded dagger, yet his voice is as calm as ever. 'Watch your tongue, *Madame*, unless you wish to have your head on a spike on London Bridge. They must perish for the safety of Arthur's reign.'

'They are no more threat to him than to you as long as they are under lock and key.'

'The Catholic monarchs think otherwise. They will not send their daughter to be queen of England unless her future as such is secured.'

He has decided. I might as well abandon my cautious lies and tell the truth as it is. 'Well, then they know how flimsy, how weak the Tudor claim is. They would not fear for Catalina's future if they thought you and Arthur undisputed. Perhaps they are right!' I turn on my heel and stalk towards the door.

'You will *not* turn your back on your king!' Tudor calls. 'And you have not been dismissed!'

'I turn my back on the grandson of a chamber servant!'

The guards let me pass, pure astonishment on their faces. I stomp out of the privy chambers and presence chamber, continuing through the palace without aim. The retort about Tudor's grandfather was true in every respect, and I have longed to fling it at him since before he even won the decisive battle of 1485. That my own maternal grandfather was of relatively humble origin is a fact I swept aside at a young age; I am still the daughter of a rightful king, and I am still descended from Edward III's second and fourth sons rather than from the illegitimate offspring of the third, as is Tudor.

Still, as the fire in me starts to cool a little, I regret my outburst. Were it not for my sister, I would be ruined for certs. Only Elizabeth's good graces can save me now… My head would look ghastly on a pike.

The trials are, of course, naught but a farce. Tudor wants the young men dead, and so they shall die.

On the twenty-third day of November, Warbeck is hanged at the Tyburn before what I assume is an ecstatic crowd. I am told he confessed with the noose around his neck, finally, to being a boatman's son from Tournai in Flanders, and not my angel brother. As if we did not know already!

Warwick's execution is a private affair on the Tower Green, as befits a nobleman, and this one I attend myself, along with the upper crust of courtiers and ambassadors. It is a stormy Thursday, the wind howling, rain cascading down into the Thames until I fear it will cause a flood.

I have not seen my young cousin for over a decade, and barely recognise him. I thought the change in his spirit and his appearance was concerning enough the day he was paraded through London to quench the rumours about Lambert Simnel's legitimacy, but that was a trifle compared to this. He was a fool to listen to Warbeck's escape plan, yet I cannot blame him when I see him. His hair is caked with filth turned to mud in the rain; he walks with padding little steps and has to be half-dragged, half-carried up to the scaffold; his eyes are dead already. One might expect a man of his rank to have been held in greater comfort, but I suspect his cell has only degraded over the years. One small mercy is that Meg Pole is not here to witness the spectacle. She knows, of course, but was sensible enough to stay in Wales with her husband and children.

The executioner strikes a single clean blow with his axe and it is over. I squeeze my eyes shut when he bends down to retrieve my cousin's head and hold it by the hair for all to see.

John of Gloucester is dealt with within the walls of the Tower, just as my brothers were. I do not know if he has already perished by the time of the other executions, or if he is the last to meet his saviour, but there is no doubt Tudor keeps his word of doing away with him. People have begun to forget him, hence it suffices to deal the blow behind closed doors and thereby avoid an unnecessary show of cruelty, but to let him live would be too dangerous in the eyes of the paranoid Pretend-King. I hope Gloucester's final resting place is more suitable than that of his father, but the chance is slight.

With the death of Warwick, the Yorkist line of legitimate male descent is extinguished; with Gloucester's, so is the illegitimate, save for Father's bastard son Arthur, who has been prudent enough to keep away from court. Now, every claimant our house can put forth is either a woman—the most obvious being myself, my sisters, and Meg—or bases said claim on the inheritance of a woman, namely my paternal aunt the Duchess of Suffolk. The latter's sons, the de la Poles, are, at least in Tudor's eyes, a growing threat.

Edmund de la Pole, Lincoln's younger brother, has come of age, and appears to be itching for revenge. At the time of the Lambert Simnel uprising, he was slightly too young to be an active participant, but he has not reconciled with the defeat. In all fairness, it is as much Tudor who has not offered reconciliation: Edmund fought the Cornish rebels on his new liege lord's behalf, yet the favour he was shown is scarce indeed. It reminds me of how Father pardoned Buckingham a long time ago but refused to treat him to the influence his status would have required, keeping him for decorative uses only. However, just as Buckingham turned first on my brothers and then on my uncle, Tudor has good reason to fear Edmund will turn on him. He has degraded Edmund from Duke to Earl of Suffolk, and made him pay the staggering sum of five thousand pounds to keep any title at all. Furthermore, a year ago, he charged him with murder and had him beg forgiveness. Although it would not surprise me if my cousin was guilty—he is even more hot-headed than Lincoln was—others were acquitted despite being involved in the same brawl, and the trial was most peculiar, the charge making no mention of Edmund having dealt the fatal blow. He fled abroad but was persuaded, or rather coerced, to return around a month ago. Lord only knows how long the truce between him and Tudor will last. Even if Edmund chooses not to act on his claim to the throne, he has two brothers still living: Will, twenty-one years 0f age, and Dick, nineteen. My aunt was far too good at producing sons to be convenient for Tudor.

For what feels like the hundredth time, I am torn between love for my oldest sister and my nephew, Prince Arthur, and loyalty to York. If any of the de la Poles were to be king… But no, I am fantasizing once more. Tudor will guard his throne again and again if needs be. How many have died in order for his reign to prosper? My brothers and Edward of Middleham—although Buckingham acted on his own accord and Middleham was snatched by illness before Tudor could lay hands on him. Uncle Richard, Lincoln, Warbeck, Warwick, Gloucester. Another three de la Pole brothers will surely follow unless they guard their backs and curb their ambition.

Her skin is chalked grey, glistening with beads of water. Her lips, like bruises, form delicate sounds, words I can barely discern. She reaches for me, the bones in her fingers protruding, but I cannot feel her touch.

The water is rising around us, yet Annie does not try to run from it. The current carries me upwards. I float while she sinks, and her outstretched hand fades.

In that moment, her words are clear at last, echoing louder and louder: Why did you let me die, Mother? Did you not love me? Why did you let me die, Mother?

I press my palms to my ears and curl up by the stack of pillows. I am as cold as if the water had indeed flooded me, and my heart beats like that of a frightened little bird. She is right. I let her die. How could I ever have pitied myself, when I was the architect of my own misery? What if I had kept her by my side that day in the garden, or run faster, or learnt how to swim? Our lives might have been very, very different. For months, I have managed to quiet these thoughts, trying to stem the guilt by ignoring them, and thought about my youngest daughter every waking hour of every day to keep her out of my nightmares. It does not work any longer—perhaps because I have been

262

momentarily caught up in the intrigue around me, and now Annie claims my nights instead. She is right to do so, for I let her precious life slip away after vowing to never let her go. Her dripping wet ghost will haunt me until the day I myself die, and although it terrifies me, I cannot wish for the ghost to leave me. It is all I have left of her.

It is not solely Annie but, to a degree, her sister as well. Sickness does not strike and kill unless it is God's will, and I was not pious enough to avoid his wrath. Perchance he sought to teach me a lesson, though I am not much better now than I was before. It appears to me that loss strengthens faith in some people, while others merely grow resentful, and I belong to the latter group. Nonetheless, had I not been so blasphemous to begin with, the Almighty might have spared my eldest, and had I not committed a thousand tiny mistakes on that July day at Tattershall, my youngest would be with me also. This must be how Mother felt having let Dickie go to the Tower, but her guilt was not justified, since she had no other choice and the soldiers would have taken her son by force if she had persisted in her refusal. No, this is different.

I consider waking my maid if only to have *someone* to confide in, but decide against it. The weight on my chest will suffocate me unless I rise and breathe fresh air, though. I slide my legs over the edge of the bed and let my toes touch the icy floorboards. Once I have crossed the strip of bare wood, my feet sink into the lush carpet while I wrap a robe around me and tie the sash tight around my waist. I open the casket on my desk, Queen Anne's casket, searching blindly with fumbling fingers until I feel the smooth clusters of diamonds against my fingers. With the broach clutched in one hand and a taper in the other, I trip out of my room. The diamond broach is more to me than a mere symbol of my Yorkist affinity, for it has been with me more than half my life, and represents a simpler time. If not simpler, then at least happier, because I was yet nearly unscathed by heartbreak. If I had known at fifteen where I would be now—childless, motherless, the widow of a Lancastrian, the subject of a ruler I resent—I would have wept.

I resume my nightly sojourn. When I reach the great hall, I freeze on the spot. A dark silhouette is sitting on one of the high chairs, legs crossed and feet on table. I force my own legs to move forward, and in the light from my taper I can now discern a face I hoped to have forgotten long since.

The man in the chair twitches and snaps around as I step on a creaking floorboard.

I wrap my robe tighter around me, my voice a barely audible whisper. 'Hello Thomas.'

Chapter XXVI

WE TALK THROUH the night. If it is possible to know a person after twelve years apart, I daresay I know him. I recognise his speech and manners like I would recognise my own reflection in a mirror, and I must have thought about him more often than I realised or cared to admit. The lines around his eyes when he smiles—he *does* smile—are real crinkles now, and to my astonishment, I spot a strand of silver in his hair in the candlelight. Still, he is younger than Welles was when I married him, a boyish twinkle ever-present in his eyes.

At first, our conversation is slow, trickling forth in awkward phrases and muddied words. I do not know where to begin. I scan my old friend's face and voice for traces of resentment or anger, and indeed there is a guarded note, but it fades as we continue. We shall have to untangle the knot that is our past someday, however, it is night, and one can easily leave necessary topics alone in the dark.

Thomas recounts his life since I was no longer in it. He has been away from court for nigh on a decade, living off the modest income from his father's lands. To my creeping relief, he says nothing of any wife or betrothed, but a confession I could not have imagined in my wildest dreams emerges.

'Northumberland was always a good master to me, say what you will of his actions at Redemore Plain,' he says, running a finger around the edge of his empty wine cup, his feet still on the table. 'He comforted me greatly.'

I frown. 'You told him about me? He could have ruined both of us.'

'I didn't tell him *that* much. I never mentioned names.'

'Go on.'

'You must swear not to utter a word of what I tell you.'

I thrill with anticipation. 'You know I will not.'

'I was…caught up in a vice. I believe it became part of me.' Thomas stares stubbornly at his cup, then raises his gaze. The corner of his mouth curves in a smile, but his eyes remind me of a terrified animal.

'What?' I shake my head in frustration as he remains quiet. Finally, I understand what vice he is implying. 'But Northumberland was *married*.'

Thomas scoffs. 'Right. Tell me one magnate who has not strayed from his wedded wife.'

'But they do not go after their *household esquires*.'

'How would you know?'

'Well, I—' I break off. I have never thought of it that way before. Something else strikes me with a tinge of offense. 'If you practice sodomy, why did you pretend to fancy me, or any woman?'

'It was not a pretence—one fancy does not exclude another, does it? If I told you about every little dalliance I've had since you last saw me, you would be scandalised indeed.'

Little dalliances? I can only presume they included more than women alone, but I am not in the mood to be scandalised. Still, what I find the most disconcerting is not Thomas' confession, but that he had to involve himself with Northumberland of all people. It was bad enough to have been that knave's servant. I am certain now that it was treason at Redemore, because Northumberland was slain by a furious Yorkshire mob four years later, and the people in Yorkshire were always my uncle's most loving subjects. The passionate violence reported cannot have been the result of taxes only.

'You amaze me, truly. You realise you could be taken to the Tyburn for this?' I say at last.

He winks at me. 'But you won't tell.'

'Of course not.' I shake my head in disbelief.

'As long as you keep quiet, I have no cause to fret. I heard your husband passed away. My condolences.'

'Thank you. He left me ample lands and estates.'

'How fortunate for you. And are you safeguarding them for any children??'

266

'No.' I clench my hands to keep them from trembling. 'Dead, both of them. Gone, forever.'

'I—I am sorry. Truly.'

The look in his eyes tell me more than any words ever could. Ought I to pour my heart out and pray that he comforts me? No, that would not be fair, not when we have not spoken for such a long time, and he most assuredly has his own losses. My soliloquy will have to wait just a little, so I swiftly move on to another topic.

'And now? Whom is it you serve?'

'Northumberland's son, the new earl, that is. He is quite the spender, and has got it into his thick head that I am the man best suited to manage his account book.' He grimaces.

In this manner, we pass the hours until dawn bleeds through the clouds outside.

As the summer heat creeps on, it brings not only blossoms and sunshine, but disease. When the first known death from plague is reported to Tudor through a discreet message, Elizabeth tells me, he turns as pale as if he were a ghost himself. The last thing he needs now is a country or even a city ridden with fear, a people who bar their doors and whisper about their King having stirred God's wrath. Moreover, the Catholic Monarchs will hardly be inclined to send their precious daughter overseas when she might be contaminated the moment she steps on English soil. The plague is never merciful, it is never solely a ripple. Sometimes fewer men and women perish, other times every third or second soul, but one cannot know which it will be this time, and thus dread's icy claws continue to tear apart the fabric of society.

Since I am not prone to illness, I find it as difficult to start walking with a scented handkerchief pressed against my lips as I did when I was a child. Thomas, however, is of another disposition.

'I found a new recipe for rosemary perfume. It is supposed to be very effective keeping the plague odours at bay. And there is this tincture I heard His Grace himself is using—' he says as we ride across the rollicking meadows outside the Palace of Hatfield, whereto the notables have retreated to avoid the worst crush of people and filth in London. Outings such as this ride offer a privacy not otherwise found at court, and I may use the excuse that I need Thomas to help with my horse and serve as my guard, whether anyone believes it or not. It is at least half true, for he is beginning to cure my fear of horses.

I turn my face to the evening sky shifting in rosy pink and flaming orange. 'If it comes, it comes, that is all. I am not so certain your scents and tinctures and charms can fend it off any better than fortune.'

'How can you be so calm?' His voice is muffled through the handkerchief.

'Everyone around me keeps dying and I am alive so far, am I not?'

'You think yourself invincible?'

I shrug and rein in my horse. 'Not at all, I just mean...I just mean that I don't really *care* if I am struck down by the plague. Not any longer.'

'By Saint Edward's toes, you ought not to say things like that! It's tempting fate.' He flashes me a look of pure horror.

'You are often a voice of reason, Thomas, but in times like these you are much too superstitious. Remember in the abbey, when you thought you would catch Agnes' ailments yourself?'

He cracks his knuckles, his face dappled in the last rays of soft red sunshine. 'How was I to know she was pregnant and not terminally ill?'

'She did die from that pregnancy.'

'Yes, you told me. If her child had lived, I would have pitied it.'

I frown. 'Why?'

'Because I know what it is like to be the nail in your own mother's coffin. It is no pleasant feeling...it never leaves. Like a persistent itch you can't reach to scratch.'

I cannot stand the way the humorous glint in his eye, which was present even when we spoke of the plague, is extinguished as if someone had thrown snow on a burning log. I have listened to him lament over the matter before, and tried my utmost to comfort, but my words seemed as trivial then as they do now.

'Please, do not torture yourself. It was not your fault.'

Thomas shakes his head. 'But it *was*. My father never failed to remind me, not even on his own deathbed. Do you recall that eve in the gallery, when you asked me what happened upon my return to the Isle of Wight after the sanctuary? I don't think I ever told you, but he died then, and there was little love lost.'

'Then he was a scoundrel.' I purse my lips. I ought to have realised that his father had passed if only I had reflected upon Thomas being an esquire and not the son of one, the title being hereditary.

'Are you trying to convince me you don't blame yourself for the death of your daughters? It is how the human mind operates, I'm afraid.'

The sky has lost its beauty; the colours hurt my eyes. The lump in my throat nearly suffocates me. He is right. *If only, if only…* 'I could have saved her. Annie. She just…she just wanted to see the fishes. I could have said no.'

Thomas holds his reins in one hand and places the other on my arm, gently. 'But how were you to know? See, in all rationality, I understand it was not my fault my mother died, and I understand I won't catch every disease there is, but rationality rarely wins, does it?'

'I promise to blame myself less if you do the same. We would both be so much happier.'

'You have my word.'

We turn our horses back to the palace, for if we are already straining the boundaries of decency by going riding unchaperoned, tarrying outside after sundown would be to thoroughly cross those boundaries. I do not know if I will be able to keep my promise, but I have high hopes of it. We both have scars from life—no doubt Thomas has some he has not yet shown me—and I appreciate companionship in the healing process.

A fortnight later, Tudor gathers his magnates and favourite courtiers and leaves England for a brief visit to Calais across the channel. There, the party wine and dine with Philip, Archduke of Burgundy and widower of my aunt Margaret's stepdaughter Mary of Burgundy, to negotiate English-Burgundian trade. While the Pretend-King is away, tragedy nestles into the innermost circle of his household: Prince Edmund suffers from the plague for five days before passing away on the nineteenth day of June. Sixteen months old, the poor boy is chanceless. We return from Hatfield to London for his stately burial in Westminster Abbey, and Elizabeth sends her husband a letter beseeching him to return from Calais as soon as the negotiations are dealt with.

My sister is beside herself, yet maintains a mask of composure. I never hear her weep or cry out, nor does she retire from the public eye, but I know a grieving mother when I see one. I feel infinitely sorry for her, for she is convinced she must keep up a dignified facade while I could wallow in my sorrow, and still there is a tiny, vicious part of me content she is not so far above me in terms of fortune as she once was. It is cruel, I know, but I want her to understand how it feels to lose more than one can bear. After a moment of indulging in this sentiment, I give myself a slap and return to my sister's chambers to sit with her in silence, allowing her grief to fill the room while I hold her hand.

Tudor returns shortly thereafter, distraught like I rarely saw him before. I dare not ask—and in truth I care little for his emotions—but methinks he is afraid, afraid that the male line of his sketchy dynasty will go extinct. Unlike the Yorkists, the house of Tudor is not established enough to allow for cousins and other more distant relatives to step forth and make a credible claim in place of the former heir. Lincoln and poor Warwick were not unthinkable kingly alternatives, but if any of Tudor's cousins were to replace his sons, their claim would likely be even weaker than Tudor's own.

Still, the Pretend-King need not worry, for he does have a healthy heir and a more than thriving spare at hand. The chances of both of them dying before they come of age and can produce sons of their own are fairly slim, especially seeing as Prince Arthur's wedding is a mere year away.

In the autumn, another proxy wedding is held, with the Spanish ambassador Rodrigo de Puebla acting on Catalina's behalf. Prince Arthur does not look nearly as content with this swarthy older man as I am certain he would with his actual bride, and I have to hide a smile throughout the ceremony.

'It is a good thing they shan't have to kiss,' I whisper to Anne.

My sister grants me a faint resemblance of a smile. She flinches slightly when her husband, who is sitting on her right, puts his hand on her arm and says something too low for me to discern. His beak-nose and thin mahogany hair, his burnished doublet and black hat, these are attributes I have come to shun away from. Though frequently updated on the latest fashion, Thomas Howard is not a man to dress flamboyantly. His speech matches his attire: distinguished but discreet, masterfully crafted but subtle. Unlike his father and grandfather, he has gone at lengths to ensure his own political rehabilitation and assimilation into the Tudor regime, serving his sovereign with faultless prowess in the field, but his rising star is equally dependent on his words. I have watched him many times as he leans over to whisper something to Tudor under the guise of unassuming council, slowly making his way to the core of the crown, as patient and calculating as Tudor himself. They make a fine match, unlike Howard and Anne, whose intimacy I struggle to comprehend. Few can resist loving her, and perhaps the secret to capturing my sister's heart is as simple as convincing her the opposite: that he alone cares for her.

After the proxy wedding, Howard slips away to consult with the Earl of Oxford and Reginald Bray, both confidants of the Pretend-King and both men whom I loathe. Young Buckingham and Young Northumberland trot at the other men's heels, a look of poorly concealed desperation on their faces. Despite the elevated positions they occupy at court as former wards of Tudor and Margaret Beaufort, they are little more than figureheads, since Tudor fears he would not be able to continue stripping them of the income from their lands if he allowed them true influence. It serves them right for their fathers' betrayals.

I take Anne's hand and pull her with me to a secluded space in the walkway. 'Tell me how you are, and please do not lie. Your hands fidget when you do.'

She shakes her head. 'I am no worse than I've been before.'

'You flinched when he touched you.'

'You are reading too much into the silliest little things, Cecily. I love my husband—he is everything I wish for.'

I think she means it; her eyes are bright and her gaze genuine, shielded only by a strand of finely spun hair that has escaped her gable headdress.

I sigh. 'I thought you wished for a chivalric knight to sing you ballads and give you flowers.' The description is half in jest, half serious, and fits Thomas Howard like a description of a lamb fits a wolf. Anne, however, is far from amused.

'I was young and fanciful and a dreamer. He might not sing but he is awfully clever and fights bravely, and cares for no one but *me*. Is that not what's most important?'

'The important thing is he does not want you, either, to care for anything but him, and if you let that happen, you'll have surrendered everything for someone who gives you bruises.'

She hauls up her sleeve and lifts her veil to show me her arms and neck. 'Look. All gone. And there is something else, too. I am with child.'

I do not know what to say. In the end, I decide on the most dazzling smile I can summon, trying to imitate our mother, and Anne returns it, relief flickering in her face. Her only son is still the cause for some concern, being a sickly child, and four full years have passed since he was born.

'When is it due?'

'Oh, I cannot be certain, but I should think in April. I know it will be a son.'

'Everyone always *knows* their child will be a son.' I regret my snicker instantly.

Anne gives me a reprimanding look through her lashes. 'Do not be unkind, Cecily, not now.'

'Forgive me. I only meant to say that daughters can be…can be wonderful in their own right. I would give anything to have mine back.'

'Yes.'

We remain in silence for a moment or two. I cannot read my sister's expression, but my own thoughts are wholly entangled in memories: Eliza and Annie playing with a toy horse, fingers sticky with marzipan, eyes sparkling with laughter, frail little bodies I will never hold again. For the hundredth time, I wish damnation upon all who give their condolences at the birth of a baby girl and then proceed to leave the child entirely to her nursemaid and governess for the next ten or fifteen years.

Anne's belly grows rapidly, and by Advent, she already wears specially tailored gowns to accommodate the babe. I rarely see her, though. These past five years, she has made scattered appearances at court, but now her presence fades further until she has practically cupped herself up in her and Howard's nest, and I fear she might not return. Indeed, only Elizabeth and I are left as occupants of the royal palaces, Kate having moved to her new London house with William Courtenay and their three children, and Bridget as always at Dartford Priory. Still, it is not to Elizabeth I turn when I receive Anne's tear-splotched letter, but to Thomas, who agrees to walk with me as I rant.

'She writes she "crossed the boundaries", and had a "fright". The child was born much too early. They christened her, but after that there was nothing to be done but bury her. Look at her handwriting, all jagged and sullied with ink blotches and tears. She's such a terrible actress, Thomas, she thinks she can keep up appearances, she so dearly wants to fool herself and everyone else that she's happy!' I draw a deep breath. 'What does boundaries mean, regardless? And fright? He must have done something. She insists I do not try to come and visit her, says it would vex her husband.'

Thomas speaks through a clenched jaw. 'I've seen the bastard, the way he whips and spurs his horses. He may be of slight build, but he does not mind violence.'

'I know. But what can I do with such an accusation?'

'Nothing. It is his right.'

Coming from anyone else, those words would have put me ablaze with fury, but I know Thomas well enough to see how it grudges him to speak this abhorrent truth. Yes, Howard may lash his horses bloody and keep his wife as a virtual prisoner, all the while bowing and scraping at court, and hardly anyone would notice or care.

The world around us does not stand still, either. On the south of the continent, the Italian wars rage on, and in the faraway north, the so-called Kalmar Union strains under the tensions between Swedish and Danish noblemen. In the Spanish kingdoms, there are fresh surges of rebellion, and Tudor grits his teeth at the delayed departure of his daughter-in-law Catalina de Aragón. The preparations are in full bloom, the thorns of said blossoms stinging every courtier and administrator as far as I know, and little wonder, because never before have I seen the kind of extreme attention to detail that Tudor now exercises. Everything must be *just so*: the colour of a sleeve, the punctuation

273

in the marriage contract, the exact number of shillings spent on the reception. He has returned England to the practice of benevolence, the forced loans Uncle Richard outlawed, bankrupting many a merchant and minor noble to finance the affair. The sole amusing part of the spectacle is to watch even Margaret Beaufort rub her temples at her son's obsessive toiling. Most of the time, though, I spend playing cards with Elizabeth— who is accumulating quite the gambler's debt—or stealing away with Thomas, and in this manner, the months pass until summer arrives once more.

Anne writes to me again, this time to tell me that her beloved sister-in-law, Elizabeth Howard, who wed a man called Thomas Boleyn, has had her second daughter. They baptised her Anne, after my sister, who is delighted despite her own hardships.

She has these arresting eyes, almost black. I do not think she will ever be ugly, although the poor child has a rather swarthy complexion. I shall call her Annie to avoid confusion—I pray you do not mind.

I sincerely hope little Anne Boleyn's fortune will be greater than Anne Welles' was.

I am teaching Thomas French to the best of my ability, a language which he has surprisingly scant knowledge of.

'A man will have greater success in love if he can call a girl *cheri* and *ma belle*,' I tell him, and he gives me a soft shove, lingering just a tad too long to be prudent. If either of us dared utter it…

It is during one of those summertime French lessons that we catch a few startling words wafting up from below the open window.

I slam it shut with a gust of warm air so as to speak freely. 'Suffolk taken flight? *Another time?*'

Thomas abandons his sketching in the margins of the glossary I wrote for him and leans over to crack the window open again. This time, we are both on our toes, listening intently to the fragments of conversation below. Some words are swept away by the August breeze before reaching our ears, yet the message is clear enough. My cousin Edmund de la Pole has fled England to the court of the Holy Roman Emperor, and taken his younger brother Dick with him for good measure. Emperor Maximilian is a fickle man, and might well aid the Yorkist rebels despite his recent negotiations with Tudor.

'Do they pose a genuine threat, d'you reckon?' Thomas asks.

'Well, no. Not yet at least. If I could, I would lavish fortune's good graces upon them, but I do not think they have much in the way of resources.'

'I see.' Noting my sudden sombreness, he grins and tempts me to smile as well. 'A toast, then, for your unlucky kinsmen.' He reaches for the wine flagon on the table by the window seat.

'A toast for those fighting for a lost cause.'

The moment our cups meet, I realise the truth of my own words with a pang of forlorn dismay.

Chapter XXVIII

B Y THE END of that October, in the year of our Lord
1501, we receive word that Catalina de Aragón has landed
in Plymouth after an allegedly stormy crossing.

Tudor can barely contain himself, for here is his grand prize
at last, the result of all his gritty negotiating with the Catholic
Monarchs.

Elizabeth and I watch him swing himself onto a horse with
uncharacteristic vigour, then spur the animal and leave his freshly
built Richmond Palace behind in a whiff of dust. He takes
soldiers with him, naturally, suitably adorned with the Tudor
Rose badge, as well as a wide-eyed Prince Arthur. The boy has
turned fifteen but gives the impression of being both younger and
far more seasoned at the same time, his tall stature contrasting
oddly as he kisses his mother goodbye with the anxious devotion
of a five-year old.

Elizabeth hooks her arm through mine as we watch the
figures getting smaller on the road. 'Cecily, do you recall when he
was born?'

I nod. 'If he had been a girl, things would have been very
different.'

'You mean Harry would have been the one to wed Catalina?'

'That among other things.'

To my relief, she makes no further inquiries, leaving me to
join her other ladies. Truth is, if Arthur had been a girl, my sister
would have had weaker bonds to the Tudor dynasty, and the child
would not have posed such a deadly threat to anyone taking the
throne. Under those circumstances, I would have been keener to
support, say, Lincoln and Lambert Simnel in their insurgency.
Things would have been very different indeed; the rebels might

have had a better chance to succeed, but the likeliest outcome would have been my own downfall. I am grateful now that he was a boy, though I cursed it at the time.

A few days later, when Elizabeth and I are sitting in her privy chambers with a clutch of other ladies, my sister reads us the laconic note her husband sent with the flustered messenger arriving that same morning.

"'The *Infanta* is worn after her journey and was taking what the Spanish call a *siesta* when I arrived at the house where she and her retinue is staying. I demanded to see her presently and was pleased",' Elizabeth reads.

I raise my eyebrows. 'His Grace would not let the girl sleep awhile but burst into her bedchamber?'

Aunt Catherine laughs, but Elizabeth purses her lips. 'You cannot know that is what happened.'

'I am merely assuming.'

'Go on,' Catherine says.

"'Our son was most charmed to meet his bride. We are traveling to London and will proceed through Southwark and the Borough to London Bridge."'

The party is due to arrive in the capital on the twelfth day of November. London is vibrating with the final preparations for the lavish festivities, the display that is to show the wealth and grandeur of the Tudor state to the whole world. There are even men walking along the streets carrying sacks of sand to cover the cobblestone in order to soak up and conceal the filth. It would not do to expose the *Infanta* to the nasty reality that is English paving combined with a lack of public hygiene.

When the twelfth day of November arrives, six pageants are placed along Catalina's route from London Bridge to her lodgings at the Bishop of London's palace. The shows are crafted from a swirl of history and myth, reality and propaganda. The actors stand on elevated platforms and perform passages from legends and Christian truth alike, meant to allude either at the legitimacy and glory of the Tudor dynasty or to sing the praise of Catalina herself. I wish I could watch them up-front, but I am not one of the English courtiers selected to be part of the procession together with the Spanish. The tens of thousands of commoners—poor and rich, old and young—however, are free to watch, forming a crowd as large as I ever saw, pressing up against the princess's entourage. Fortunately, there are banisters in place to keep the lowliest lot at a proper distance.

Elizabeth, Anne, Kate, and I are among the courtiers embarking from Richmond Palace in Surrey to Baynard Castle in London, where we are to greet our new family member the following day. The castle is a peculiar choice considering Tudor's anxiety to convey his own line's legitimacy, for it was the London stronghold of York during the early years of the civil war. My grandfather kept four hundred loyal men there during his pursuit of the throne, and my father was crowned in the great hall after the battle at Mortimer's Cross. The building lies east of Blackfriars, the south range and turrets appearing to rise out of the Thames, fishing boats gliding past the stone. On the opposite side is Saint Paul's Cathedral, a short walk away—perhaps that is the reason for Tudor's choice.

The next day, the triumphant Pretend-King receives the Spanish ambassadors at Baynard, after which he presents Catalina to his wife and the rest of us ladies closest to the crown.

The fifteen-year-old *Infanta* might have been English judging solely by her appearance: light hazel hair falling in soft waves down her back, twinkling blue eyes, skin the colour of fresh cream. She calls to mind a doll, with her petite build, round cheeks, and snub nose. I suppose she is beautiful—yes, very beautiful, but I am starting to become numb to beautiful women these days, having seen so many. I would rather see too much beauty than too much ugliness, though, as no doubt the common people do.

What strikes me first about the Spanish retinue is the bell-shape of Catalina's and her ladies' gowns. Whereas our English skirts are full yet flow naturally from the waist to the feet, the Spanish model sticks out from the hips, as if held out by a rack of sorts. It looks terribly odd to me, but fashion is often progressive on the continent, and I have long since swallowed the dreary fact of being at an English disadvantage when new trends emerge.

Once I have soaked up enough of Catalina's clothes, I turn my attention to the four Spanish ladies flanking her at a respectful distance, a tiny part of the entourage she has brought. Two are of a slightly darker complexion than their mistress, while the other two women must be Moors, their skin glistening dark brown. Their hair is black like charcoal and curly in a way I have never seen before, the tiny ringlets gathered in cauls ready to burst for the volume they hold.

I try not to stare, but it is near impossible. I have heard stories about this strange people before: they worship a heathen God and write with foreign letters. I do not know how common they are in Spain, or how civilised they are, yet Isabel de Castilla must hold these particular ladies in very high esteem if she chose them as her daughter's chief companions.

I assume all Catalina's attendants speak Spanish alone, perhaps Latin also, and I cannot make myself understood in either tongue. Unless Tudor sends them back to Isabel and Ferdinand after the wedding, they shall have to learn English so I can converse with them and find out more about all the lands overseas. Surely, any worldly Spaniard or Moor must have a repertoire of thrilling stories to tell, as well as exotic customs to share. Nothing as piqued my curiosity as much since, well, I cannot even recall.

In mid-morrow on Sunday, the fourteenth day of November, the wedding procession emerges from the bishop's palace to cross the square and continue towards Saint Paul's Cathedral. This break with the tradition of holding royal weddings in Westminster Abbey smells suspicious to me. Perhaps Tudor wishes to mark how he considers himself a monarch of a new age. If so, the insult at his predecessors appals me., because traditions such as these were made to be adhered to.

Catalina is a splendid figure on her mule, a dot of white silk and satin in a sea of colourfully dressed nobles. Her dress is hooped and pleated in what I have learnt is the Spanish fashion, her dollish face veiled. By her side rides ten-year-old Prince Harry, already a treat for the crowds, waving and grinning. Judging by her expression, the bride is growing mildly irritated with her new brother-in-law, as one can easily be with a boy his age, but Harry takes no notice.

With a few exceptions, everyone who is someone is part of the procession; even Thomas might have joined if he had asked nicely. English and Spanish courtiers alike amass under the crust of grey clouds on the November sky, as if on our way to a light-hearted picnic in springtime.

If his father was a toad, the new Duke of Buckingham is a rooster. We have all donned our finest garments, but he? He has bought himself a coat allegedly worth *fifteen hundred pounds*, which is half the yearly income of a wealthy duke and more than all six pageants cost together. I grit my teeth as I watch him ride in front of me, the coat handsomely draped over his broad shoulders. How dare he outshine not only me but every member of the royal family, even the *Infanta?* He must be as vainglorious as his father was, and I confess I cannot muster any cousinly love for him. At least his mother, my aunt Catherine, is at long last happily married. Jasper Tudor passed away some time since and Catherine's new husband is a scandalising fifteen years her junior.

We arrive at Saint Paul's in a whirl. As the groom's senior aunt and a princess of the blood, I have been designated to carry Catalina's train during the ceremony. Although carrying *anyone's* train stings a little, I am fully aware of the prestige this role holds, and if Tudor had disregarded court custom by choosing another woman to perform the service, it would have been a bitter offense. Thus, as the Spanish princess dismounts her mule and approaches the gates of the cathedral, I bend down to pick up her white train, the fabric smooth and cool against my fingertips.

The cathedral has been hung with enormous tapestries to create a more welcoming atmosphere, and the aisle is covered in red cloth. Stalls have been erected in the nave for the most notable guests, and a high wooden platform placed near the altar, which is where the bride and groom are to speak their vows. The nobles scramble to take their rightful places.

Dressed in white just like his precious bride, my poor nephew is wringing his hands, forcing his eyes to stay pinned to the gold decorating the altar below the platform where he stands. The young couple has been exchanging courteous letters in Latin for years, yet rumour has it they were unable to speak to each other upon their first meeting, having learnt vastly different dialects of the language. Of course, they should both count themselves lucky to be wed to someone highly born and their own age, and without any obvious irredeemable flaws.

The ceremony, too, passes without incident. Prince Arthur maintains the grace of his mother and the remoteness of his father, speaking his vows with rehearsed meticulosity. Said mother and father, together with Margaret Beaufort, watch in privacy behind the latticed windows of a discreet closet adjoining the stage.

Catalina's voice contains the confidence and passion of one who knows she has arrived at her destiny. She may have had all of Europe at her feet, princes begging her parents for her hand, but the way she talks, I am convinced her heart is set on being Queen of England. It is a desire I understand all too well, but she is closer now than I ever was.

After the ceremony and the celebratory mass following it, Arthur retreats through a side entrance while Catalina and Harry—and I, carrying her train once more—retrace our steps down the aisle.

As we emerge from the cathedral, we encounter another of Tudor's spectacles: a green mountain covered in precious metals, the previous Earl of Richmond's "Rich Mount". At the top are three trees and three kings: the King of France, the King of Spain, and in the middle King Arthur, whose tree is adorned with red roses and a Welsh dragon. A spring of rippling wine erupts at the base of the mountain so that the commoners crowding forward can drink to their hearts' delight.

After a moment of praising the Rich Mount, we proceed to Lambeth Palace for the wedding feast and the rituals following it.

One advantage of my marriage to Welles was that I avoided the ceremonial bedding, which Catalina and Arthur have to endure that same night. Raised to duty since they learned to walk, the process still requires ways of coping. While Catalina pulls the covers up to her chin and refuses to look at the bishops and other spectators, her young husband does not have to think a great deal, since his well-meaning friends have coaxed enough wine down his throat him to render him dazed. They both appear almost tragicomic where they lie side by side, the canopied bed surrounded by ecclesiasts and courtiers alike.

After the customary blessings and toasts, the onlookers trot out in a single file. I am the last to exit, closing the door behind me, leaving the young couple to their marital duties. I hope Catalina's wedding night proves a more positive experience than mine was.

On Tuesday afternoon, almost the entire court, along with a throng of London dignitaries, continue upstream to Westminster on no less than forty gorgeously adorned barges. The skies are at last clearing after a day and a night of rain whipping roofs and beating against windows, and now the thick ash-grey clouds slowly creep away towards the horizon. The air is still damp against my skin, and it does not require a genius to understand why Tudor initially wanted the wedding to take place in summertime.

Nevertheless, the week of festivities that await us could not be dulled even by a snowstorm. We go through a shameless, seemingly endless chain of banquets and pageants, balls and games. Few things I have ever experienced can rival this display of finery—and, of course, that is the whole point, to outshine the past for everyone to see. What one does not have in terms of lineage, one compensates for in terms of propaganda.

The most outstanding event is by far the jousting tournament. I nigh on hurt my neck trying to see every detail of the competitors' costumes at the entry from my spot on the bleachers. This must be the most imaginative, not to mention expensive, apparel worn on English soil for decades.

Young Buckingham, who is the chief challenger, enters with his horse inside a wheeled pavilion of white and green cloth covered in red roses. After him comes Young Dorset—my nephew, who has inherited the title after his father died in early September—also in a pavilion, this one golden and a striking contrast to his ink-black armour. If my late half-brother could see his son now, he would be over the moon with smugness at how handsomely it paid off to join Tudor in exile all those years ago, regardless of the limited position he himself endured afterwards.

Kate jumps to her feet, eyes shining with merriment, as Courtenay enters clad in red, his horse styled to look like a red dragon. The colour and the mythical creature are clear references both to Lancaster and, more specifically, to the Welsh Tudor dragon, the same emblem that sullied Redemore Plain. Kate does not appear to make the connection, or perhaps she does not care, because she claps her hands and fastens a token handkerchief on her husband's lance. Their relationship is peculiar to me. Both are young and bursting with energy, both have a lurking capacity for recklessness but lack sharp intelligence, both are handsome beyond reason, and thus they are remarkably well suited. Still, I fail to spot any genuine romance. Rather, it is as if they were children thrilled to play a game with one another.

The magnificent entrances and parades resume before the jousting itself commences. The combatants crash together in a mash of splintered lances and buckled plate armour time and time again. I cannot help but instinctively shut my eyes at the moment of collision. I am uncertain as to whom I ought to cheer for since none are men whom I have any great love or trust for—there are very few of that kind in general nowadays. In the end, I decide on my kinsman Lord Rivers, simply because I like his costume the best: he arrives in a pretend ship with a firing canon.

I turn to Kate, who has sat down again. 'How do you think the newlyweds are finding married life?'

'I'm sure Arthur is pleased. Guess what he said the morning after?'

'What?'

Kate smirks and clears her throat to produce an awful imitation of a young man's voice. '"Willoughby, bring me a cup of ale, for I have been tonight in the midst of Spain!" Or some such nonsense.'

I swallow a laugh. 'That sounds too crude to be sweet little Arthur.'

'He's a fifteen-year-old boy. Did you expect him to tell his friends he stayed up playing chess and dicing the whole night?' She is right, of course, and she should know. Sometimes I forget the age gap between her and Arthur is closer to that of siblings than that of aunt and nephew.

'I suppose not. I do like the *Infanta*—the Princess of Wales, I mean. Don't you? She respects the English throne and wants it,' I say.

'Then you must be jealous.'

283

'Only a little. I am heartily tired of being envious.'

'She's too…too *clever* for me! She tried to speak Latin to me when we were preparing her for the bedding. It was so very odd.'

'Her English is improving. Methinks she is quite the learner.' A notable absence in the tiltyard catches my attention. 'Edmund de la Pole ought to be here.'

Kate crinkles her nose. 'Billie likes him. I don't. His brother was always touching you when we were little, at Sheriff Hutton.'

I close my eyes at the bleak memories bubbling up to the surface of my mind, feeling queasy as if I had eaten something rotten. 'I did not think you noticed…you really *were* little. Suffolk is not Lincoln, though they are sprung from the same bed. Did you say your husband is a friend of his?'

'I cannot tell, except I heard them talking once, over supper.'

'What about?'

'Stop nagging me!'

I abandon my attempts to extract any juicy information from my little sister. Perhaps there was nothing to it, despite the oddity of the man riding in on a Welsh red dragon and the latest Yorkist claimant being on good terms, and frankly, I have little by little lost my appetite for courtly intrigue. Some people, like Margaret Beaufort and Mother, become both more enthralled with scheming and more skilled at it as they age, but I fear the opposite is true for me. The more I think about it, the more I am overcome by a desire for peace, away from court, like those golden days with Annie in the early summer of 1499. Ever since Tudor took the crown, or at least ever since I married and moved away to Tattershall, I have started to become detached from the world I grew up in.

Once the tournament ends for the day, I manage to sneak away to meet with Thomas in the stables, where I know I will find him tending to the destriers on his own accord. We are fortunate, for the actual grooms have long since completed their drab duties and retired to an evening of revelry admittedly humbler than the celebrations that their masters enjoy at this hour.

I stride through the rushes and dust on the floor to rest my hand on the glossy, warm hair of the mare Thomas is mumbling pretty words to.

'Whose is this?' I ask.

He smiles. 'The Earl of Essex'. Her name is Heloise.'

I stoke Heloise's mane. 'This wedding has made me too nostalgic for my own good. Did you know none of my husbands proposed to me?'

'Surely you did not expect them to.'

'You did.' I bite my lip. We have been on the verge of this conversation so many times but never delved into it.

Thomas shakes his head. 'It was foolhardy of me to ask you to wed me. I know that now.'

'Ask me again. Please.'

'No. I meant what I said that day—I asked twice and I shan't do it again. I think...I think I wasted my youth on you. All the years I spent wishing you were with me, all those years are time I won't get back.' His voice trembles, not with bitterness but with tears.

'But I *am* here now,' I say.

'Yes, yes you are, and I'm glad, but you will leave sometime soon, like you did before. And I'm sorry, but I refuse to suffer for it once more.'

'You do not understand, Thomas. I am not leaving.' I round the horse and lace my fingers with his, my jewelled rings unwieldy. I take a deep breath, blood rushing in my ears. 'Well, if you still cannot bring yourself to ask me, I shall ask you instead. Will you marry me?'

To my despair, Thomas scoffs. 'How foully you mock me.'

'No. Don't be the blithering idiot I was. If you truly want me to stay, all you have to do is say the word. I did not treat you right, I understand that now, but I had hoped you would forgive me, if not for my sake then for your own.'

'What of your ambitions? We would not be wealthier than my father was. The King would banish you from court, perhaps even confiscate all your lands. How could you be satisfied with the life of a common gentry woman?'

'I would have *you,* just as you told me that day in the woods, and that would be enough. Mayhap we could even have a family, for my mother had children when she was older than I am now. And I am a widow with my own means—I could wed you if I chose to.' The words spill from my lips in a stream I cannot control, and there is more yearning to emerge. If my daughters, God rest their blessed souls, taught me one thing, it is that there are many ways to be happy. A massive land grant and a fancy title is one kind of happiness. The purer kind, however, is based solely on affection, as I learnt when I held Eliza for the first time and as I suspected each time that I lost a loved one.

'You wouldn't regret your choice?'

'Never. I am so weary of all this, the infighting and intrigue, the death. Living in a place where I used to belong but has not for years. All I want is a quiet life, filled with *love*. Real love, not the way I loved Welles, and not the sisterly love I feel, but the way I love—' I have to pause not to stutter. 'The way I love you.'

Thomas stares at me. 'I thought you would never say it.'

'And will you?'

'I should have fourteen years ago. I love you shamelessly, ardently, for certs too much to rise in the mornings without you.'

After he takes me in his arms to sweep me off my feet, he makes a quick turn and we both tumble down in the haystack by the stable backdoor. My stomach soon aches from laughing, although we compose ourselves enough to share first one kiss and then another until I lose count. It is the first time I have ever fully indulged in my romantic instincts, and I am glad I do, because they have haunted me.

Chapter XXVIII

THE FIRST PERSON I dare share the secret of my liaison with is Bridget, who has come to court for the wedding celebrations. She has been here two or three times since she was spirited away to the priory all those years ago and even a week after the wedding, she appears like a plain blackbird among prancing peacocks. I trust Elizabeth has provided her with the means to purchase fitting attire, but Bridget dons her nun's habit and veil every day without a glance at the luxurious fabrics the tailors try to tempt her with. I admire her for it but I do not understand it. If I were her, I would never want to return to my old priory again; I would cling to all the dashing clothes I could lay my hands on and discard my habit at once. Saying naught of these thoughts, I instead spill my secret to her in eager little trickles of truth, truth I know she will guard well.

We have ventured outside, away from the festivities for once, to walk along the Thames. A thin crust of ice glints in the sunlight, stretching from one river bank to the other like a sheath of silver. The men and women hurrying down the streets and alleys are as unlike the cheerful crowd I witnessed upon Catalina's arrival as can be: grim, bleak-faced, dressed in mundane woollen cloaks, their day of glory and show already a distant memory.

'Do you love this man, Cecily?' Bridget says at last. I need not caution her to speak low enough to ward off prying guards, for her voice is soft as swan's down.

I cannot keep myself from smiling. 'I do, I truly do. If Lady Mother could hear me now, or Elizabeth, or myself only a few years ago—'

'Then you must not let it go to waste.'

'I have no intention to, that I can promise you. I shall wed him, be it at the expense of my lands and my honour.'

Bridget is silent for a long while before saying: 'I feared for you. I feared you might never experience the delight of having a beloved.'

'What do you mean? Have I been so lacking in affection before?' I take a deep breath to calm my temper, feeling as if the air is turning to ice crystals in my lungs.

Bridget gives a gentle shrug with one shoulder. 'Oh, no. Not at all. But you would not have risked all.'

'Well, no, I suppose I would not have. Would you?'

'You forget the vows I have taken.'

I cannot resist the urge to tease with a sprinkle of blasphemy. 'Can't a nun fall in love? Or does Christ refuse to share your heart with any other?'

'Do you recall Alice?'

I knit my brow, leafing through the images of faces in my memory without success. 'Alice?'

'The woman I mentioned when you last came to visit at Dartford.'

'What of her?'

'You asked whom I could give my heart to. It is true I'll never marry, but pray do not think me without emotions of my own,' Bridget says, as if these were the most natural words in the world to utter.

'I never thought such a thing!' I take her naked hand in mine, marvelling at how she can reject even the simplest of luxuries that is leather gloves in wintertime. Should I inquire further, implore her to elaborate? Every fibre of my being is yearning to know whether my youngest sister speaks of friendship or of a more intimate bond, a kind of bond I have previously only heard Thomas discuss openly—yet that was in the dark of night. Perhaps it is best not to ask and not to know. I may have a talent for safeguarding secrets when I so wish, but I have my hands full with my own at the moment. Moreover, I am not certain Bridget can put it in any clearer terms for me.

I cast a glance over my shoulder to ensure the guards we brought are still ambling fifteen feet behind, out of earshot for our low discussion. Then, I turn to the third matter of the heart that day.

'What do you know of Anne's marriage?'

'Nothing. Has it escaped you, sister dear, that you are the only one in this family who still cares to speak with me at length?' There is no bitterness in her voice. 'Years of estrangement will do that.'

My breath forms puffs of white smoke in the cold. 'Mayhap. Then I'll tell you now that Howard is not fit to polish her boots, let alone share her bed. She had a babe who was born much too soon and died this spring. By God's truth, if he did not beat it out of her, it was the pain I know he so often inflicts on her psyche.'

Bridget crosses herself in silence.

I continue. 'She says he still loves her. I think he still has passions for her, is still fond of her, and for all I know he has no mistress. But that does not change his cruel nature.'

'"The Lord tests the righteous and the wicked, and the one who loves violence, His soul hates."'

On that note, we turn to resume our walk back to Westminster. The sky is grey marble, streaked with gold, somehow unforgiving. Rarely has London been so quiet, so void of bustle and life, so eerie.

Thomas and I have a certain difficulty staying sane now that the only thing ever keeping us apart are social obligations. Despite my sobering walk with Bridget, I am flushed and love-crazed again within the hour of returning, eager to give in to passions I did not know I was capable of.

One of those winter days, Thomas and I have the rare luck of stumbling upon an empty solar at Westminster, and he bars the door to ensure our privacy. Bursting with giggles I ought to have abandoned with girlhood, I let him pull me onto his lap in one of the armchairs. Perhaps this is the kind of silly escapade I would have spent my time on if I had not been whisked away to Tattershall with Welles—I have much to catch up on.

Thomas' lips are warm against my temple, my mouth, my neck. He is in the path of the sun, the light painting his silky hair brighter than I know it to be. The thrills edging up my spine and to my fingertips are sweeter than honey.

'I've longed for you too many years to ever let you go now,' Thomas murmurs against the curve of my shoulder. 'I hope you realise that.'

'I don't mind one bit.' I think I have never spoken truer words.

I reach up to knock my headdress off and pull out the hairpins, allowing a cascade of burnished gold locks to fall like a curtain around our faces and shoulders. What happened in the stables might have happened again there and then, were it not for a thread on Thomas' sleeve getting caught in my diamond broach.

'Let me untangle it,' Thomas says and sets about the task, narrowing his eyes. 'You still wear that thing? You don't think it is time to…let go? Much too sparkly.'

I muster a glare. 'Do not dare mock my broach. You might as well mock my very person.'

'I would pick something more imaginative, then.'

'I *like* sparkly.'

'I know.' He seeks to part my lips with his again but I pull away ever so slightly, thrusting a hand in the pocket hidden between the folds of my gown.

'Speaking of jewellery, I have something for you.' I extract a small gold pendant, studded with bands of tiny pearls, and slip it over Thomas' head.

He takes it in his palm, studying the precious stones. 'Fine craftsmanship,' he says with a grin. 'But don't you know I have no need of pretty gifts and tokens?'

'You do if you want to keep a lock of my hair.' I unsheathe the dagger in his belt, wind a few strands around two fingers, and make the cut. The garland fits perfectly in the pendant.

'Thank you, sweet Cecily, for finding me again on that night.'

I could stay forever in the solar, and I nearly do, mindless of the dancing that has begun in the great hall. Only when the first notes of lutes and virginals fleet into the room where we are sat does it strike me that the entire court must be marking my absence.

'Say you had a headache and took to your bed. That latter part does not have to be a lie, right?' Thomas whispers with a wink blatant enough to make me laugh.

290

'I could say that. Or you could let me change into a fancier gown and come dance with me.'

'What, before everyone?'

I shrug. 'Why not let them grow accustomed to the sight before I spring the news of our marriage upon them?'

'Our marriage.' He savours the words like a delicacy. 'You do know how to persuade a man.'

'I like to think so.'

Tudor's howl carries merciless through the April night. I never went to sleep, but I can imagine the horror of those waking to that inhumane sound, a sound containing a chilling note of madness. Minutes before, the Palace of Placentia was still and quiet and dense with sleep. Now it appears all Hell's demons have risen to make merry in the gloomy halls.

I rise from my bed, abandoning the seven-page letter from Thomas, sweep myself in a frock, and scurry towards my sister the Queen's chambers. Upon arriving, I find she has already gone to her husband, and I am left to wait with a cluster of ladies trying to rub the sleep from their eyes and suppress their yawns. Some of them have slept in Elizabeth's bedchamber to help maintain the heat in the room; some have, like myself, come tripping from their own chambers to investigate this most harrowing of commotions.

We wait a good half hour before my sister returns. Only one person before has brought my thoughts to a snuffed-out candle: Anne Neville, embalmed days before her funeral. Elizabeth's cheeks are not just waxy white, though, but have turned an interesting shade of green, her eyes glazed, unseeing.

I take two steps forward and grab her arms, perhaps too roughly, disregarding all ceremony and titles, making use of the nickname I have not uttered since we were little. 'Tell me, Beth. What, in the name of the Holy Virgin, has happened?'

Her knees buckle and she would collapse on the floor were it not for my grip. I need not say anything, for two other ladies hurry forth to assist me in coaxing her to the bed. No candles are lit at this hour, and I have some difficulty discerning the women's faces, but I believe I spot Aunt Catherine and Bessie Tilney both.

If only Anne were here, or Mother… They would know what to say to remedy this sorry state.

'Beth,' I whisper for my sister's ears alone. 'Tell me, at least.'

At last, a breath of a voice: 'Prince Arthur. Dead of the sweating sickness. *Dead.*'

I pull away abruptly, feeling my own face drain of colour and a sour taste on my tongue. Not only do I know the pain of losing children, but I know the blow this is to everything Tudor has built, everything he has fought for. His Tudor Rose Incarnate is dead. The boy with whom all our hopes rested—even my own, because I had begun to find some small comfort in knowing that England would still be ruled by a king half Yorkist. Arthur…Arthur who demonstrated a sense of duty rarely seen, Arthur who did not hesitate to let his little cousins Eliza and Annie borrow his most treasured manuscripts. Prince Arthur, who sealed the most prestigious marriage alliance in England, who was supposed to be the link to the royal House of Castile.

My thoughts have already darted on to Catalina de Aragón, now a widow in a foreign land, when the sobs come. Unhinged, strangled sobs, mingling with short cries and gasps for air. Even at this hour of her greatest need, I feel mildly awkward with my oldest sister, and leave the others to sooth her while I set out to find Tudor. Of course, I should not venture into the open corridors and galleries dressed thus, but I doubt anyone will notice what I am wearing at a time like this.

I find the Pretend-King in the outmost part of his privy chambers, staring blankly through the high window as if awaiting dawn. For the first time in my life, I pity him. I pity the man who shattered the world as I knew it, for he is in shatters himself.

'Your Grace,' I say in a low voice. 'The Queen needs you.'

He does not move. 'She told me to take heart in God's mercy, because we still have one prince and two fair princesses. She told me we are still young enough to have more children.'

'All very well, Sire, but my sister is in dire need of comfort. You must tell her what she told you. Come now!' Under other circumstances, it would have given me immense pleasure to watch Tudor heed *my* command and follow me back to Elizabeth's privy chambers, but I am not capable of joy tonight.

I am proven right: her husband alone can calm my sister. Not until this moment did I truly believe he loved her, yet for all his domination of her, there can be no other explanation. Perchance his love is similar to Welles' love for me—sprung out of necessity and many years of companionship—although her own affection was kindled before they were wed. Regardless, the scene offers me a peculiar glimpse of humanity, vulnerable, raw humanity that I did not expect to ever find in the remote Lancastrian ruler.

Two years ago, Tudor had three healthy sons. Now he has one, a single thread upon which his dynasty's future hangs, and his paranoia grows by the day after Arthur's death. Before his eldest has even been buried properly, he issues a tangle of new arrests: William Courtenay, Young Dorset, Exeter, and Will de la Pole, who is Suffolk's younger brother.

Kate catches me just as I am about to seek her out. She is flushed pink, bleary-eyed.

'Have you been crying, Sister?' I ask, stunned. 'I did not think you cared for your husband in such earnest ways—'

'Never mind him! He'll manage. But what if the King pursues *me?* I swear he has gone mad!'

'Hush!' How queer, that I should be the one to caution against slandering Tudor, considering my own record of doing just that.

Kate finally manages to stop flitting around like a trapped bird. 'Remember I told you Billie supped with Suffolk once this last summer? The others did, too, the other men that were arrested, and…'

'And now Tudor think them to be conspiring against him,' I finish for her. 'Are they?'

'How would I know? Billie can be so wondrously impulsive!'

I pull her with me to sit on a velvet-clad pallet. At twenty-one, she looks almost identical to the little girl who used to wail and rage and giggle without any consideration for our mother or our nursemaids. However, this time she is not in a fit over a toy or a scolding. This time, the blood-soaked block on the Tower Green is surely as foremost in her mind as it is in mine.

'Bless them all if they have put themselves in this quagmire for the sake of the White Rose. As much as I regret it, Suffolk stands little chance. You know that, don't you, Kate?'

She nods zealously.

'I think Tudor knows it, too, but he wants to root out every Yorkist, however small a threat they pose. Lord only knows how many more men he means to seize.'

'There is more.' Kate's eyes have returned to their usual colour and contain a flicker of the delight that she takes in knowing more than others for once, a kind of delight I am familiar with myself. 'A man named James Tyrell has been in the Tower awhile now. Tortured, I'm sure! The King had him fetched from Calais because he, too, had been corresponding with Suffolk.'

I frown. 'So? I do not recognise his name.'

'Does not matter, Cece, what matters is what I've heard. Rumour has it…' She makes a deliberate pause. 'Rumour has it he confessed to more than he was charged with. He confessed to murdering the princes.'

'What princes?'

'*Our* princes.'

The magnitude of Kate's words dawn on me slowly, so slowly that it hurts all the more. On the few-and-far-between occasions she mentions our angel brothers, she simply refers to them as 'the princes'. Like Bridget, Kate was too young when they were taken away to remember much if anything. To her, they can be naught but hazy figures, faraway phantoms of tragedy.

I grapple for words. My tongue is unwieldy in my mouth, my throat dry like caked mud.

'Cece?'

'What says this man…Tyrell?' I manage at last.

'I know not. The trial is less than a fortnight away, though. I bet we will find out then.'

'Yes. Yes, I suppose we will.'

The paranoia continues. On the last day of April, two common Londoners have their ears slashed off for daring to speak ill of the Pretend-King and his council.

Two days later, on a Monday heavy with rain that never falls, the show-trial of Tyrell and three of his associates takes place in London's Guildhall.

Thomas insists on going with me. I do not mind the scandal of it, fearing I will bite off my own tongue unless I have a warm hand to clutch. Naturally, the sight of the Queen's sister and the man whispered to be her immoral paramour raises eyebrows, but it is not we who are the main attraction, not in this spectacle.

James Tyrell is a robust man, thick as a tree trunk and equally coarse by the look of his weathered skin. His tawny beard is the colour of withered grass; his broad nose blends into the rest of his face without distinction. His legs are close to failing him, and one arm is lodged in an improbable angle: traces of torture, perhaps the rack.

I believe…I believe I do know this man. I saw him a few times in the company of Uncle Richard, especially at Nottingham Castle, a trusted servant if I remember correctly, knighted by my father on the battlefield after Tewkesbury. Though his own father was Lancastrian to the bone, Tyrell was a loyal Yorkist until Tudor took the throne and coerced the man into his service—up till now. Could he have murdered my brothers? Buckingham would likely have had access to him…

The trial commences. I listen with half an ear as the jurors read up the charge of treason and the intelligence gathered by Tudor's network of spies, facts proving Tyrell did lend support to Suffolk in Calais. As the trial draws to a close, I snap out of my trance.

'Do you stand by your confession regarding the sons of the late King Edward IV?' one of the jurors says.

Tyrell meets the other man's inquisitive gaze without blinking. 'I made no such confession. I did not lay hand on the wretched princes. This I swear on the Bible.'

To my astonishment, the jury does not press Tyrell in this matter, does not even ask him to take the oath he offered. I cannot hear what they whisper among themselves, but there seems to be a revelation of sorts, and this particular charge is dropped flat, as if it had never been spoken.

I turn to Thomas. 'Why do they let it go so readily?'

He squeezes my hand. 'No doubt they remembered how it would wretch the King if they condemned Tyrell for the murders.'

'I thought Tudor was only too eager to lay the blame on my uncle's trusted knight.' I cannot disguise the bitterness in my tone.

'Maybe he is. But you forget, that man has been in Tudor's service these past sixteen years. How would it look if a sovereign had favoured the perpetrator of the crime of the century?'

I shake my head in disbelief. Before I have time to reply, the jury pronounces their sentence.

'Sir James Tyrell, you have been found guilty of foul treason by means of aiding the exiled rebel Edmund de la Pole. You are to face a traitor's death four days hence. The law has condemned you to be hanged by the neck, taken down alive, disembowelled, have your private parts removed and burned, beheaded by means of axe, and quartered, according to the pleasure of His most august Grace King Henry VII.'

Tyrell emits a choked sound from the base of his throat. Finally, his stretched and tortured legs give way. He cannot have expected any other outcome, yet the death sentence appears to weigh on his shoulders like a yoke of led, and he has to be dragged from the Guildhall back to his cell.

When I ask Kate where she heard the rumours of Tyrell's confession, she merely crinkles her nose and says: 'A young lawyer said something about it. Thomas More, I think his name was. Smelled like rotten fish.'

Fortunately for Tyrell, Tudor shows a twinkle of lenience and allows his prisoner to be beheaded rather than face the traitor's death allotted him. Tyrell makes no last speech, and I do not think I shall ever find out the truth.

Perhaps he was indeed the man the toad Buckingham tasked with the filthy deed. Perhaps he made a false confession when pained by the rack cracking his bones. Or mayhap this was all a fabrication of the lawyer Thomas More's mind.

Honestly, it matters little to me.

Chapter XXIX

PRINCE ARTHUR WAS buried in Worcester Cathedral on Saint George's day, late in April. The choice puzzled me before I remembered that Tudor likely wishes to downplay the disaster, insecure on his throne as he still is. When I dress in my mourning garb every morn, I cannot help but wonder how many days I have spent in black these past twenty years.

Mother once said the death of Edward of Middleham was divine retribution for her own boys. Naught has yet convinced me that this was the case, on the contrary, but I wonder if not Arthur's passing so shortly after his marriage was retribution for the three young men who met their maker on Tudor's command to pave the way for said marriage.

What I do know now, though, is that John of Gloucester's death can only have been Tudor's personal decision, a bonus execution for the sake of retaliation. Father's son by a mistress has been called to court and installed as Elizabeth's cupbearer. He lacks all ambition, true, but his bloodline is no sketchier than Gloucester's was, yet he does not suffer for it.

The court is grief-stricken after Prince Arthur's funeral, but as I suspected, a political crisis is looming as well. We wait under tense whispering as Catalina is brought back to London, she herself recovering from the same sweating sickness that took her young husband. If she is with child... But no. The Spanish princess is not carrying the heir to the throne, which is all the worse for her, since she is now a redundant commodity to her father-in-law.

Prince Harry, now the new Prince of Wales, must be reined in and begin his tutelage as the future King of England. His sprightly manners, which delight me so, often border on reckless, and the carrot-headed young boy has the character of a crowd-pleaser rather than a sensible liege lord. It would not surprise me if Harry grows up to be every bit as self-indulgent as my own father was late in life, God rest his soul. For once, I hope Tudor lives another five or ten years. No one likes a boy-king, and no one likes a regency.

Once more, my thoughts stray to poor Catalina. Her father, Ferdinand de Aragón, is one of the most stubborn men I have heard of, and refuses to pay the rest of her dowry now that her husband has been ushered to heaven. Tudor, meanwhile, negotiates for the money with an iron fist despite his personal sorrows. While they squabble back and forth, the sixteen-year-old widow remains in England, practically penniless, Tudor refusing to grant her the revenue of the dower lands that are hers by right. How dearly he loves his gold! To him, she has gone from invaluable to a nuisance over a night.

It is then that the question of the wedding night arises. If the marriage was indeed consummated, Ferdinand and Isabel ought to pay the rest of the dowry whether Catalina stays in England or returns to Spain; if it was not, they could even demand that Tudor return what he has already received. Catalina alone knows what happened that November night.

Still intrigued by her exotic retinue, and stung by pity for my nephew's widow, I ride on my barge downstream to Durham House on the Strand to pay her a visit.

The *Infanta* receives me in the solar of the fairly grand house, where she and two of her Moorish attendants are occupied with needlework.

During the six months since she entered London on that most glorious of days, Catalina has added several years to her appearance. Where once her face was doll-like, cheekbones now protrude under milky skin; where once her gowns amazed me, black damask now dulls the impression. I hope grief has not aged me in a similar manner. However, as I approach closer, I discover much to my relief that a new set of clothes and a few weeks of hearty meals ought to be enough to transform her back into the priced treasure of Christendom.

'Welcome, Lady Cecily,' the Dowager Princess of Wales says as I dip into the slightest of curtsies.

'My condolences, Madam. You have recovered well from your own illness?'

'*Gracie Deo.*'

'Yes. Forgive my bluntness, Madam, but what do you intend to do when your period of mourning has passed?' I can stem my curiosity no longer.

Catalina gestures for me to sit with her by the table, and calls for a servant to bring us mulled wine and a plate of sweetmeats. The princess touches none of it, claiming she is fasting for the Ascension and proceeds to answer my question with zeal.

'*Mi padre quiere que me case con el hermano menor. ¡Qué locura!*'

I picked up enough of the Spanish ladies' native tongue during the week of wedding celebrations to discern a few of the words, and I can only stare. 'Prince Harry?'

Catalina nods, her black veil swirling around her head in an ominous gauze cloud. '*Es mi destino ser Reina de Inglaterra.*'

'Madame, my Spanish is not what I wish it to be, and I am no canon lawyer, but Harry cannot wed his brother's widow, surely?'

Catalina takes the trouble to return to her fragmented English. 'I know more *sobre la iglesia* and God than you do, Lady Cecily,' she reminds me. '*El Papa* decides.'

Her words ring true: a papal dispensation can make almost any marriage legal in the eyes of the church. There is something else, though, something emerging from my mist of memories, something Margaret Beaufort once said.

'Does not the Bible tell that a man who beds his brother's wife shall be childless?' I feel quite smug about my sudden mastery of the scripture, though I may be paraphrasing, until I see Catalina's eyes darken like a stormy sky.

'It is…*grosero* to imply I was Arthur's wife in the flesh. Doña Elvira can tell you I was not. I am maid. *No me toca la mano de un hombre.*'

My cheeks burn. 'Pardon me, Madam. I've no doubt you understand my curiosity.'

'I know many speculate. They should not. It is between me and God, and the Almighty knows I am virgin *en todos los sentidos.*'

So, this girl truly does believe it to be her destiny to be Queen of England. I can make little sense of it, still, there is no denying she cuts a figure not easily trampled to dust. I have seen my fair share of English queens: my mother, who was the most beautiful woman ever to wear the coronet; Anne Neville, who was the bravest; and Elizabeth, who has accomplished everything expected from a king's obedient spouse. If Catalina de Aragón was to join their lot, she would be the queen to command the greatest respect.

I cannot bring myself to question her further on the consummation of her marriage despite the suspicions that Arthur's words after the wedding night give me, because if I were in her shoes I would be mortified, embarrassed beyond reprieve. It is only my own curiosity that suffers, for I do not believe every single word in the Bible is necessarily a prophecy, and the possibility of Prince Harry having a childless marriage is so distant to me both in time and likelihood that it feels imagined.

The brevity of Catalina's marriage to Arthur, and indeed the reminder of the brevity of life that his death is, has spurred me towards the rash action I have been intending since November last year. Thomas and I must be properly wed in a church before some obstacle or other comes in the way, or I fear it will never happen. Our union is already sealed, for we have been betrothed and shared a bed, but without a witnessed ceremony, others could claim it was not so.

My decision will shock not only the court in general, but Elizabeth in particular. Is she aware of the change in me?

I find my sister alone in her privy chambers, seated by the card table, dressed in black for her son. The lines carved around her eyes by grief's iron chisel is not nearly as distressing to me as the strands of grey I spot in her strawberry-blonde hair, strands I am certain was not there six weeks ago.

'I am to be married,' I state, careful to keep my tone as neutral as if I had commented on the weather.

Elizabeth does not look up from her cards. 'You always had such bawdy humour.'

'I mean it. I am to be married, and soon, to one of Northumberland's esquires, Thomas Kyme.'

My own spark of irritability has lit an unexpected fire in my sister. She shoves her chair back and stands, dropping the cards on the table.

'Have you lost your wits?' She grabs me by the shoulders in a way she has never done before, then pity creeps into her eyes and extinguishes the flame. 'Oh, Cecily...You have already taken him to your bed, have you not? Are you with child, is that it?'

I pull away from her. 'Do not look at me like that. You and Tudor...I remember well enough! And it's not as if I am the sole sinner in this world. I remember Father's fancies, also.' Mayhap it is unwise of me to jump to this last topic, which is still as sensitive as a raw burn, but it is among the first defences that spring to mind.

'We do not speak of *that woman*.' Elizabeth's voice is cool, her response pure reflex. Jane Shore's name has not crossed anyone's lips for years, not since she wed a lawyer and settled. 'His fancies never harmed his reputation, Cecily. He was the *King.*'

An incredulous laugh escapes me. 'Never harmed his reputation? Are you hearing the words coming from your lips? If he had not made a plight-troth to Eleanor Butler—'

'You cannot know that. No one knows, not even Mother did.'

'Uncle Richard thought he knew.'

We stare at each other for an agonizingly long moment. My sister has bitten her nails down to the skin on three fingers already.

'You never...never told me what *you* truly thought.'

'Well, I wanted to believe as Mother and you did, that we were legitimate princesses. I wanted to believe it so much and for so long. But I...I always suspected deep down it might not be so.' As soon as I have uttered these words, they resonate with me. I could not have been more honest with her.

'Oh, how can you say such a thing? You shan't convince me.'

'I have no desire to. In truth, I...I care little myself, for I'll soon be gone from court, away from slanderous tongues wagging.'

'You may not leave me, not when Arthur—' She clasps a hand to her mouth and I fear she will start to cry. Then, as so often before, she smothers her emotions, smoothing back her glossy facade.

I take a step towards her. 'You know I grieve for your loss, Beth, more, I daresay, than you grieved for mine. But I am so weary of adjusting my life to what others see fit and proper, what they require and demand.' Forcing the hint of disquiet from my voice, I bend forth to brush my lips against her cheek. 'I won't part with you in an argument, but know this: I mean to be gone within a fortnight, and I mean to be *happy*.'

Just as I am about to leave my sister to gape after me, she stops me in my tracks, saying: 'Tell me one last thing. Did Gloucester ever confess to the murders? Did he confess directly to you?'

'Do not believe everything Mother and Tudor has told you, Beth. It was Buckingham's deed. There.'

'You have no evidence.'

I shrug. 'Perhaps not evidence as clear and hard as would please you, merely a brief letter and an oath that lives in my memory alone, but frankly, you need not heed me. I am finished with this infighting.'

Next on my list is the person who, believe it or not, is essential for the ceremony to take place.

'Thomas,' I whisper, putting my hands over his eyes. 'Do you have a minute or two for me?'

The question is perfunctory and he twists around in his chair, only too happy to put down the pencil in the account book. The numbers blur before my eyes.

'God Almighty, this is dull!' He intertwines his fingers with mine. 'Can you guess how much Northumberland spent on ribbon garters this past fortnight?'

'A pound?'

'Five pounds!'

'For whom, his mistress?'

Thomas grimaces. 'I do pity the lass, whomever she is.'

I stifle a laugh and put my hands on his shoulders in as serious a fashion as I can bring myself to. 'I did not come to talk about that boy or his expenses. I came to ask if you will wed me.'

He grins. 'I thought we agreed on that already. Or did I misinterpret the past six months?'

'I mean wed me *soon*. We never decided on a date, but I do not care to wait any longer.'

'Right you are. I will wed you this very night.'

'Tonight?' Not until now did I fully comprehend how quickly my life is to change, how drastically. We will surprise the lot of them—I can imagine Tudor going into a fit once he finds out.

'Unless you have something else demanding your attention.'

'Fortunately, I do not. And Thomas? Do take a bath beforehand.'

He laughs and wraps one arm around my waist. 'You think I stink?'

'No, of course not! It tends to calm the senses, though. I bathe twice or thrice every month myself.'

'We'll see—I would not want to gamble my good health when the best part of my life has only just started.'

After supper that evening, I retire early and dress in my finest gown: scarlet velvet stitched with gold and silver thread, the square neckline cut low to reveal my saffron-coloured kirtle, the sleeves slashed and folded back for yet another peek of rich yellow. I search for the silver caul Thomas gave me that Christmas in sanctuary, but to no avail. I have to make do with a simple coiffure pinned to my head; for this time alone, I let the veil remain in my clothing coffer. After all, there will be none but my betrothed and the priest to see me thus.

Of course, this is not entirely true, since Thomas has tasked two trusted friends to accompany us to Westminster Abbey and serve as witnesses. It is no safe endeavour to be outside in London after darkness has fallen heavy over the city.

Lanterns do light our way to a certain extent, though, sprinkled like fireflies. Upon entering the abbey, we are engulfed in the sheen from hundreds of candles lining the nave and the high altar. I fathom this must be a special order for tonight, because I cannot recall there was ever such warm splendour during my days in sanctuary unless there was something to celebrate or to grieve for.

'How lovely,' I whisper to Thomas.

'Come.' He steers away from the aisle and leads me by the hand towards the cloisters and smaller chapels.

'Where…?' I get no further before we have stepped into the Chapel of the Pyx. 'You sly weasel.'

'I knew you would like it. Let's pray you do not trip during a dance step and bang your head against the wall this time.'

I hardly even notice the priest officiating the ceremony, so caught up am I in casting stealthy looks at my groom. To my joy, he has dressed himself in finer clothes than I have ever seen him wear. In his fashionable midnight-blue doublet and hose paired with shiny leather boots, he could almost be mistaken for a high-ranking nobleman rather than an esquire managing his master's account book.

On our way back, I tilt my head back to take in the needle-stitch-stars against the night sky, marvelling at what I have done. 'I feel like a criminal!'

'Believe me, you're no worse than a scandal.'

Once we have parted with our bantering companions for guards, it is I who lead him by the hand, hastening through the palace towards my bedchamber.

I dismissed my women for the night before the ceremony and God only knows what they must think, but I have no need of their assistance, especially since Thomas has quite the extraordinary skill for unlacing gowns and locating hairpins. His kisses are light, flitting from my palm to my wrist and my eyelids like the grazing wings of a butterfly. I allow my kirtle and chemise to slip from my shoulders, tugging at the lacings of his doublet with one hand.

I did ask Joan, my favourite maid from Tattershall, for one service this eve. The bath is still steaming, fragrant with lavender and a softer note of vanilla.

'By Saint Edward—' Thomas mumbles between the kisses. 'Are you now intent on having me wait for you to wash?'

'I thought I might convince you of the delights of bathing, beloved,' I tease. 'You cannot refuse me now.'

He laughs at that. My own laughter turns to a small shriek the moment I stumble on the bath curtain and we are on the verge of plunging backwards into the water, breaking bones against the marble rim.

'Sorry, silly, but it seems to me that the bed is safest for now, until you can clear your head, and I mine.' He discards his doublet on the floor, still laughing, and helps me step out of the garments that are now a circle of scarlet and saffron around my ankles.

My bed has never before been this warm, this accommodating, this longed for. When I rise again, hours later judging by the burnt-down candle on the nearby table, the bath water has long since cooled and is mild against my skin as I lower myself into it. Specks of lavender drift on the surface, gilded in the candlelight. The soap is slippery in my hands, hence I quickly abandon it and merely lean back with my feet propped on the smooth rim.

I have not bothered to draw the curtain, and Thomas pushes himself up on one elbow, head cocked, watching me with an amused twinkle in his eye.

I close my own eyes and sink further back. 'What?'

'Have I told you what a sight for sore eyes you are? Your hair is all…floaty, like a fan around your head. Or a halo.'

'I am thirty-three.'

'Really? You could have fooled me you were twenty on the day.' The irony in his voice is unmistakable, but I do believe he means it, too. He was never one for empty flattery, and thank God for that.

'Well, I am glad I am not truly that young,' I concede with a smile. 'I was not so wise then. I…I could not see the things that mattered most.'

It would be beyond sacrilege to describe the sins we engage in that night, though now it is not adultery. And, surely, most of Christianity would be doomed if a plain old confession could not remedy these things.

Slated beams of early summer sun peek through the window. I pull my knees up to rest my elbows on them, the silky sheets tangled around my waist, my tousled hair loose around my shoulders. Outside, a bird is chirping, soon joined by another and a third. It is still early and only the bustle of servants stirs the palace outside my firmly locked door. *Our* door. My glance wanders to the figure beside me, sleeping on his stomach with his face buried so deep in the pillow I would have feared he might suffocate, had it not been for the steady rise and fall of his back. The sight of Thomas clutching the embroidered blanket in one hand lures a tickling smile to my lips. He can be such a child sometimes.

I do not know what this day will bring, or where we are to live. I do not know if there will ever come a time when I regret what I have done.

There is such a wealth of things I may never know the truth of. What would have happened if Tudor had been slain before he usurped the throne, who I would have married. Whether my mother or my uncle was in the right about Father's plight-troth to Lady Eleanor Butler, whether my sisters and I are indeed illegitimate. Who carried out Buckingham's orders to murder my brothers. There was a time when these uncertainties kept me awake at night—but not any longer.

What does any of it matter now? My brothers are dead and buried regardless. I have been considered legitimate, baseborn, and once more legitimate in the eyes of the world, and whichever interpretation was correct will not impact my life henceforth. Tudor did win on that bloody battlefield, and there is no use in speculating and wishing.

Naught of all this can change that I am a daughter of York. I am a daughter of York, and this once, I look not to past glories and grievances, but to the future: my future, who is sleeping soundly by my side as morning wrestles London from night's grip.

Epilogue

THE LEAVES OF the trees clustered around the East Standen Manor have already begun to shift to russet and vermillion. In every direction, the landscape stretches towards the sea, the steep white cliffs clashing with the waves below. Seagulls glide above, squealing, like stains of bright paint against the cornflower-blue sky. We rarely go to the shore, though, and I have taught my daughter to never, *never* let go of my hand when we are near the water.

There are dimples in her cheeks as she smiles and swings our hands back and forth while we stroll towards the great oak towering on the south side of the manor house. The wind whisks her dark hair—inherited from her father, whose own hair is increasingly tinted with silver at the roots—around her chubby face. She is no Eliza or Annie, but she does not need to be, because she is a treasure in her own right, and every treasure has its charms.

Thomas sticks up a hand in the air for greeting. He leans comfortably against the rough oak trunk, legs stretched out and crossed before him, resting the baby on his one arm with ease.

'Mama?'

I release Margery's hand. 'Go on.'

She sprints ahead of me to tell her father all about the rabbit we saw a short while ago, a flighty animal that made her eyes wide like cups.

Out here, on the Isle of Wight, I am not 'Lady Mother' or even 'Mother', but simply 'Mama'. I have not been Lady-anything for more than four years. Tudor did what was in his power, confiscating my lands and property, banishing me from court, likely with a look of glee in his cast eye. He must have rejoiced to see the back of me and thus having one troublesome in-law less to keep watch over. Fortunately, I found rescue in the most unexpected person: Margaret Beaufort. At last ridden with guilt over the way she treated me once upon a time, or simply afraid to face her maker without as clean a slate as possible, she persuaded her son to return what was mine by right. It is for my lifetime only, but I do not mind greatly.

I follow Margery to the oak and sink down next to my husband, resting my head against the trunk, studying the green lace-pattern-foliage above.

Margery runs off again, skipping through the high grass, careful to stay within my sight.

I turn to Thomas. 'I received a letter from Kate earlier this afternoon.'

'And how is the dear one?' There is a note of genuine interest in his voice, for since we wed, he and my younger sisters have grown to be good friends.

'Excellent, I should think. She says she misses her husband, but I've no doubt she finds ways to amuse herself while he is in the Tower. You know, Thomas, I never liked the man better than I do now.'

'How so?'

I flash him a smug smile. 'He grew in my affections first when he aided Edmund de la Pole. Foolish, of course, but it proved he was not the whole-hearted Lancastrian I thought. And now…now he's rather agreeable merely by staying imprisoned.'

'I suppose you wish the same of your other brother-in-law, too. I would, damn him.'

'Yes, yes I do wish it. Anne still writes nothing of his rough ways, but how am I to know whether he has truly made amends? She is as smitten as she was ten years ago, and I cannot search her for bruises when she persists in secluding herself from me.'

The thought of Anne, as fragile as a butterfly and yet strong as granite, steals the mirth from me, and I know it shows on my face. My favourite sister is one of the few concerns I find myself stuck with. When Elizabeth died in childbed on her thirty-seventh birthday, less than a year after I abandoned her to wed my beloved esquire, it only served to increase my guilt over Anne and all the others whom I have failed to help, as well as ignited my own fear of dying. Mother Nature has a certain vicious tendency to deny old age to members of our family.

Thomas shakes his head. 'I do believe the world has cast a shadow over your eyes, sweet Cecily. Leave the brooding to me, or better yet to our elders. The summer has not yet retreated—surely, we can still enjoy a day such as this without turning it irksome.' He slides the baby over into my arms, places a kiss on my temple, and pushes himself to his feet. With a splash of sun on his face, he catches Margery and lifts her high until she shrieks with delight.

Their laughter rings in my ears, convincing me that Thomas is right: we can still enjoy a summer day such as this.

The infant is sleeping soundly, a trickle of drool in the corner of his mouth. I press my nose against his downy head and inhale the dearest scent I know, a mild autumn breeze tickling my cheek.

I named my only son Richard—after my valorous uncle, yes, but foremost after my angel brother, who is still a child himself, living forever in my memory, frozen in time, as are Eliza and Annie. That is the lovely aspect of memories: they never change unless one lets them.

I have my lovely memories and my lovely present woven to a single gilded fabric. I have two new, thriving lives to care for, and a husband with whom I can laugh at misery and smile at blessings. At last, I have peace.

I have longed for it so much. *Tant le desiree.*

Author's note

The War of the Roses and the dawn of the Tudor reign is too intricate, too complex, to treat in a single novel without omitting certain events and details. I have aspired to remain true to source material and not stray from facts unless it was vital for the purpose of the story, because I believe accuracy is key when writing historical fiction.

However, there are parts of history where the records fail us and guesswork is necessary. For example, all we know with certainty about the fate of Cecily of York and John Welles' daughters, is that they died young and never married. It is possible that these children died in infancy, but it is generally accepted that Elizabeth Welles died in 1498 and Anne Welles in 1499.

As for the liberties I have taken in this novel, there is no evidence of Thomas Kyme being at Westminster Abbey or at court at certain times; I have also left out his first marriage to an unknown woman and the son said marriage produced. Furthermore, I have omitted Edward of Middleham's burial at Sheriff Hutton.

The matter of fact versus fiction is, of course, relevant when talking or writing about any aspect of history, but perhaps more so than usual regarding the War of the Roses and in particular Richard III. Sources from the Tudor era are often heavily biased and eager to reproduce the slanderous rumours that benefitted the rulers of the time. The contemporary author and debatably historian John Rous dedicated his *Historia Regum Angliae* to Henry VII, in which he claims, among other things, that Richard III emerged deformed from his mother's womb after two whole years.

When most people today hear about Richard III, they at once think of Shakespeare's play with the same name. The image of Richard as a devious, deformed usurper and child-murderer has, sadly, come to be seen as more or less true. What we have to remember is that William Shakespeare wrote this play during the reign of Elizabeth I, a Tudor monarch who wished to separate herself from a less glorious past when her grandfather's rival ruled England, as well as the fact that Shakespeare worked in the entertainment business, not with historiography.

In fact, Richard was frequently noted for his unfailing loyalty to his brother Edward, his strong morals, and his courage. Moreover, he was a patron of literature, education, and the church. During his brief reign, significant reforms were passed. He outlawed forced loans (so-called benevolences) and established the practice of allowing poorer subjects to petition the King directly in order to access justice otherwise too expensive for them. Moreover, he translated the laws of the land from Latin and French to English in order for commoners to understand them. These are only a handful of many examples.

The myth about Richard's physique is just that: a myth, or rather propaganda developed shortly after Henry VII won the crown at Bosworth field, a place that contemporaries called Redemore. The "hunchback and withered arm" described in Shakespeare's play are pure fiction; in the middle ages and early modern period, outward deformity was perceived as both a punishment for and a sign of inner evil. After the discovery of Richard's skeleton under a Leicester car park in 2013, we now know that he did suffer from scoliosis, i.e. a curvature of the spine. However, the only visible effect of this would have been that his right shoulder was slightly higher than the left, and this barely showed at all when clothed. The condition likely caused pain, but obviously it did not limit his daily life or prevent him from participating in rigorous exercise and battles.

Other characters are also largely portrayed such as I have concluded from recorded behaviour and contemporary descriptions, yet it was necessary to invent or enhance certain traits for the purpose of the narrative. While I approached my research with an objective perspective, the main character's family ties and personality resulted in an intensely Yorkist novel. I sympathise with many but not all of the protagonist's views.

Few historical murder mysteries are as timeless and as passionately debated as that of the princes in the tower. Countless people believe they know the answer, yet it is unlikely that anyone ever will, and perhaps that is for the best, considering the asset a mystery provides for fiction writers. We lack the evidence needed to convict a suspect in a modern law court; we can only speculate in if they were killed at all, or spirited away.

To me, what marks Richard III as partly or wholly innocent of the crime is the question of motive. It does not take more than a second glance at the situation to realise that Richard stood the most to lose by the deaths of his nephews, as can be seen from how his reputation suffered, and the fact that their disappearance meant that Henry Tudor could claim the throne for himself. Richard's single reason for wanting them dead would have been to remove them as rallying points of rebellions, but if this was the case, why did he not make their deaths known to the public? He was no fool, and would have understood that the princes were more dangerous to him dead than alive.

Except for the princes, Richard had another seventeen nephews or nieces upon his accession to the throne, not including Edward IV's children by his mistresses, and none of these suffered any harm during Richard's reign. While their claim to the throne was not as strong as that of the princes, especially in the case of girls descended from the female line, it was by no means trivial despite various circumstances, as is shown by Elizabeth of York's significance to Henry Tudor and the threat her cousins later posed to him. Why do away with two nephews and let another seventeen claimants live?

The second main suspect(s) is often regarded to be Henry Tudor and/or Margaret Beaufort, since they both had a clear motive. I believe they had a far less opportunity and means than other suspects, although they may have been involved in planning the deaths. If either Tudor or Beaufort knew what happened to the princes' bodies, it stands to reason that they would eventually have produced the bodies to lay the blame on Richard in more precise terms than they did, as well as to ward off pretenders such as Perkin Warbeck. The identity of Warbeck cannot be established with a hundred percent certainty, but it is widely thought today that he was not the younger of the princes

Finally, there is the third suspect. I am convinced that the Duke of Buckingham did have both motive, means, and opportunity, but I do not have a conclusive view on every detail surrounding the mystery—such as whether they died before or after Buckingham's rebellion, which is related to why he made the decision and to what extent other nobles were involved. He had his own claim to the throne through his descent from Thomas of Woodstock, he was Lord High Constable of England which gave him authority over the Tower, he spent time in London during the summer of 1483 after the King left on progress, and, unlike Richard, he appears to have had the character required.

The only substance for the rumours about Elizabeth considering a marriage with her uncle comes from a letter written by historian George Buck, in which he summarises a note allegedly from Elizabeth to John Howard. Neither Buck's letter nor Elizabeth's note survives, and even if both of them did exist, which is improbable, the content could be interpreted in several different ways. In addition, Richard may have been considering marrying Elizabeth off to a Portuguese prince. In my opinion, a match between Elizabeth and Richard would not only have been political suicide for the King, but wildly uncharacteristic for both of them.

Cecily of York died of unknown causes on 24 August 1507. Tudor historian Edward Hall writes in his *Chronicle* that she is buried in Quarr Abbey, Isle of Wight, but any records confirming this were destroyed along with the abbey in the dissolution of the monasteries.

Thomas Kyme was in all probability dead before 1530 and certainly by 1535.

Cecily's and Thomas' children, Richard and Margery (or Margaret), can be assumed to have reached adulthood and married, since they are mentioned in a 1602 copy of the heraldic *Visitation of Hampshire* (1576). However, they were never shown any royal favours such as land grants or titles, which demonstrates how detached from court Cecily became after her unconventional last marriage.

Henry Tudor died in 1509, possibly from tuberculosis, and was buried in Westminster Abbey next to his queen, Elizabeth.

His son succeeded him as Henry VIII, and married Catherine of Aragon (here referred to with her Spanish name, Catalina de Aragón) that same year. In this novel, I have left out the early rumours about Henry VII considering a match between himself and Catherine after Elizabeth's death.

Cecily's sister Anne died in 1511, leaving no surviving children, and her husband Thomas Howard married the much younger and reluctant Elizabeth Stafford, daughter of the 3rd Duke of Buckingham (here referred to as Young Buckingham). There is little to no evidence regarding Howard's relationship with Anne, but his second wife testified to both physical and emotional abuse, and he later flaunted his mistress Bess Holland for all to see. Howard became an enormous influence at the court of Henry VIII, both in his own right and as the uncle of Anne Boleyn and Catherine Howard.

The 3rd Duke of Buckingham was not so lucky, but was executed for treason in 1521.

Bridget died in Dartford Priory, 1517, and was perhaps the most obscure of the York sisters.

Katherine (here referred to as Kate) remained in royal favour and was the godmother of Princess Mary (later Mary I), before dying in 1527, having outlived all her sisters.

Margaret Pole (here referred to as Meg) was made Countess of Salisbury in her own right, but was executed in 1541 after she and her son Reginald Pole fell out of favour with Henry VIII; Kate's eldest son was also executed for association with Reginald Pole. Margaret is considered to have been the last Plantagenet princess, although neither the Plantagenet bloodline nor the House of York was entirely wiped from existence. It is sometimes tempting to forget that Henry VIII himself was as much his mother's son as he was a Tudor, and he is said to have self-identified with his more glamorous Yorkist ancestors and their military prowess.